slug

hollie mcnish

slug

FLEET

2021

FLEET

First published in Great Britain in 2021 by Fleet

3 5 7 9 10 8 6 4

Copyright © Hollie McNish 2021

The moral right of the author has been asserted.

*All characters and events in this publication, other than those
clearly in the public domain, are fictitious and any resemblance
to real persons, living or dead, is purely coincidental.*

A CIP catalogue record for this book
is available from the British Library.

ISBN 978-0-349-72635-9

Typeset in Garamond by M Rules
Printed and bound in Great Britain by Clays Ltd, Elcograf S.p.A.

Papers used by Fleet are from well-managed forests
and other responsible sources.

Fleet
An imprint of
Little, Brown Book Group
Carmelite House
50 Victoria Embankment
London EC4Y 0DZ

An Hachette UK Company
www.hachette.co.uk

www.littlebrown.co.uk

CONTENTS

For my grandmothers,
who'd most likely have disowned me
for most of what is written here,
but whose conversations, time and tellings-off
have inspired at least half of it

and for my mum,
who is such a good mum
who told me so much more than her mum told her,
who was told almost nothing by her mother

SEVEN WAYS TO READ THIS BOOK

You don't need to be told how to read a book. I imagine this isn't the first book you've ever read. If it is, then I'm very honoured that you're here, and wish you the best of luck. I've been told I'm an easy read so hopefully it'll be all right.

I am writing this because the book you're possibly about to read is not only fairly long, especially for a poetry-ish book, it's also quite an odd mixture of memories in prose and essays and then poems and some short stories in between.

Thing is, I love poetry – poetry is what I write the most – but I also love chatting and, amongst other hobbies, chatting is probably what I do the most. In terms of reading, non-fiction is what I read the most. I like it all.

If a poem is 'good enough' it should manage to stand alone without the reader or listener being given any back story or explanation to it. I believe this, and hope the poems in here can stand by themselves if needed. Despite this, when I read a poem written by someone else, I really like knowing a bit more about it. At live readings, I sometimes like the intros to the poems as much as the poems themselves.

When reading poetry books, I tend to delve behind the scenes first, or rummage around a bit in the poem's history, partly because I find it interesting and sometimes, in all honesty, because I have no idea what the poem is about and I want to know. Sometimes poetry makes me feel a bit stupid. Sometimes I like this and let the words wash over me; sometimes I just want to know what is happening.

I also like to know other things about poems; why a poem was written, when, even where if it was in an exciting place or a pub I can then visit and sit in. I've stayed in Brown's Hotel as part of the Laugharne Festival in Wales and I swear the rosé, despite being the sort of luminous pink hen do syrup that I still order even though it gives me the worst hangovers, had just a hint of Dylan Thomas's pen ink to it.

One of my favourite poems in the world is Wilfred Owen's 'Dulce et Decorum est'. For me, it's significant to know that whilst he wrote this war poem from personal experience as a young soldier, a poem supposedly drafted in Craiglockhart War Hospital in Edinburgh after he suffered shell shock in the Somme, Lord Tennyson wrote 'The Charge of the Light Brigade' (which is one of my least favourite poems) after reading a newspaper story in *The Times* whilst he was Poet Laureate.

So this book is a mix of poems I've written and some of the memories, thoughts or research that inspired them. It is sorted into seven themed sections with a short story between each section. There is no real reason for these stories other than that I also love writing stories and sometimes when I'm reading non-fiction or poetry I crave a story.

So I hope you enjoy reading this book, however you choose to do so. Here are some possibilities:

1. **From start to finish, in that order, if you have the time and desire.**
   For the most immersive read – as in, if you fancy doing the thing I love to do and read books in the places where they were written or set or thought of, perhaps even drinking the drink that was being drunk whilst the writing took place, then you might read this book either on an uncomfortable stool by an old metal desk next to your bed; in your bed between 11 p.m. and 2 a.m. when your kid (or pretend kid) has finally gone fully to sleep; on the train journey between Peterborough and Edinburgh staring at the east coast cliffs drinking tea sucked up through a Twix; in the Box Café in Cambridge slurping the best lentil soup the world offers;

in Dukes Bar in Yorkhill, Glasgow drinking rosé or Prosecco with someone you want to either kiss or play chess with, or both.

For the most immersive experience reading the 'Blood' section of this book, I'd say wait till the heaviest, most cramping day of your period, or, if you don't have periods, then read this section whilst punching yourself lightly in the womb area whilst staining your pants with tomato ketchup or brown sauce. For the most immersive experience reading the 'Masturbation' section, just take your time and choose the bits you like best.

2. **Read the poems as you would in a book with just poems in it.**
If you're only here for the poems and want to read them without all the intros and outros and explanations and stories, then there's an index of poems at the back that you can use instead of the contents page.

3. **From start to finish but skip the poems.**
I wrote another book called *Nobody Told Me*. It had prose and poetry like this one. I was told by a lovely audience member after a gig in Cardiff that they really enjoyed it, but *of course skipped all the poems*. Of course. They said it just like that, almost like it was a given; a compliment even. I was slightly insulted but then remembered I also used to do this with Roald Dahl books I read as a kid. I hated when poems in *Charlie and the Chocolate Factory* 'got in the way' of the story. I angrily ignored them all.

I really love poetry so I'd be slightly sad if you did read the book this way, without at least trying a couple of poems out, but it's also OK if you want. Just don't tell me at a gig.

4. **Dip in and out as you wish.**
There is an underlying order to this book and I spent quite a long time working it out. That said, it's in no way vital. All the sections can be flicked through on their own.

So if you fancy a poem about pigeons or rainbows one minute and then a short story about birth the next, then just have a little leaf through the pages or the poetry index and see what jumps out at you. My titles aren't too obscure. The poem about pigeons is called 'dublin pigeon'. The poem about rainbows is called 'rainbow'. The birth story is called 'Push'.

5. **Pretend to read it but don't actually read it.**
   You might not have chosen this book yourself; you might have had it bought for you. As far as I can tell from book signings after gigs, this is often done by well-meaning parents, carers or aunties passing presents to teenage children. Sometimes a friend to a friend.

   Perhaps the person who gave this book to you said, 'You'll love this poet,' but you don't think you will. Perhaps they used my mum's most dreaded word 'should' when they gave it to you, as if reading this book is a moral necessity.

   If this is the case, and you don't really want to read it, but don't want to insult your friend/dad/auntie, then I'd recommend reading the first prose bit of each section and then the following poems: 'magic show', 'fingering to ed sheeran's shape of you', 'pink or blue', 'when i am dead, will you finally shut the fuck up?' and 'like otters', because these are the most commented on online and at gigs and therefore statistically the ones whoever bought this book will most likely have heard.

6. **If you're just here for the fingering poems, and all good if you are, then you will find these near the end of the 'Masturbation' section.**

7. **If you're mainly here to read about my grandmothers, which I would also understand, then the section entitled 'Endings' unfortunately contains most of the stories about them.**

ENDINGS

Dying and Buying Stamps

Mostly it is loss that teaches us about the worth of things.

ARTHUR SCHOPENHAUER

youth

today i am the youngest
i will ever be again

younger than each lick of sea
each sigh of wave on beach
each pebble skipping stream
each kiss of ticking rain

today i am the youngest
i will ever be again

tomorrow –
and the next day

– the same

and so she died, having never tried quinoa

on her deathbed, my granny did not say:
i wish i'd spent more time comparing my face
to other people's faces

on her deathbed, she did not say:
i wish i'd spent more time gazing in the mirror
sucking in my cheekbones
to see if i'd be slightly more appealing
with slightly higher cheekbones

on her deathbed, my granny did not say:
i wish i'd spent more time poking the fold of flesh
which puffs against my breasts
when my hands hang limp

i wish i'd spent more time listening
to people who suggested
i'd look prettier with a fringe

i wish i'd spent more time likening
our unused wedding china
to the richer neighbours' unused wedding china

i wish i'd spent more time
dusting flames on the fireplace
as my children, tucked in blankets, slept,
dreaming they could fly

on her deathbed, my granny did not look me in the eye,
whisper in a final gasp, my hand grasped by her hand:

6

i wish i'd owned that kitchen island
i wish i'd seen fewer shooting stars
i wish i'd mown a neater lawn
i wish i'd tried quinoa

POTTERY

I paint flowers so they will not die.

FRIDA KAHLO

My maternal grandmother died during the coronavirus pandemic. She was my last surviving grandparent and one of the people I've felt closest to on this small, spinning planet. As with many other people grieving loved ones, I watched her funeral on a live stream.

As the allotted time grew closer and a looped video of a calming waterfall assured me that my internet connection was working, I began panicking about what to wear, where in my house to sit, whether to have a glass of Prosecco or a cup of tea, as if these decisions were important. I was watching it on my own. I wondered what other people across the world were wearing and eating at funerals now that no one could see them disrespecting traditions.

In the end, I stayed in tracksuit bottoms, put on a jumper I think she liked and sat on the couch eating a Tunnock's Wafer dipped in very sugary tea, listening to the story of her life whilst staring at a coffin and the back of my mum and auntie's heads two metres apart above the top of wooden pews.

I also, half by accident, half because I was busy crying, forgot to switch off the live stream once the funeral was over. I assumed it would cut off by itself. So I also watched the cleaners disinfecting the crematorium, the local reverend and organ player taking off their jackets, unwrapping and eating sandwiches and chatting about the care home possibly reopening to visitors, and then I watched half of the next person's funeral.

The speeches about my grandma were beautiful. Some of the lines from the reverend, such as, *We would normally sing now, but because of the virus we are not permitted to sing in public* or, *Before we run out of streaming time,* made it feel a little like a dystopian sci-fi film.

After the funeral ended, it felt horrible being on your own. I thought it would be fine. Nice even. Calm. My gran hated funerals. I'm not a massive fan either. Is anyone? Like most people, I'm also not too big on others seeing me sob. But it was shit. No number of lovely text messages and phone calls from family and friends could replace a quick hug. I watched my mum walking out of the building and all I wanted was to be there. I didn't think I'd crave seeing other people's faces in the flesh so much.

I made another cup of sweet tea and wrote some poems.

There's a comfort I find in writing that I don't get from much else: trying to find desirable words to frame thoughts onto a page; playing with metaphors; deciding which silences merit line breaks or commas or dashes or just a little more blank page all to themselves. Like moulding and carving clay. Like that scene in *Ghost* where Patrick Swayze sits behind Demi Moore and kisses her neck while she tries to make some sort of vase on her pottery wheel in the middle of the night because she can't sleep.

I guess in this metaphor, Patrick Swayze's hot, half-naked body behind me represents the comfort and excitement that the writing process gives, and the clay lump spinning in my palms are the scattered ideas which at some point I can hopefully mould into whatever poetic shape I am able.

I really like the idea of poetry as pottery, but thinking about that particular scene more carefully, it is maybe not the best metaphor.

Demi Moore is actually a very skilled potter and when Patrick

Swayze comes and sits behind her, he fucks up the vase she's already almost completed so that instead of finishing her creation they end up rubbing wet clay into each other's hands, abandoning the vase altogether and undoubtedly having the sort of sex that Aphrodite's clitoris was created for. Nonetheless, the thought of that scene is a nice tangent from grief and one which I think my gran would have approved of because she fancied Patrick Swayze in that scene as much as I did.

Writing is distraction and focus in one. A hot-water bottle pushed directly onto cramps. It also seems a bit sick sometimes: selfish, self-centred, narcissistic. Like, *That's a good line about your grandma's funeral, yeah, nice, Hollie, keep that bit in the poem.*

In the end though, I love it. The writing. The editing. The reading back. The reading of other people's poems sculpted for various other reasons and in various different ways.

So most of the poems and memories and stories I write are primarily for myself: to ease pain; to paint; to heal; to reorganise anger; to giggle; to think more clearly; to convince myself of feelings that maybe weren't quite true; to have fun; to play with language; to imagine alternative realities; to wallow; to question; to reconsider; to remember; to give some sort of shape to things that overwhelm me.

Like death. Like birth. Like how it feels watching a funeral live streamed into your living room. Like the desperate yearning I now have, to mould a pot out of a chunk of moist clay whilst being tousled from behind by a horny lover.

similes about how much i miss gran

like spring, when winter runs over, and strangers agree, shivering in bus stops, despite the comfort thick woollen jumpers can initially spark, that they've all had enough of this cold now; like youth, when you're too old to plan; like unbroken bones when they break; like waking to decaf; like blood when it's due; like fat on a newborn; like earrings post-partum; like offers on foods you can only afford while the offer is on; like popcorn, in those ridiculous cinemas that refuse to sell popcorn; like clouds blocking sun in a park when the light is too fierce for the echo of white on the page and the story, the story was getting so good so you sweat and you swear and you squint

– i miss you like this

chasing ceremony/convincing myself

i'll not get to your funeral.
that's fine.

i know you'll not make mine.
you hate the fussing anyway.
your favourite colour's yellow
not black.

on your street, when next door died
too soon before you did
neighbours clapped the passing hearse
as if the corpse were on a royal tour
you turned towards your daughters

here –
don't you dare do that for me

hair cradled into rollers
each night until the night you left
still lifting life with curls

the laws do not allow me
to stand and watch a lifetime
exit puppet-show-sized curtains
as tears try to console each other
two metres apart;

the only good things
are the sandwich platters
afterwards, anyway,
and we can't even have those

12

so i'll celebrate you here
three hundred miles from home

wear that butter-coloured jumper
you once said made me pretty
wallow in self-pity
as if your loss is all my loss

let lips tremble all they want
eyes swell to embarrassed red
too obvious a grief to meet with any friends
even with the recommended
coffin space between us

no need for all that, huh?
who cares about it, right?
i already said i love you
so many times in life:

each time i said i love you;
each postcard that i sent;
each nightie that you lent me;
each evening that we wasted
watching prerecords of *countdown*
at a volume that i'm almost sure
has pierced some of my eardrum;
in refining just that splash of milk
to slightly hint your tea with
till you looked inside the cup again
and smiled, and said *that's perfect*

deficit

written before coronavirus literally stopped us from touching

when newborn babies' cords are cut
from mother's blood, the heartbeats split
skin to skin is held as high
as milk to mouth, as breast to lip

waves crash;
we clap them for their constant flow
the moon pulls slow, the cliff face purrs
us babies grown to adults now
still skin for skin our skin still yearns

but *no!* we warn – a dirty word now
do not touch the signs keep guard
red ropes round the precious nudes
art collections kept in darkness

hark! the morning birds declare
berries passed from beak to beak
sheep huddled tight in hillside frosts
make saunas of their body heat

not us! we're not such basic beasts!
shivering in single file
a handshake to greet our neighbours
elbows off, use fork and knife

husband must touch only wife
do not hug that child in need

to stroke yourself, still ancient sin
let grandpa sit alone to grieve

rubs reserved for v.i.p.s
massage parlours, highly priced
our body's biggest organ stifled
depression rates are on the rise

no wonder we fill homes with fur
purring skins upon our laps
calming creature comfort blankets
outlets for our wanton pats

oh precious pets to rub to rub
cuddle to our hearts' content
newborn babies passed like snacks
oh let me have a snuggle next!

to be that cat for just one day!
to be that baby rocked again!
to be that dog brushed and brushed!
to hug to hug to hug to hug!

but no! let's hoard that precious touch
convince ourselves of scarcity
rip shadows from the feet they cling to
monogamy of tenderness

as if breathing too much love
into too many choking lips
will mean one day our hugged-out hearts
have no more heat to give

but tides! keep kissing sand and rock
but sun! spills hot on naked lands
but winds! run never-ending laps
palms always warm when holding hands

like telling stories
like singing songs
like drying sheets in midday sun
like kneading knots from backbone aches
like moonlit walks
like jumping waves
like arms round waists
like stroking skin
there's nothing lost!
there's nothing lost!
however much we give

our single human superpower
whilst hope still cradles bones

infinite; renewable
until the sun explodes

r
a
in

drop

unleashed

from full-bellied sky

for the briefest of solitary flights

now splashed into sea, river or stream
on the palm of a child catching cloud petals
pierced on the tip of commuters' umbrellas
dripped into footprint, puddle or gutter
flimsy skin ruptured teardrop released
backintoborderlesslife

lucky

for you, gran, who, more ill than you'd ever been, kept saying you were 'so lucky'

one day it might be us
neighbours come to visit
knees creaking as we stand up
farting as we walk

we
who cannot shower any more
washing at the sink
teeth separate from our mouths

one day it might be us
nurses gather round
children frightened by our sunken face
hair the shade of cloud

right now
we sit with you, gran
clasp your cooling hands
you say you feel *so very lucky*
i find it hard to understand

grandchild

for anyone who has loved and lost this label

i'm no longer anybody's grandchild now
just a daughter and a mother and i know
how much i'm blessed with these but as pure
enjoyment goes, i liked being a grandchild
best of all: who will spoil me rotten now?
who will feed me sugared drinks when i've
just brushed my teeth for bed? who will
put the fire on when i am towelled from the
shower? yes, yes, i know and i am grateful
for all the time we shared; some people
never meet their grandparents at all; so many
people don't; but i did, so let me mourn
and let me moan

DISCUSSING ORAL SEX WITH GRAN

My gran used to go into hysterics when she recalled the time she went into the local hairdresser's and asked for a 'cut and blowjob'. I like to give myself some credit for this. We had been talking about this particular sex act that week because my gran had been told that blowjobs were a myth: *Why would anyone want to do that?* She was also made to believe, until her third child, that babies were born out of the anus, because that's where the doctor told her to push and, to be fair, that's how it often feels. It did for me.

'In those days you did not ask any questions or talk about those aspects of the body. You weren't told anything and you didn't ask anything.'
 'How crap.'
 'Yes. It was, my darling.'

After birth, she said it was seen as unladylike to mention anything about the tearing or the bleeding, so many women just sort of pretended everything was fine, which meant they got a lot less sympathy or help with their body's post-birth healing and had 'little excuse' not to have penetrative sex the minute their husband fancied it again.
 I've spent a lot more time talking to my gran about bodies and senses and sex than I hear most grandchildren do. It was one of the most unexpected and enjoyable treats of our time together.
 I loved both my grandmothers to heights that I hope will always

dizzy me. I didn't speak to both so openly. Just my mum's mum, Gran: about sex, passion, about why I should've learnt Latin; about word derivations; about tight bottoms and dancing and travel. She only started going abroad when she was in her seventies. She met my grandad just as he was back from war. He never wanted to go abroad again after what he experienced whilst travelling as a soldier. Fair enough, it sounded horrific.

So, in her seventies, after my brilliant grandad had passed away, largely thanks to my mum and auntie and dad, she finally stretched her legs around Europe. One place she didn't get to was Italy.

My other grandmother – Granny – I mainly spoke to about soup recipes, the dangerous staircase, what the neighbours were up to, how to ignore conversations you couldn't be arsed joining in with and, nearer the end of her life, how tiring it was being very old.

My gran lived longest, and I called her at least once a week.

Whatever the reason for the call, within about five minutes Gran would be saying, 'How did we start talking about this?' as the conversation drifted to bottoms and dirty jokes once again and I'd get the blame for apparently having moved the discussion on to these topics when, hand on heart, it was more often her. Or at least a solid, sordid half-half.

Having talked to my gran about these things makes me both very thankful and very angry. Thankful for myself, angry for the past.

She said once that she and her friends were born into the wrong generation and would have much preferred to have been born when I was born. When people romanticised the past, my gran always pulled them up. 'No, no, it wasn't better in the fifties. No, really, it wasn't.'

Once when I was visiting we read a newspaper article together, the headline of which claimed that women's libidos were lower than men's.

A survey had found that the women studied enjoyed a hot bath or a massage as much as or more than having sex, whereas the vast majority of the men asked preferred sex to the massages or baths. For the newspaper, this finding was enough to garner the implication that women's libidos were lower.

After we'd read the article, my gran nodded and said, 'Of course,' as if it were totally obvious; a true, incontrovertible fact. She told me that many women just don't really like sex that much and certainly not as much as men do. I have had this same remark made to me by many other (heterosexual) women, as well as a fair number of other women whose sexualities I knew nothing about, whilst chatting, pissed, in book signing queues post-gigs.

Obviously, what the research had defined as 'sex' was p in v (penis in vagina) sex; anything else was excluded.

I disagreed with my gran and with the article. Not about the enjoyment of massages and hot baths, but about the lower sexual appetite proposal resulting from it. For me, the best sex is pretty much all about massage. Lips massaging lips, hands massaging skin, genitals massaging genitals. A kissing of skin to skin until all skin feels like marshmallows oozing, melting in the microwave on top of a digestive biscuit.

Simplified study aside, my gran and I then talked for hours about this article and about pleasure and we ate a lot of Galaxy chocolate squares and Turkish delight and by the end of the hours chatting we had worked out that many women of her generation were told that the orgasm was a myth for anyone without a penis, and I said I was happy that wasn't true and she said, 'Trust you to be so crude,' and we both blushed awkwardly and giggled a lot.

She then told me something which has marked my mind ever since: as young girls, many of her peers had devoured romance novels and because of these novels they had been so looking forward to having sex. Then they had sex. Then they had it again. It was, she whispered, 'Such a disappointment for so many.'

I don't think many women then had much of a chance of anything else. When my gran got married, she said her mother told her two things about sex, by which of course she meant p in v. Nothing else was ever mentioned. I think that's why my gran made so many jokes once I was old enough to hear them. In her words, I was fair game to laugh with about these things, 'what with all the dirty poems you write'.

She told me her mother, in true romantic fashion, had told my gran, a nineteen-year-old woman about to move away from home for the first time, two things.

Firstly: sex was an obligation; one of her duties as a wife. Not only would she vow this before God, it would also legally be true. As late as 1991 in Britain, husbands were exempt from raping their wives because, legally, marriage meant implied consent to sex at any point post vows.

This legislation sprang from a seventeenth-century statement by a man called Sir Matthew Hale, which was subsequently passed from Britain and adopted into the common law of many Commonwealth countries:

> The husband cannot be guilty of a rape committed by himself upon his lawful wife, for by their mutual matrimonial consent and contract the wife hath given herself up to her husband, consent which she cannot retract.

Despite the criminalisation of marital rape in 1991, a recent survey shows that people, especially the over-sixty-fives, are still 'iffy' about the idea of consent being needed in marriage.*

Secondly: my great-grandmother told my gran that sex was not only 'rather unpleasant', but also dirty and sinful, a sin that she none-theless would have to commit because of the God-blessed union.

What a sexual pep talk that must have been. *Dear daughter, both God and Law now bind you to have sex but it'll be shite and you'll likely go to hell for it.* I'd like to see anyone find vast physical comfort

---

* YouGov Attitudes to Sexual Consent Survey, 1 December 2018

in life with an opener like that.

After my gran told me this I asked her lots more questions. She chatted. We ate more chocolate. I thought of the poem by Liz Lochhead called 'Social History'. It is about all the sex her mother didn't have. The second verse begins with:

The sex my mother could've had
but didn't
sounded fantastic

Despite often having loving and happy marriages, so many women seemed to have lived without having felt many of the lovely, safe and complimentary feelings my body offers me, and the fact that the reason for this was not their or their husband's fault – I was assured that most of the husbands she knew of never forced their legal right and were almost as uneducated as the women were about their own bodies – but purely that of the cultural and political climate they lived through, is quite shite.

I never imagined it would be early conversations with my gran (and later, often hysterically, my aunty, mum and gran together) that would have catapulted me into questioning so many things about my own body; about my turn ons and offs and all the historical factors that have gone and still go into inspiring, silencing or shaming those.

Perhaps in the not too distant future, I'll be the one shouting 'for god's sake mother, what *are* you and your granddaughter talking about!' as I stumble into a blowjob joke or power shower chat between my daughter and my mum.

Perhaps there's something about that skipping of a generation that allows more freedom and less embarrassment between grandparent and grandchild.

Perhaps I just got lucky. Perhaps it was that dash of brandy in the milk.

lie back and think of scotland

and she jokes   *in our day it was just*
                            'lie back and think of england'
and she jokes   *for scottish women that was even worse*

and she jokes   *oh you young ones, so provocative*
and she jokes   *we were told it was normal if it hurt*

and i sigh, say   *that one hasn't changed*

and she jokes   *we weren't told that we could crave things too*
and she jokes   *sex was like another set domestic chore*

and she jokes   *the clitoris, we thought it was a herb!*
and she jokes   *shopping in our heads whilst we were bored*

and i sigh, say   *that one hasn't changed*

and she jokes   *how much we loved to read romantic novels*
and she jokes   *the wedding night; how excited we were then*
and she jokes   *the disappointment once the deed was done*
and she jokes   *if only we could live that part again*
and she jokes   *it's a pity that we can't*

and she jokes

and neither of us laugh

culaccino

*(*Culaccino *is an Italian word, which has no direct English translation. It has several meanings, my favourite of which is: 'The mark left on the surface of a wooden table by a sweating, wet, ice-filled cold glass'.)*

the scent of a story still clings to your chair
unaware the narrator is gone
your nightgowns are folded and boxed for collection
your pots of fake flowers act like nothing is wrong

on my knees, on the rug, still glittered with skin
i pocket the daydreams you dropped
your longings so locked in by duty and place
let me flick past the page where you stopped

ink those stockings again up the backs of my legs
let me stride through the almosts that tittered your lips
shame has lessened its cuffs now
your ladylike scars, mere marks on my wrists

one last clink to you, gran, italy calls
they say the poems are gorgeous this time of year
yes, i promise to press at least one red poppy
yes, i promise to dip all my toes in the shore

then i'll sip on espresso; scoff all the ricotta;
melt mozzarella; lap up the days
from the plate; lick gelato; sip on prosecco
let glitterball moons keep the night-times awake

so come away with me, gran, let us dance in this dusk
those jezebel jokes were too good to waste
let's take up the hems you politely declined
spin topping stars till our anklebones break

let me scream all the screams your times turned to sin
waltz all the waltzes your fingers forbade
let us hang out our hearts in this hot lashing rain
till we are both of us drenched, our bodies opaque

and yes,
i am picking my favourite laments
from your never dids, never wills, too little, too lates
but figs ripen too fast for the sunday times crossword
and i'm not bothered to learn how to bake

so vieni con me, a Italia, gran!
feel the healing of heat on uncensored soles
let's laugh in piazzas, sleep face down in pizza
i miss you, amore mio

kiss

> *for saints have hands that pilgrims' hands do touch,*
> *and palm to palm is holy palmers' kiss*
>
> SHAKESPEARE, *Romeo and Juliet*

for lovers; for all kissing

palm already kissing palm
we lean a little in

timid lips to timid lips
the air between them crushed
until they kiss

now, lips kissing lips
our lips begin to part
tongues searching in the dark
two torchlights passing stars
until they kiss

now, tongue kissing tongue
and lips still kissing lips
chests lean a little in until they kiss

now, chest kissing chest
and tongue still kissing tongue
hands kiss hair kiss neck kiss skull
hands kiss cheek kiss breasts kiss breath
crotch kisses cocked-out leg
legs kiss legs kiss feet kiss toes

lips kiss cock kiss tongue kiss throat
tongue kiss clit kiss lips kiss clit
kiss fingertips kiss tongue

our bodies bundled sweating
into kissing heaps of heat;

contented, we release;
unravel breath from breath
toes unkissing toes
legs unkissing legs

lips unkissing nipple
chest unkissing cheek
hands unkissing heart

till giggling, we fall apart
just palm still kissing palm

fill your basket

for Violet

only so long
bones will be covered
by muscle, muscle
covered by flesh

only so long
limbs will be able to stretch
ears and throat
fill up with song

only so long
skin will be able to hold
a hug; a kiss; a caress

till then, let us cram
these baskets of body
with what life
we are lucky to get

stamps

for Vim, Helen, Tammy and Lj

on that afternoon
when i wrongly thought
i would die

the empty bucket
did not bother me

✓ never climbed machu picchu
✓ never gambled in las vegas
✓ never swam in tanks with dolphins
✓ never walked the wall of china
✓ my spanish is still shite

did not cross my mind
that mind too full instead   with

✓ friends not called for months
✓ hugs unravelled much too rushed
✓ words we did not say
✓ a gift i never gave to mum
✓ reflections never lingered on

a postcard filled with soppy thoughts
crumpling in my bag to send
when i remember to buy stamps

MIMICKING THE VICAR

Every one of us has a skeleton beneath our skin. Like, right there. Almost exactly like the skeletons you see hung up at Halloween or on bracelets on Buddhists' wrists or on the flags of pirate ships. Just there, in our bodies, close enough to touch. I have never been able to get over this fact.

There is a place called the Sedlec Ossuary in the Czech Republic. It's also known as the Bone Church. Inside, there are said to be between forty and seventy thousand people's bones used as decorations: there are bone candelabras, bone coats of arms, bone mounds, bone bunting – if you can call it bunting when it is made of human skulls. I'm not sure what the rules of bunting are.

I went to the chapel when I was seventeen with my friend Hanna. I'm glad we went. I'm not glad we went hungover.

The chapel is the most amazing and gruesome thing I've ever seen. I still don't know how I feel about it. The artist (or maybe in this instance, interior designer) who created the decorations was a woodcarver called František Rint. His signature is on the wall near the entrance to the chapel. It is written in bones.

Rint was given this artistic commission in 1870 by the Schwarzenberg family. Before his transformation of this chapel, the bones had been simply stacked inside the ossuary by a half-blind monk during the early fourteenth century.

The overabundance of bones for such a small site stems from 1278 when the abbot of the Cistercian monastery in Sedlec is said to have travelled to Golgotha, the site on which, according to the Gospels, Jesus was crucified. He returned with Holy Soil, which he is believed to have sprinkled over the abbey's cemetery, turning this hitherto largely unknown chapel into a five-star burial site.

Its popularity became particularly problematic during the Black Death in the mid-fourteenth century and the Hussite Wars of the early fifteenth century. Quite simply, the graveyard was too popular to contain all the bones. Eventually, I guess, bunting seemed the most suitable solution.

Before this unexpected visit to the Bone Church, I'd had few actual conversations about death whilst growing up. Nobody talked about death in any depth. I was fortunate enough not to have anyone close to me die until I was in my twenties. I am still trying to be OK with the idea of my own death, but, like many people, I'm absolutely not.

Occasionally, people around me will start talking about death and they often say how they'd hate to live for ever because they'd watch their friends and family getting older and dying and wouldn't that be awful and sad? In these moments, I nod my head like, *Yeah, yeah, absolutely agree, that would be horrible, I'd rather die*, because I don't want to look like an unfeeling bitch but inside I'm mainly thinking, *No fucking way. I'd still rather live for ever than actually die*.

The only close reminder of death during this privileged childhood came once a year at Halloween. To this day, the sight of a skeleton hanging in paper chains around October time, all jangly-limbed, occasionally wearing a top hat, compels my fingers to begin immediately prodding my own flesh.

First, I examine my hands. I pinch the fingers of one hand with the thumb and index of the other, feeling for the bones, connected by the knuckles, up to the fingernail tips. My fingernails are already dead, I'm told. Like hair, which we can cut painlessly because it's dead. I find this weird. Growing up, I was sold so much crap about how important my hair was to my appearance and my 'femininity' or 'prettiness', and which new must-have product I should buy to make it more shiny than the last must-have shiny hair product did, that when I learned that it was dead already, that hair, I started to find it a bit freaky. Just dead cells spilling out of holes in your head. Just a big heap of dead atop your head.

I feel all the bones in my hand and I wriggle my hand, then I swap hands and feel the bones beneath the other. *There is an actual hand skeleton there,* I think, *just like the one I am about to hang on my wall to scare the shit out of my friend with when she opens the door.*

Then I feel my ribs and I think of ribs and barbecue sauce and that story I was told at primary school about Adam and Eve and how women come second to men because they needed a guy's rib to be made from and then got damned for ever with labour pains and periods, all because they tried to make friends with animals and eat healthily.

Then I feel for my backbone.

If I am feeling brave, I go to my eyes. I find this part the scariest of all. I feel the bones around my eye socket and think of that hole that, for me, makes skeletons so frightening. Perhaps I watched Hitchcock's *The Birds* too young. Perhaps I watched *every* horror film too young. Perhaps I stupidly thought that watching horror films made me cooler and more mature whereas in reality they just left me scared of the dark for the rest of my life. I have banned myself from watching any more. I still cannot leave the shower curtain drawn without seeing a psycho blade, I cannot walk down a corridor at night without seeing two tricycles ridden by child ghosts. I panic when driving alone in case one of my daughter's dolls has come to life and has a creepy vendetta against me.

So I outline my eyebrows with my thumb and feel under the ridge a bit and try to imagine the day this is all that will be left of me. Just bones with holes where the eyes used to be. Just holes where everything I've ever seen in the world entered my consciousness. I also try not to imagine this ever.

I often then think of vultures pecking eyeballs out and then I think of what happened in India when they tried to cull the vultures because they thought there were too many of them, so they shot a load of them, or poisoned them – I can't remember – but *then* they realised that the vultures had actually been super helpful at stripping animal carcasses clean and now, because they had been culled by the clever humans, there were fewer vultures chewing all the meat off dead animal bones meaning all the meat was left on rotting animal carcasses, which *then* meant that the wild dog population increased because of all this extra food that they were finding and because of *this* the wild dog numbers went up so much that there was a rabies outbreak and us clever humans realised that nature was an intimately interwoven wonder which we should maybe have stopped fucking with quite so much until we better understood the true talents of vultures. Then I think of skeletons again.

Despite this fear of my own bones and my increasing inability to watch any scary movie with my eyes open, I always loved Halloween as a child and still do.

Halloween was a big thing in my family. I grew up in England, but my parents are Scottish. Halloween is nicer in Scotland than in England. Not always, but a bit.

For a start, when you knock on people's doors in Scotland, you don't call it trick or treating. In Scotland, it's called guising and the point is to earn your chocolate or sweets or money or (sigh, fuck's sake) fruit rather than simply threaten or demand these things. A song at the door. A poem recited. I'm not saying there are no eggs thrown in Scotland.

The costumes in Scotland are also different.

The one time I spent Halloween in Scotland I was seven and my older cousin Tracy came out dressed as Minnie Mouse and handed me a Rudolph the Red-Nosed Reindeer costume. We were going to a party with her friends where I'd be the only English one there and I thought she was trying to set me up.

Here's my English cousin, she thinks it's fucking Christmas, twat.
But she wasn't.

35

In Scotland, you dress up as anything for Halloween. The idea isn't so much to dress up as vampires and scare the living crap out of people who have gone to bed early, lights off, pretending they're out. I can understand why people hate Halloween.

The party was great, my cousin and her friends spent a lot of time, in between dancing and parading our costumes and stuffing gigantic marshmallows into our mouths, getting me to repeat lines about the Queen, for them to attempt to copy in my accent before falling about laughing.

Back in England, our house was Halloween headquarters. Under the stairs we had a huge bin bag stuffed with masks and cloaks and face paints and fake blood. Sometimes during the rest of the year, if I wasn't too scared to look in the back of the cupboard, I'd peek in the bag just to get excited again. I loved the game where Mum hung jam doughnuts from a string and all the kids in our village came over and we had to eat the doughnuts with no hands or lip-licks, blood jam dripping down our chins within minutes.

I also loved being allowed outside at night to go walking in the dark. I loved knocking on the neighbours' doors, having a little glimpse into people's lives, saying hello to people you never otherwise got the excuse to say hello to.

There was nothing else in my upbringing, other than freezing your toes carol singing at Christmas time if you were forced to by the school, or maybe taking an occasional pack of biscuits over when someone new moved into the street, that actually involved saying hello to my lesser-known neighbours. I loved going from door to door, saying 'Trick or treat' and then judging them on what level of confectionery they handed to us.

One old woman across the street used to give bubblegum. She was a favourite. Another middle-aged couple handed out whole packets of chocolate buttons. Also excellent. One household of 'do-gooders' gave satsumas. Not our favourite.

What a strange insult the term 'do-gooders' is; to berate people who are trying to 'do good'. I'm not sure whether our irritation at this sort of Ned Flanders *Simpsons* stereotype is simply to appease our own guilt for not attempting to do similar amounts of goodness in life, or if people who are always constantly kind or helpful or healthy are genuinely very irritating regardless of our own guilty conscience. Either way, I didn't work that hard on my scary costume for a fucking satsuma.

One Halloween, when I was nine, I ran home sobbing after just fifteen minutes of trick or treating. It was the first year we had been allowed to go on our tour of the neighbourhood without any of our parents and the first year I had created my costume without their supervision.

The group of us kids had collected sweets from a few houses and said thank you to a few neighbours when we arrived at number 29. (For anyone who knows where I lived as a kid, don't go egging that house. It might not be number 29. I can't actually remember the number, I just thought it sounded better to pretend I remembered it.)

We knocked on the door of number 29 and stood back. The local vicar answered. I recognised him from school assemblies.

We chorused, 'Trick or treat, happy Halloween,' and smiled at him and waited for another round of sweets to fill our pumpkin baskets. He looked at me, stared silently for what felt like much longer than it likely was, then called me despicable and slammed the front door. Maybe he called me disgusting. Maybe he just tutted. It was horrible enough that I immediately turned and scarpered away from my friends, up the hill back home.

When my dad answered the front door, I began to sob, blurting out the story frantically between snotty sniffs, my coat still wrapped around me. When I took my coat off, dad looked at me and said, 'Oh shite, Hollie, let's change your costume, love.'

I had dressed as a vicar. Buttoned-up white shirt, black tie attempting to mimic some sort of dog collar and a giant wooden-cross necklace my friend Caroline had given me around my neck.

I didn't know that Halloween was controversial. All the

Christians in my family celebrated it in a similar way to how many of the non-Christian families in my school still got presents from Santa Claus and dressed up as a pregnant virgin in the school nativity.

I didn't know about the different types of Christianity or that some Christians might object to Halloween.

My school was Church of England and we didn't talk about Halloween but I'd never really noticed that. My cousins' schools in Scotland were Church of Scotland and they spent October making witch's hats and pumpkin masks. My daughter's school is Church of England and they do not celebrate Halloween at all, whereas her Scottish cousins' Church of Scotland school still has a Halloween disco. We are both very jealous of this.

Perhaps it's a Scotland–England thing; maybe because Halloween is said by some to have originated from ancient Celtic harvest festivals. Perhaps it was just those four particular schools. Perhaps Scottish Christians just like making paper ghosts.

I didn't know that the house I'd knocked at aged nine, dressed up as a vicar, was the house in which many of the village church goers, including the vicar, gathered in anti – or alternative – Halloween celebrations.

After a few minutes wiping my tears as my parents explained the vicar's possible objections to my costume, my friends knocked on the door to see if I was coming out again. I nodded and then looked down. I was still in full clerical clothing. My mum ran to the toilet, grabbed all the loo rolls she could and my parents frantically wrapped them around my head and body while filling me in briefly about Ancient Egyptian traditions. It's the closest I've ever got to a 'you shall go to the ball' Cinderella moment.

At twenty years old, I worked as an assistant teacher in the French Caribbean for a year. As October approached, I was asked to teach some classes about Halloween and Bonfire Night. 'British Autumn Traditions' the teacher called it.

I was in Guadeloupe. There, the main festival during these months was All Saints' Day, which is the day after Halloween. I had never heard of it before and I found the celebration of it incredible. Hailing originally from the Catholic commemoration of saints who had died and in the Catholic view 'achieved heaven', it had, on this island at least, been extended into a celebration of not only Saints, but anybody you loved who had died.

On All Saints' Day, I was taken with one of the teachers to the local cemetery, where food and drink vans lined the streets. There were no graves, only large, cement-topped family tombs; the whole place was packed with families and friends sitting atop these tombs, picnicking and playing music loudly and drinking Ti' Punch and telling stories all day about their loved ones. It was very beautiful.

The next week at school, the pupils did class presentations about their All Saints' Day festivities. It was then my turn to speak about my own 'Autumn Traditions', which, I realised at that moment, had consisted mainly of begging sugar, and celebrating the capture and torture of a Roman Catholic by watching a puppet burn slowly on a big pile of flames, while families of hedgehogs legged it from the pile of wood they'd thought was their new home for a couple of days.

I'm not condoning what Guy Fawkes was trying to do when he placed barrels of gunpowder in the basement of the Houses of Parliament, but standing in front of a classroom of kids who had just described a day's feasting in memory of their departed loved ones as I told them about Halloween and Bonfire Night felt a little lopsided.

Afterwards, arms were raised:

So, what have sweets got to do with the devil?
When do you celebrate family you've lost?
Are the fireworks meant to look like the gunpowder exploding?
Do you actually put a man on the fire?
Do you like the royal family?
Have you ever had tea with the Queen?

I left that classroom thinking how messed up my traditions were and how I was determined to take some of the All Saints' Day ideas home with me. I now celebrate All Saints' Day in part by eating the favourite foods of the ones I've loved and lost while chatting about them round dinner. So far, this consists of cheese toasties (with mustard) and cream of celery soup for my paternal grandparents, a fried breakfast from Morrisons for my maternal grandad, a sticky toffee pudding for a close friend and a Fruit Corner yoghurt, Galaxy chocolate and bean burgers for my gran. I have purposefully ignored any of my grandparents' love of liver and onions, mince and potatoes and tongue sandwiches.

My friend told me about a bookshop in London where, as you left, the elderly woman who worked there would shout, 'Thank you, remember you die!' as the little bell tinkled the door closed. I try to do that to myself every now and then.

I still watch the fireworks on Bonfire Night and I still go trick or treating with my daughter. I tried to hang up doughnuts like my mum used to but I couldn't work out how to and so just tied all the kids' hands behind their backs as they plummeted their faces into plates of jam doughnuts. Perhaps I'm kidding myself that these festivals are only traditions and are doing no harm any more. Perhaps this is true. I still poke my face with my fingers after hanging paper skeletons across my living room every October.

Saying all this, neither Halloween nor Bonfire Night seem to provoke as negative a bout of emotions as Christmas does for many of those around me. It seems skeletons and satanic worshipping and Catherine wheels and gunpowder plots exploding in the sky do not incite as much self-hatred and sadness as the idealised notions of family life and flamboyant present-giving that the commercial hijacking of Christmas has brought. *A Christmas Poem* by Wendy Cope springs to mind here.

flash

when autumn comes to strip my bones
please fling the ashes somewhere warm
i pass this graveyard every walk
the headstones look so bored

don't bother with that burrowed mud
for blossoms plucked to wilt upon
as children, scratching moss from stone
count up my years, and carry on

go mourn me (if you want to mourn)
somewhere we have worn with love;
grab two porn star martinis
gulp each floating passion cup

go search the forests' thickest trunks
mourn me from the highest branch
blow raspberries at the grinning moon
legs paddling the stars

go mourn me in the cinema
scoff popcorn long before the film
go mourn me in a daytime bath
let bubbles overspill

fill your palms with nyjer seeds
watch the goldfinch flock
clamber up the campsie fells
flash the whole world far below
yours tits or arse or cock

i promise i'll be with you;
can't promise i'll not watch

salad bowl wisdom

for Granny

you taught me not to worry; how to save a celery soup with salt and cream; how to smile and nod and move on when the battles are not worth the screams; i have mastered that technique, imagine you beside me as i turn away from shouty cunts; you taught me how to spy unseen behind a half-closed curtain when the neighbours' routines change; that life is short; that nothing good is certain; that nothing bad is certain; that days are long when you're alone; you taught me how to fill up the smallest bowl at the salad bar at pizza hut in such a way that while paying for the small bowl you actually get the same amount as the top-priced large container: raise the base up first with coleslaw, potato salad next, cold pasta at the end, overlap cucumber slices all around the edge hence creating extra wall space, fill this engineering masterpiece from the sides up to a central peak, two times higher than the bowl itself;

walk slowly to the table, winking to your friends

the whole world in your hands

POWDERED DIPS

One of the things I love about being oldish – at least old enough to be viewed without doubt as an adult – is being able to go into shops that offer free testers, and take the testers. I mean food testers. I'm not bothered by sachets of hand creams or squirts of perfume. Testers you can eat.

When I was younger, there was an annual farmers' show in the next town. Amongst all the 'who has the biggest sheep' competitions, candyfloss stalls, 'win a goldfish you'll likely let fall to its death on your journey home' games; in amongst all of that was a food tent.

In this tent were endless lines of wooden tables and on them sat opened jars of jams and sauces and pickles and dips and chocolate spread and crackers you could soak it all up with, before moving on to a dessert of broken-up pieces of fudge and biscuits and brownies.

There was one stall in particular that sold different sorts of creamy dips that you bought as powders and then added water to. We never bought any of the powdered dips (they were, if I am to believe my mum, about £200 a jar) but I do remember them being the most delicious thing I'd ever tasted, scooped up with crisps from the baskets waiting at the edge of the stall, just at the right height for my thieving hands.

Together, Mum and I trailed these stalls, she passing me free testers, me shovelling in each one until we walked out the other end of the tent, smug and satisfied.

When I'd reached the golden age of thirteen, I was allowed off with my friends at this farming fair. To save money on lunch, I took them all to the food tent, going on and on all the way there about these dips and crisps and chocolates you could just take for nothing.

'For nothing?'
'For nothing, I swear to you.'

We went in and looked around, realising immediately that we were fucked. The hands grabbing the testers were all adult hands, much larger and more sensible and more sure of themselves than our wee chipolata fingers. We were intimidated, but determined. A few rules were quickly established:

1. *Look like you're interested in buying it.*
2. *Talk about how much you're wanting to buy something.*
3. *Put your shoulders back.*
4. *Be confident, just go right up, just right up, and just take a cracker and just dip it in the jam, all right?*
5. *I'm not going first.*

We stood back a little, practising our stares and nods and adult-like conversations about why we intended to buy chutney that afternoon. We walked slowly up to the dip stall first, perusing the wares as convincingly as we could.

I pointed to a pot of pink mayonnaise and started telling my very interested friend about how my mum would love that one for her birthday. My friend nodded back like, *Mine too, for sure, for sure, shall we try it though, yeah, just to see, like?*

I stuck out my arm to grab a cracker, and was immediately spotted and stopped by the bastard stallholder. We tried a few more stalls and reached the end of the row without so much as a morsel of a broken chunk of bread, not one of the stallholders persuaded of our intentions to smother our parents with chutney hampers, if only we'd been able to have a tiny taste of the produce, please.

From that day on, I romanticised adulthood as the age when I would be old enough to test all the free dips at the food tent without anyone holding me back. I would never have to pay for a meal again. I'd be minted.

This flair for freebies runs in my family. My dad's side mainly. A quick thank you to my Aunty June here for my unapologetic doggy bag demands.

My dad himself is fairly gifted at this too, though his obsession is less focused on free testers and takeaways and more on the very cheap home-made cakes you get at local school fetes and church dos.

Holidays in Scotland. We'd be merrily driving along until my dad would suddenly swerve as he saw a makeshift cardboard sign pinned to a tree advertising a local school fete or village hall festival. He'd pull up outside a local building – a school we had absolutely nothing to do with was the most embarrassing – and get us all out of the car to go find the tombola, lucky dips and stalls of 20p sponge cake slices made, I now realise, by mothers guilt-tripped into raising money for underfunded educational establishments. My dad loves home-made cakes.

My granny was less focused on cheap and more on free; that ability to take an adequate assortment of treats without it spilling over into actual theft.

When friends came up to Scotland for the holidays, we'd go to Loch Lomond, where my granny would discourage us from entering certain souvenir shops that lined the loch and direct us instead into others. All sold the same Scottish tourist tack – tartan tea towels, Nessie teddies, tins of shortbread biscuits – but I realised after a few visits that the solid differential between the shops was based on which handed out free testers of tablet and shortbread as we walked in; and which didn't.

It was proven to me that I'd passed on this family skill when my daughter, at eight years old, asked, 'Should we disguise ourselves and go in again?' after I told her it might be a bit risky to go for a third hot chocolate sample from Whittard on the same trip to town. She didn't agree and made me put on sunglasses and go in again, as we chatted to each other about which of the expensive coffees we were apparently thinking of buying her nan for Christmas that year.

Although I'm sure these sorts of chain shops have hoards of profits and don't give a damn about how many testers are taken, I still feel the need to do this elaborate role play about what I am planning on purchasing. I don't remember my gran doing this. My memories are of her striding smiling in to shops, showing us where the assistant with the tray of tablet was and telling us to take a tester, before we all walked out again. Perhaps you get more confident with age. Perhaps my gran was just a don.

My monthly trip to town with my kid now consists of: multiple free hot chocolates at Whittard; free shortbread (when you buy eggs from the market woman on the second stall down); free fudge samples from the fudge shop; free cheese and ham crumbs from the Spanish meat man, and occasionally, if it's the right day, free tea and biscuits from a clothes shop called White Stuff.

I find this last one the hardest to feign genuine interest in. Firstly, because I have never purchased anything from that shop and still find it intimidating to go into because it sells expensive wrap dresses. Secondly, because the free testers are so readily available – there is an area where you can actually pour yourself a cup of tea from a teapot and there are plates to put the biscuits on – it almost feels like a trap.

Two more recommendations.

Waitrose: This isn't a sure thing but the first time I went to Waitrose was with my boss at an office job I had after leaving university. She took me there to get supplies for a meeting and I left having sampled half of the cheese and chocolate produce and with two free lip balms. The richer you are, the more free shit you get it seems.

Topping: this is a brilliant and beautiful group of bookshops with stores in Bath, Edinburgh, St Andrews and Ely. They offer you a cup of tea or coffee when you go in, so you can browse the books and sip your free drink and basically feel like the queen of some sort of underground, secret writers' club from nineteenth-century Paris. The Topping bookshops are all in the UK, I just still associate exciting writers' things with dingy Parisian bars and bookshops.

I've only been to the Topping in Ely. The first time I went, I made a day trip of it with my kid because I was so excited. We went for a fry-up first in a café close by and I refused to buy a cup of tea with my breakfast because I was saving it for, in my daughter's eye-rolled words, 'that bookshop you're going to get the free one in'.

I can't mention Topping without a quick wink to some of my other favourite bookshops. I don't know if these ones give you anything for free. Mr B's Emporium in Bath; Heffers in Cambridge; the Portobello Bookshop in Edinburgh; Lighthouse in Edinburgh; Rough Trade in London; Charlie Byrne's Bookshop in Galway; Shakespeare and Company in Paris and Massolit Books in Budapest.

I've recently been taught by my city-grown boyfriend that most art exhibition openings are not ticketed and have loads of free alcohol at them. I'd never been to one until he took me. Despite genuinely wanting to see the exhibition, I still felt like I was going to get huckled out for taking the wine. There were peanuts on offer too, but after watching a programme about peanut bowls on bar counters often containing traces of piss, hair, skin cells and semen, I've been put off that a bit.

In 2019, I did a gig in York. It was the middle of quite a long tour and I was telling one of the other performers there about how I hadn't bought any tea bags for a whole month, I'd just stolen them all from the rooms or breakfast buffets of the hotels I was in.

She didn't even crack a smile, just immediately told me that it was *actually really bad for the environment when people nick those sorts of things from hotel rooms*; tea bags, shampoos, soaps. 'They are always individually plastic-wrapped and the more people steal them, the more they're produced, you see?' I nodded.

The next morning, as I left that hotel in York empty-handed, I found myself gazing wistfully at a basket filled with a pretty decent selection of tea bags and shortbread biscuits, as if I were leaving a part of my soul behind in that small bundle of offerings.

the day i stopped nicking tea bags from hotels
(or granny, forgive me)

this is your fault granny that i am like this:
i cannot leave the tiny shampoo bottle in the hotel shower
which i do not need to take i do not need to take it
it will just sit in my bathroom cupboard unused for years
but i cannot leave it or the shower gel or the body lotion
i don't even use body lotion i've never used body lotion

this is your fault granny

i cannot leave the tea bags in the basket for the next guest
i cannot leave the biscuits in the packets in the basket
for the next guest, i cannot leave the alcohol in the glasses
or the barrels or the bottles at all-you-can-drink parties
that you pay set fees in advance for, this is your fault granny,

that night i ended up in a car park in a tutu thinking the
car park was my bedroom because i had to get my money's worth
you have to get your money's worth Hollie at all-you-can-drink
pay-in-advance parties which was only five pounds to get into
don't worry granny, i wasn't hurt, my friend found me,
explained that the car park was not my flat the car park space
not my bedroom but granny,
remember,

you used to order twenty packs of sugars with your tea
on the train down from glasgow just so you could steal the
packs of sugars with the excuse that they would have thrown them
away anyway after being on your saucer, you never even ordered tea
just a mug of hot water and twenty packs of sugar

slipped a tea bag from your handbag so you did not have to
pay full price for a cup of tea
on the train today i left a hotel room
for the first time in my life without taking a single tea bag

not one

you do not need to take the tea bag hollie
you do not need the tea bag hollie
the war is over

but now i'm on the train back home staring out the window
and i can feel you on my shoulder
looking down on me disgusted
frowning at the loss *what has happened to your family?*
what has happened to your grandchild?
whispering *traitor   traitor   traitor*

selective hearing

i'm not sure granny was as deaf as she made out;

she seemed to hear the birds fine
recognise the songs they sang
the foxes searching stones
for chicken bones we snapped for luck

it was only when she had to greet us
get up from that wicker chair
in her tiny porch that caught the morning sun

it was only then, when visitors arrived:
put her kettle on, made each other tea;
turned down her central heating;
advised her on new tv channels;
proposed the use of internet;
coaxed her to the car, said
a run would do you good;

only then, she'd shrug;
tap her ear, proclaim
hearing aid must not be working

then, sitting on her own again
tv off; heating back to tropic warmth
in the wicker chair in the tiny porch
that caught the evening sun

the world sprung up again
foxes rummaged bins
birds sang

disappearing act

i remember your face
less and less each day

when i try
i just get memories
of photos of your face

and that doesn't
feel the same

as far as you can paddle

today i'm not ok
yesterday i was i think
grief, it comes in waves
today, i'm underneath

crests pace the floor above
meticulously regulating
punch on punch on punch
each surface breath attempted
another skull thud comes
as underwater currents
whip the clouds off kilter
feet somersaulting face
seaweed swarming limbs
seasalt flooding lungs
nostrils burn seawater sharp

tonight i'll reach the shore
vomit out the sobs
hang tearducts up to dry
crawl back into bed

tomorrow,
paddle out again
see how far i get

IT'S LIKE THEY KNOW

In the hospital this bleak mid-winter
You were just an old woman
You were just an old man

JACKIE KAY,
'April Sunshine'

The final days of my grandad's life, he made jokes about the lack of sex in hospital. My gran scolded him. I loved watching them like that.

His body was in tatters. An old coat. Worn and weathered and protecting him from neither wind nor rain any more. Storms would be impossible to bear. When he died, I thought of this coat coming off. Finally, an unzipping of such a heavy burden. It helped me to think of it like that. I was twenty-one when he died.

I'm almost sure my grandad waited to see everyone he wanted to see before he died. I hear a lot of stories like this and it's hard to know which ones are your heart pleading truth from fantasy. I met a woman who worked in a care home once and she said that this happened a lot. Elderly people who were dying slowly hanging on until some final end was tied up in ribbon.

When my grandad went into hospital for the last time, an influx of grandchildren flocked to his bedside. Myself included.

I was sitting in my room at university, three hundred miles away, at 2 a.m. the day before. Just finished an essay. I started to get ready for bed and thought, *What the fuck am I doing?*

I panicked, booked the next flight to Glasgow, shoved any clothes that were clean into a bag and ran out of the college rooms, through town, to the bus stop.

I know cheap flights are the environment's kryptonite, but in this case, I will always be grateful for the low-budget fare.

I'd never run through town in the witching hour so sober before. Without the usual cider blanket it was freezing cold, but refreshing to breathe in deep ice breaths. The people spilling from the clubs looked less glamorous than I remembered the week before. Mascara more smudged than smoky. Lots of vomit on the pavements.

When I arrived at the bus stop, flushed, begging a ticket to the airport, I received so many sympathetic looks from people I think they must have thought I was fleeing sadness not running towards it. Maybe I made that up. I often make up stories about other people I see and assume people are doing the same about me, but it's more likely they were thinking of other things.

Eight o'clock the next morning, I got to the hospital in Glasgow. My mum prepared me for the difference in my grandad's appearance. I went in and hugged what was left of his body and he apologised for the hassle and we swapped 'love you's.

All my grandparents did this when they were dying. Apologised for the trouble. *What a shame*, they said. For us. *What a shame.*

When my grandad hugged, the knuckle on one of his hands always dug into my back and the tighter he wrapped his arms around me, the more it hurt. He had arthritis and by the time I knew him one of his knuckles was stuck, permanently sticking out. I was so glad that when we hugged in the hospital my back got jabbed again. It's the most physical memory I have. Sometimes I stick my thumb into my backbone when I miss him.

Afterwards, I sat in another room and cried and my mum hugged me. My grandad died that night.

Perhaps he hung on. Perhaps we were just lucky. Perhaps I would have made up some sort of story no matter how it happened. Perhaps if I hadn't gone up to Scotland and seen him, I would have said it was intentional so as to remember him in better form. Perhaps I would have thought that true. Perhaps it would have been true.

I think of that rush to the bus stop if I ever need motivation in life.

The only downside of this rush to say goodbye to grandad was that I had no suitable clothes for the funeral and ended up going in a skin-tight brown woollen dress, purple tights, knee-high boots and a long, fur-hooded jacket. The clean clothes I'd shoved into my bag were the things I never wore. Saying this, my grandad had given me strict instructions about his funeral: *not to cry, and not to wear black.* So at least I managed one of those.

My granny was similarly old and ready to die by the end of her life. When she was ninety-two, she told me she'd started eating more cheese. The doctor had told her years before that cheese was bad for her. *Raises your cholesterol.* Despite all the free tablet and sugar sachets, she was too healthy.

It was weird speaking to someone who seemed fairly happy for life to be over. Not from pain particularly, more a feeling that she was done. Aching body, yes. But she'd had a beautiful life and was grateful for this. Her husband had died ten years before. She had had enough now. She couldn't do a lot of things she liked to do any more. Ready to go.

I cannot imagine ever feeling like this but I hope one day I do.

I saw my granny three weeks before she died. My daughter skipped school to visit her. The trip to say goodbye was noted as 'unauthorised absence' under government school regulations. The trip for the funeral was noted as 'authorised absence'.

She was still totally 'with it' and when my daughter asked her how come she'd lived so long, she breathed in a silence similar to Yoda's when Luke Skywalker asks him whether Darth Vader is his father. She then answered, slowly, 'Soup and pudding.'

On her deathbed, my granny said *eat soup and pudding.*

My shopping bill is about £7 a week because of those final words.

I have been very lucky to know my grandparents. I am selfishly thankful that many of us in the family got pregnant 'too young' and were privileged enough health-wise that we managed, for a while, to squeeze four generations into a living timeline.

I tend to write only in prose about people I love who died in old age like this. Younger deaths are reserved in my notebooks for poems. I can't deal with them so well in full sentences.

back up for the funeral

driving up the road
as pinks and blues collide

a sky like sleeping beauty's dress
in the best part of the film
– colours flicking back and forth
between the fairies' magic wands

the left, a fading scarlet sun
scorching pink the whole night air

the right,
a cool, calm stoic blue

driving through the middle
the whole sky feels like you

role play

can we pretend
for just one day
that we are fine,
please?

make love, as if
your best friend
in the world
is still alive?

paint the sunrise
neon stripped again
across this
looming grey

force the daylight
through the rain
as if a rainbow
never fades?

can we pretend
for just one day
that we're ok,
please?

because soon enough
i know this lie
will tumble
to its knees

you'll need
to spend the day
in bed again;
childhood duvet cave

till then
let's take a walk
let sunset warm
this wet-faced sorrow

tell tears
not to refill
until tomorrow

loss

the joke was meant to be over by now
but your clothes are still empty
your friends are still grieving
the river's still spitting up sea-glass and bark

it's almost a year
the spring's coming up
come back now
we get it; ha ha

SHORT STORY: PUSH

for the girl, tagged slag in the classroom
for the teenage parents tutted at on the bus by a stranger while
*   their kid cried*
for the girls who've given birth but never orgasmed
for the girls told they 'only have themselves to blame'
for the new young parents' group telling their stories as the
*   babies bounced*
for the meticulously tidy bedsit and cup of tea
for the giggles you shared over pizza and crisps
for your cursing and stories and kindness

girl, fifteen years old, one birth story amongst many

and i'm breathing like there's a breathing race and i'm
        fucking winning it
and the midwife says to keep breathing but not to push
because if i push now it is likely to rip my arsehole apart
she doesn't say it like that but i know that's what she means
but my whole fucking body is telling me 'push, bitch, fucking
        push, bitch'
and you have no fucking idea what it's like
when your whole fucking body is telling you one thing
and this woman is telling you to ignore it and just keep
        breathing

and i scream so loud to stop me from pushing but it's not me
    screaming
it's my mouth screaming by itself 'cos it is a fucking idiot
and it thinks that if it screams loud enough some of the pain
    will escape
but the pain just gets worse and i keep screaming and not
    pushing
and the pain comes and goes and comes back and i scream

and i remember my sister's scream when she was eight and i
    was five
and i said *the rag doll is mine now*
and i took the scissors we used to cut scraps of newspaper
and make messages out of words for the grandma we liked
and i cut my sister's doll's hair and said *your doll is a boy now*
and you can't call your doll Stacy now and she screamed
and said she could too and my mum ran upstairs and
    screamed at me too
and i cried because the whole world was my enemy

and i'm crying now too because there is not one thing i can
    change now either
to turn things back
to avoid having to do this now
and i'm screaming again
and they offer me to squat in this water pool
and it looks like our old paddling pool which burst when i
    was ten
but i'm getting into it between contractions hunched over
like how i think i'll look if i live till eighty but i probably
    won't
and i think about the girl at school who called me a fat slag
    last month

and i hate the world even fucking more

and i take my pants off, of course
'cos how the fuck is a baby gonna come out if you've got your
    pants on
but i don't take off my bra 'cos i don't think about taking off
    my bra
'cos why would i

and i'm screaming and i'm not pushing
and in between the screaming and not pushing
i'm thinking i sort of wish i'd taken my bra off too
'cos now i'm in a paddling pool in a hospital with bits of
    blood all gooey
floating around on the surface of the water
and i thought it would be cleaner than bits of blood
floating around the fucking surface of the water
and at least i haven't shit myself
and i wonder how many women have shit themselves in this
    pool before me

and i'm in a bra but no pants and it feels so fucking weird
'cos no woman ever walks around in a bra and no fucking
    pants
maybe pants and no fucking bra but not bra and no fucking
    pants
now i feel like a fucking idiot and there's a bunch of students
    watching us
and i don't want to look like a fucking idiot with people
    watching us

then she's saying *push now push now* 'cos now my fanny is
        wide enough
less likely to rip the skin in half
and that's the thing i've been fearing the most all these
        months
is the ripping
and yes i've been rubbing fucking oil between my arse and
        fanny
i can't remember the name of that place
even though they kept saying it all the fucking time
and no my fucking boyfriend hasn't been helping me
and no i didn't fucking ask him to do it even though he'd
        probably find it quite funny and anyway the oil is
        expensive
but i'm still happy that it's slightly less likely
because i used it right
i won't have my arse ripped apart

and she says *push through your bum* and it does feel like that
like you're pushing through your bum
and when she says *push through your bum*
it reminds me again of the fact that i might shit myself

and i am pushing

and i can't fucking believe that this is what i really have to do
and all he did is fucking jerk off in me what a fucking cunt of
        a world
and he asked did you cum, did i cum, of course i didn't
        fucking cum
and i look up in between the pushing and some fucking
        students are in the room now because my water bag
        hasn't burst

and one of them says to the other one that it's good luck if
    your waters don't burst
and starts fucking talking about sailors and shit
and how water bags that didn't burst were sold to seamen to
    keep them safe at sea
and i shout at them that i don't feel very fucking lucky right
    now
and could they please stop talking about seamen
and i'm not selling any fucking sailors my fucking water bag

and i feel like an earthquake
and i am screaming because there is no other way to push
    hard enough
through my whole entire body than screaming it out
and i need to keep pushing otherwise i will die
and the baby will die or the baby will die and i won't
and how the fuck do you recover from that
and i think of that woman in the pregnancy group
that i didn't want to go to
and one of the students who was going on about the sailors
is wearing a white top
a white fucking top with no stains on at all
a white fucking top
and i am covered in bloody water and the water has got colder
and someone is topping it up with warmer water
and i can't believe that this is not going to kill me
and i can't believe that this is what other women do
and i can't believe this is what my mum did
and i try to breathe calmly
and it helps for a bit
and i take a sip of lucozade that i'm handed by someone
and i think fucking lucozade as if i'm doing a fucking
    marathon

and one of the students says something to the other one and
     they look at me
and i wonder how much the tickets cost to watch me
no fucking pants on
screaming my arse out of my face

and it's not working is it?
no it's not working
why's it not working?
and they heave me out of the water
and i forgot how heavy my belly was
and now i'm just standing soaking wet with a damp bra and
     my fanny on show
for all those fucking students
and they bring me a towel and she says *you're doing well*
and she says *we'll try a different position*
and i ask *why isn't it working?*

and she brings a chair which looks like a toilet
and i don't want to fucking give birth into a toilet
but i don't want to argue
and i sit until the pain comes again
and out of the water everything's heavier
and the seat that looks like a toilet is slippy
and i scream and i scream and
i try to push an entire life through my fanny and

the head is coming she says
what? i say
and *the head is coming* she says
and *keep going* she says so politely she says
you're doing so well she says

and i doubt it 'cos i've never done anything fucking well in
    my
ahhhh and i scream and i scream
in my ahhhh in my
fucking ahhhh in my life
and she tells me *keep going keep pushing*
and i'm ahhhhh and the head is out
and i think fuck fuck fuck i have a head sticking out my
    fucking fanny
a human head sticking out my fucking fanny
and a bra but no pants and i wish i'd taken the fucking bra
    off

and there is blood seeping over the floor like slime now
and i don't know if that's normal
is that normal? i scream
please let that be normal
but how can blood everywhere be normal i think
is that fucking normal i scream
and she says *it's normal don't worry*
and her hand on my back feels like life
and it didn't look like this in the fucking brochure i say
and she smiles and it's so nice when she smiles
and i scream more and more
and when the shoulders come out of my fanny
it feels like flames are burning the edge of my skin
i have an exploding volcano erupting between my legs
and if i go to hell now
i don't think the flames burn your fanny like this
and i push and i scream and a feeling like burning slime slips
    from my insides
and stops.
and the pain changes

and i don't have to push
and i don't have to push
and i don't have to push
and i don't have to push
i don't have to
i don't
i

silence

and the pain eases
and a baby cries
a baby is there
the baby, crying
is put in my arms

and i hold the baby

and i look at the baby

and i don't have to push

and i don't have to push

and i wonder if i am alive
because there's blood round my feet
being soaked up
by people with blue tissues
and i look at the baby
and from the baby's belly
the cord is grey
like a mouldy carrot
i follow it

it is still inside me
fuck, it's still inside me
that's so fucking weird
we are still together
and the midwife smiles
and the cord is still pumping blood between you, she says
and she tells me i have to push the placenta
i have to push out the placenta
and the word push sounds like the word death
and the word push sounds like the word torture
i didn't know i'd hear the word push again
i didn't want to hear push again
i don't want to push again, i say
you have to push she says
please don't make me push again, i say,
it's ok, she says
if i don't push out the placenta
it can kill me too
and i scream but the scream comes out as tears
and the students are all watching me cry now
and i thought that i was past being killed now
and i look around the room
and the baby is breathing
and i wonder if i'd rather die now or push again
now the baby's ok
she says *push* so politely
you have to push it's ok
and i push and i push again
and i cry
and the placenta flops to the floor in the blood puddle
and it wasn't that bad
the pushing this time
and it's huge

the placenta
it's fucking huge
purple spilt jelly
and i feel faint

and the midwife smiles at me again and says *well done* but
  not *congratulations*
and for a minute i almost forget and i look at the baby
and i look at the blood on my thighs
and the blood round my feet
and my fanny is still out
and i look at the skin on my belly below
and it's empty and wrinkled
and i think i'll never put on a bikini again
and i wonder how to hide this skin from my friends when
  they're in their bikinis
and i wonder what my boyfriend will say when he sees
and i think of the belly tops i'll throw out
except the ones i can wear with high jeans when i go back to
  school maybe
if i can face school again after this
and i look back at the baby
and i feel my tits ache
they don't know, do they?
and i'm all right with the bra now
and the midwife comes over
and i apologise for my potty mouth
and the midwife smiles at me it's so nice when she smiles at
  me
and she tells me it's fine

and she tells me i'm no worse than anyone else
and i think of the adults i know and i imagine them
      screaming like that
and i think of the teachers at school and wonder if they
      screamed as loud
and i can't imagine our history teacher ever screaming like
      that
but she has three kids
and i look at the baby the baby
and i look at the midwife the midwife
and it's so good not to feel so much pain any more
the pain is easing
and we sit for what seems like the rest of my life is beginning
and i realise the cord has been clipped
and they pass me a tea
but i don't drink tea
and they take her away.

GROWING UP

Short Skirts and Arseholes

Just because I look sexy on the cover of Rolling Stone *doesn't mean I'm naughty.*

BRITNEY SPEARS

NAUGHTY

The first time I remember properly arguing with someone in a position of power was in sixth-form. It was about my skirt. The length of it.

I hardly ever argued with adults when I was younger (parents excepted), but by this point, I was so sick of being pulled up for the length of my school skirt that I couldn't hold my tongue. I remember feeling both petrified and pissed off at being asked into the head of year's office, again.

I watched this teacher's lips moving, mesmerised by his thick beard, as he awkwardly discussed the effects of thighs on show, reminding me 'for the hundredth time, Hollie' about school uniform standards. I was to set an example to the younger years, and this was not a good example.

I remember staring at the floor silently, wanting to tell him to go fuck himself up the arse.

I realise 'go fuck yourself up the arse' isn't a phrase we really use in English, but at that time I was studying French and had just learned a collection of new swear words that I found pretty interesting.

In French there seemed to be a lot of derogatory words related to sex work and sex workers. Like, instead of saying 'what a mess' or, I guess, 'what a fucking pigsty', I was told that in French people say 'quel bordel', which literally translated means 'what a brothel'. It can be used for a messy room (which I don't think there's much evidence a brothel would be equivalent to) or a really confused scenario. Some examples:

Quel bordel!
Literally: What a brothel!
Idiomatically: What a shambles! / What a fuck-up!

Ça va être le bordel!
Literally: It'll be a brothel!
Idiomatically: It'll be chaos!

Or my personal favourite:

Foutre le bordel dans quelque chose
Literally: To fuck the brothel in something
Idiomatically: To screw/bugger something up

Looking into all those phrases also made me realise that I had had no idea that bugger was actually about anal sex, using it throughout my childhood, as in 'to bugger something up', which I imagine is what it's like for kids using '*bordel*' more and more as they grow up speaking French.

Similarly strange: in English, when we drop our keys or trip or something like that and might say 'oh shit' or 'oh bollocks', in French, as well as saying '*merde*' (shit), they say '*putain!*', which means 'whore'. Like 'oh whore, I've forgotten to take my pills' or 'oh whore, I left my kid in the supermarket'.

If you want to make it stronger, you can say '*putain de merde*' which is like shit-whore. (You can also say '*bordel de merde*', as in 'shit brothel'.) I'm not saying I like these phrases, I just find it amazing how swearing has evolved slightly differently in different cultures. In general, it seems mainly about toilet habits and sex, but with very intricate variations.

Swearing is one of the trickiest things to get right and the most likely thing to make you sound like a cunting fuckbag if you get it wrong in a foreign language, even just a little.

To me 'oh whore' sounded ridiculous (and later, sexist and

generally wrong), until I realised that English-speakers went about saying 'oh testicles' whenever we made a mistake, which is also pretty sexist, I guess, dissing these squidgy semen-loving carriers.

In terms of the insult I was silently whispering to myself as I stood in the office that day, it was my attempt at translating the French word *enculé*.

Thinking now, it probably translates best as 'up your arse' which I guess we do say in English. Or 'up yours' which I never really thought meant 'up your arse' until writing this just now, but I guess it does. At the time, I'd recently got back from the French Exchange and had asked Elsa, the excellent girl who I was paired with and who was actually French, what *enculé* meant and she said, 'Well, uh, it is like fuck you but with the fuck in the bum.'

So in my head at that time, standing in my immoral skirt, staring at that teacher, I had translated it as 'go fuck yourself up the arse'. Sir.

I said none of these things to the teacher. I've always been fairly polite out loud. Or perhaps just not always confident enough to speak up. I breathed in, adamant though that this time I was not going to just smile and say sorry, sir. I calmly argued my case, hands sweating profusely. I said that my skirt length surely did not actually affect the boys' grades and that below-knee-length skirts were very difficult to move in, sir, and that, in terms of the distraction, it worked both ways: I found lots of the boys' uniform distracting, specifically their crotch bulge in tight trousers.

The meeting was not a success. I was being *totally ridiculous*. Uniform policy was there for a reason. Rules were rules.

I left the room shaking in that way I still do when trying to calmly discuss anything I feel very strongly about, especially with people in positions of power. I wonder at what point in history we might ever stop correlating female morality with amount of thigh skin on show.

I don't make the point about crotch bulges lightly. They really did distract us (me) a lot.

And it wasn't just the other students that were a problem. One of

81

our science teachers used to wear his trousers very high, and when he stood at our desk in science, those benches that are a little higher than the desks in other lessons, it was like his penis, outlined by folds of thin, light beige material, was just right there at eye level. I don't think he did it on purpose. He just had a penis, which was not his fault, and I just liked the idea of penises, which was not my fault either.

What annoys me most about my telling-off that day was that it was implied that I was the problem, by having the skin above my knees 'on show'.

I understand the toing and froing of a system that wants to protect pupils in short skirts from the sort of taunts and reactions that may unfortunately accompany them wearing these short skirts. So, in that way, however irritating it is, I understand a uniform policy that has a limit on the height we could jack up our skirts to.

However, not once were the 'lads', whose grades I'm almost a hundred per cent certain had never been proven to be directly related to the inch by inch measurement of other pupils' clothing, given a 'how to concentrate while there are people around who you might fancy looking at' talk. It was our thighs, and those alone, that were described as the problem. There was to be *no further discussion*.

At that point in my school life, those of us with vulvas were not and had never been allowed to wear trousers. For this reason, as well as new difficulties attempting to walk, run, skip or play at breaktimes in below-knee-length skirts, our joy in handstands and cartwheels was dismally crushed in Year 7.

I think it was at this point in my school life, standing in my illegal skirt, feeling like a distracting slag, that I started to question these sorts of tellings-off; to query ideas of naughtiness and disobedience and what was actually wrong and right and why things like, I don't know, my knees, were being so demonised.

I knew I was becoming increasingly attractive to people. I don't mean everyone. I just mean, it's a natural progression as you grow up: the slow realisation of those more sexual feelings, in yourself and in others.

I feel I could've owned that; grown into it as safely and confidently and comfortably as anyone can, considering the amount of change taking place physically at that stage in life. Instead I, and every other girl I knew, was continually scolded for our skin, told not to go out wearing certain clothes.

Not once did anybody say to me: *Just so you know, it's absolutely not your thighs or your chest or your shoulders that are the problem here, it's people who might treat you like less or, at worst, attack you, because of their inability to understand that you are not, in or out of any outfits, something they have a right to.* No, I was just told off. And I hated it even more once I didn't agree with it. My boy friends had other rules applied to their appearance – long hair, for example, was banned in school. Scruffy trousers or shirts untucked are less controversial examples. But they were never 'not going out dressed like that' for any supposed sexual reason.

As a kid, I hated being told off in general. Of course.

Looking back, however, I feel that most of the times it happened in early childhood were pretty justified. Then, I was mainly told off for things I still think of as fairly naughty. Kid naughty, as in, a bit dangerous – like running around the swimming pool or putting my thumbs in wet cement or telling my friend's mum that my friend had died so that she didn't have to go home after a sleepover.

I also got the tellings-off for stuff which was a bit more subjective. Like farting.

The first time I remember being properly told off by someone other than my parents, I was five. I ran in the primary school canteen.

I was clutching my empty lunch tray, plastic plates shifting across the surface like that air puck game you get at bowling alleys and seaside arcades and always try to keep playing once the money has run out and the air stops flowing, and it still sort of works because you've got one chip that hasn't been battered into the slit goal yet.

So I was running with my tray, more quickly than normal;

canteen whispers had confirmed that British bulldog was on that day. Stuck in the mud too perhaps, if time. I was understandably excited to get the fuck out onto the school field.

My best friend Jodie and I had just finished our lunch. We'd sponged up every bit of ketchup with our burger buns and sipped the last loud sucks of liquid and air up through the straws of our Um Bongo cartons, discussing whether or not it was actually drunk in the jungle. We made our way across the hall, busting to escape into the playground of Bucklebury Primary School.

Halfway across the hall, the head dinner lady started screaming at us. I'll call her Mrs Rivers here because I never knew her name.

First my name, followed by a slower than usual 'aaaand' before Jodie's name, was hurled across the heads of gaping fellow gobblers. We were called to attention and made to 're-walk' the walk from the seats on which we had been sitting, to the tray drop-off point towards which we'd been running. Run-walking I'd say. Mrs Rivers said running. I didn't argue at that time.

Before we did this re-run-walk, Mrs Rivers announced to all of the school pupils still eating their lunch that they were to *stop eating, put down their forks and spoons and watch as Jodie and Hollie now demonstrated how to walk properly, because it seemed that they had forgotten*. I still hate this sort of sarcastic shit from adults. I try not to do it. Like, I haven't forgotten how to walk, you arsehole, I just want to go and play bulldog.

Giggles spread like head lice across the canteen. Jodie and me were petrified because for some reason the pupils of our school had concocted a fantasy about this particular dinner lady being a witch.

We often made up stories about the older women being witches. The woman who lived in the house opposite on my street was a witch. Whenever our ball went into her garden – a very well-kept garden for a witch – during a game of kerby or forty-forty, we would spend ages arguing about who would dare go and fetch it.

This lady wore a neck brace. I now realise that this is where all of our witch ideas began. I also realise I have no point of comparison as to whether witches' gardens have generally been deemed tidy or not. The only one I can remember is the witch in 'Rapunzel' and she had an allotment with lettuces in.

The stories we made up at school about the male teachers were different. We used to say things like, 'He probably still lives with his mum and wears train pyjamas to bed.' We couldn't think of a rude equivalent to witches.

After Jodie and me had proved our ability to walk correctly in front of a sea of smirking children – I see this as my first of many so-called 'walks of shame' – we were told that our class teacher, Mrs Danvers, would be informed of our naughtiness. We were also petrified of her because she had grey hair and didn't smile as much as our other class teacher, Mrs Cornwall, so was obviously secretly a witch too, although she didn't wear gloves like in *The Witches*, but Roald Dahl wasn't always right, we concluded.

Once in the playground, we ran to the very end field. We were petrified. Both being Roald Dahl readers, we wondered if the chokey was a real thing – the child-punishing school cupboard from *Matilda* which had spikes inside the walls so you'd have to stand bolt upright unless you wanted spiked all over your body. We also wondered whether, thinking of the book's headmistress, Miss Trunchbull, children might really be whizzed around teachers' heads like shotputs.

Taking all of these issues into account, we decided the most sensible thing would be to hide from our teacher. The only object available was the netball post. I stood behind that post with Jodie all lunchtime long, bodies bolt upright like bean poles, hands flat to our hips, hearts pounding pinballs, sneaking glances around each side of the post, despite the fact I could obviously see around it anyway and that my body was three times as wide as it.

At that time, we were past the age where you genuinely believe that you can hide in hide and seek by covering your own eyes but, I guess, only just coming up to the age when you realise you can still be seen when hiding behind an object thinner than yourself – even if you cross your fingers and close your eyes really, really tight.

As an adult, I still breathe in when I'm driving through a tunnel, as if my inhaled breath will shrink the car width to less frightening dimensions. In my heart, I know this doesn't work, but I just can't risk that sort of shit.

At the end of lunchtime, having unhappily watched from our ingenious hiding position the game of bulldog unfold without us, we walked jelly-legged into the classroom.

And nothing happened. Nothing at all.

I still don't know if Mrs Danvers was ever told about our canteen running, or whether perhaps, as a teacher of an underfunded state primary, she had better things to do than search for two kids during her lunch break, but the constant suspense of waiting to be told off was like Hitchcock at his best.

Second time I was told off.

With Jodie again. We were both thrown out of Brownies for this.

The Brownie hut was on the edge of our local woods. I never really wanted to go to Brownies and got about as far as saluting the Queen when I started misbehaving. I blame my grandma for teaching me a solid lack of respect for the royal family. I never got any badges on my sash. That includes the hostess badge, which still exists in Brownies but not in Cubs.

The main reason we got in trouble was for changing the direction of the stick arrows in the woods. If my memory doesn't fail me, they were mainly set up by the Girl Guides in preparation for our walks. Jodie and me learned that these arrows could be changed with a light, inconspicuous kick. The fact that such confusion could be caused simply by kicking a twig on the floor must have given us a lot of amusement, because we continued to play this game on our walks.

The final straw came on a special outing into the woods that the

Brownies were to make. On their own. Jodie and me knew the local woods better than the others. Maybe because they weren't so local to the village or maybe because they weren't allowed to roam so freely with older brothers all summer. I miss making dens in the forest.

On this occasion, the outing was an orienteering challenge. No leaders. Just us Brownies and some volunteering Girl Guides who didn't really know the woods either. The task was set: instead of stick arrows, bits of blue wool had been hung from tree branches in a long path leading from the Brownie hut to some sort of treasure chest in the middle of the woods. I can't remember what the treasure was or why everyone was so excited about finding it. Perhaps there was another badge at stake which I'd not be getting again. With the help of the Girl Guides, we were to follow the blue wool, find the treasure, and follow the blue wool back. Easy peasy (pudding and pie, kissed the girls and made them cry – not all right any more).

I don't remember whose idea it was to do this, but Jodie and me gradually trailed to the back of the line of more eager Brownies, until we were about three metres behind the others. As we reached each dangling blue wool signal, we quickly whipped it from off the tree branch and stuffed it into our pockets.

Once we all reached the treasure, Jodie and me gave the others a head start before we shimmied off into the trees and darted back along our well-known route to the play park by the Brownie hut, leaving the others lost in Narnia. I can still picture them walking in front of us as we dragged behind them further and further until escape was possible.

Thinking back, it was a mistake to go straight back to the play park near the main hut.

As soon as we were there without the others, we were seen by the terrifying Brown Owl, more terrifying probably because she was slightly muscly and didn't look pretty and frail like Miss Honey and all the other 'friendly female characters' in every storybook and film I'd ever read and watched as a child.

I sometimes wonder if it is Roald Dahl or Disney that is more to blame for my childhood prejudices against women who were larger than sticks and older than thirty. I don't make my daughter relive those childhood reading lists. I know a lot of parents desperate for their kids to love all the same stories they loved. I forced this a few times with Roald Dahl and bought a collection of 'The Classics' for the same reasons until I realised, rereading the books myself, that many stories written twenty years or longer ago were more often than not empty of all attempts at diversity, frequently openly racist, full to the brim with jokes about fat children eating pies and generally set in small English countryside villages. Shirley Hughes excluded. And *Jilly, You Look Terrible*.

So, I'm not saying this is true of all past children's literature, just that there are enough brilliant children's writers nowadays, who are both exceptionally talented and much less bigoted, to not freak out if your child isn't enjoying *The Railway Children* any more.

Back to the Brownies.

Miss Trunchbull looked at us and asked suspiciously where the others were. *Just behind us*, we lied.

It took almost an hour to find everyone.

Once the panic was over, Brown Owl immediately called for Jodie and me, which weirdly I found very unfair. She asked if we had caused this commotion. *No*, we both lied, our heads shaking overambitious maracas.

She gave us that final chance adults often give children to spill the truth by saying our names again one by one in that slow horror-film style before the phone rings or the door knocker knocks or a jar falls from a table near to where no one is standing. We both looked her in the face, our tan culotte pockets stuffed so full with blue wool that it was spilling over the edges. Still, we denied our actions a final time like the absolute arseholes we were.

After the blue wool incident, both of us were asked to leave Brownies. As punishment, Jodie's mum made her do Girl Guides when she was old enough. I didn't get very harshly punished. I found this odd. I later found out this was because my mum was thrown out of Girl Guides as a teenager and felt it would have been hypocritical to be hard on me for being a similarly unbadged little shit.

In general, my mum was more lenient than Jodie's mum.

This didn't stop me asking to swap mums on several occasions, because Jodie's mum not only had pink wafer biscuits and garibaldis in her cupboard at all times, she also had a soda stream. For me, the perk of living with a soda stream at Jodie's house outweighed the possible tellings-off her mum might give me.

Jodie's mum also matched the colour of her earrings to her underwear, bra straps and jewels in sync at all times, which made me feel like she was the closest thing our village had to a film star. My daughter has told me how she'd like to swap mums a couple of times and I won't lie, it hurt a bit, so I now feel bad about that. Sorry, Mum. I love you. I don't mind that your underwear doesn't match. I'd still love a soda stream, which Caroline says can turn any shit white wine into Prosecco.

Another bonus time I recall Jodie getting told off and me not was at a local pub gig.

There was a singer on stage in the pub garden of the Cottage Inn, our local. Halfway through the set, she invited any kids up to sing for a pound each (I don't know why she did this). Jodie and me immediately raised our hands. We were about eight years old and called ourselves The Chubby Brothers because we'd been told many times that we were fat and looked similar to one another.

We went up and sang loudly into the microphone the most popular song amongst us school kids at that time:

We are the teenage girls
We wear our hair in curls
We wear our dungarees

Down to our hairy knees
A boy came up to me
And gave me 50p
To have it off with him
My mummy was surprised
to see my belly rised
My daddy jumped for joy
It was a baby boy

Jodie was forced to give the money back. She was then dragged home by her parents. I was allowed to keep the pound, which I think makes that my first paid gig. Jodie is still one of my closest friends. Our mothers met at prenatal classes.

Third time I was told off. Throwing a snowball at lunch break.

I see no reason to expand on this. I realise there was likely a health and safety reason for the ban as there was a tendency for stones to be covered in snow and thrown at people's heads at my secondary school, but I am still fuming about being sent inside for throwing snowballs with Lema on the one school day it snowed in 1994.

Fourth times. Plural: laughing.

I have always had a problem with laughing when I'm not meant to. I feel that getting punished for this is really unfair because I genuinely cannot control it. Without any scientific evidence, I think it's genetic. Like the Brownies issue, my mum is to blame.

When I was about fifteen, my mum almost got us knocked out on a late train home to Glasgow by a swavering pissed guy who asked *what the fuck we were looking at* and started raging at us. Her answer was to start laughing hysterically almost directly into his face. I held up a newspaper in front of her mouth, whispering kindly, 'Fuck sake, Mum, at least pretend you're laughing at this,' but it was no use. She couldn't stop.

When she was a teenager, Mum says, she remembers being chased by a group of 'enemy kids' from the neighbouring town outside

Glasgow, and being unable to run fast enough because her legs were buckling with laughter as friends screamed at her to *hurry the fuck up*.

During my childhood, she regularly had to leave school performances because the vision of a bunch of kids attempting tunes on the recorder while the teacher frantically waved arms in time to no obvious rhythm was too much for her to bear.

I had my first taste of this when my kid was seven; at a two-hour Christmas assembly of five- to nine-year-olds playing a variety of instruments. I was nervous on the way, worried about these inappropriate laughing genes I'd inherited off my mother.

Sure enough, about three minutes into a little boy playing 'We Are The Champions' on the violin, my whole body was burning, my lungs inhaling sweaty slow breaths in an attempt to stop my stomach from lurching forth as I tried desperately to avoid being seen pissing my pants by his rightfully adoring parents. Through the majority of the recitals, my right knuckle was leant against my mouth so that I could bite into my fingers as a sort of lock on this horrendous reflex reaction. I don't know if it's the silence of those sorts of settings or the pressure to react in the exact way we are supposed to that causes such difficulty. I definitely don't find children nervously standing on stage funny. Maybe I'm just horrible. I have considered that.

I used to work as a French tutor, teaching GCSE and A level pupils, one to one. I gave this up when I was twenty-five after enjoying the work for over four years, because of a horrible lesson when I spent three-quarters of the time in muffled hysterics in front of a terrified teenage boy who had been trying his best French accent in a restaurant role play I'd suggested.

I was a waitress. He was the customer. It was terrible. Every time he began to order *une baguette*, I felt the sweats and giggles coming on and within seconds was sobbing with laughter, making up excuses about something funny that had happened just before I'd got there. The fact he may never attempt to speak French is most likely my fault and I feel awful about it. I quit the job and have never tutored anyone one to one again.

At school, laughing was the only reason I was ever asked to leave class.

In sixth form, I sat in English staring at my teacher's crotch because she had, as we called it, a camel toe in her trousers. I was staring in that absent way you do when you don't realise you are doing it. I didn't realise my teacher had noticed me staring at her crotch, or that she had been looking at me then looking at her crotch for about ten minutes. I also didn't realise that slowly, the whole class had also noticed and were glancing from me to her to her crotch and back to me again like a perverted tennis tournament.

After a while, she blurted out, 'Hollie, what *are* you staring at?' I looked up and my friends Rowena and Danny burst out laughing from across the room, which set me off. I find that type of laughter uncontrollable. I become a wind-up toy. One of those rabbits whose cogs you turn and turn and release and then they do half-arsed broken-legged somersaults that are nothing like what the advert says they do, until the clockwork stops. I was sent out of the classroom after being unable to stop laughing for nearly ten minutes and for disrupting the lesson. Fair enough. I was.

After talking myself calm, I went back to class, saw Rowena's grin unravel, caught sight of the teacher's crotch and my body melted again. I mustered a *Really sorry, miss*, left the classroom, and stayed away the whole lesson, crying in the corridor.

I felt bad about this.

My English teacher was brilliant, the kind of teacher who tried her best to bring every book we were studying to life. She was the person who got me at all interested in actually reading adult poetry when we studied *Paradise Lost*; I became obsessed with Milton's images of hell. Milton went blind while writing this epic poem and made (I assume made unless she was an extremely selfless child) his daughter write down the entire book as he dictated it to her. Last week my kid wrote down the shopping list as I read it out to her and I felt a bit like John Milton.

I was really annoyed with myself after the laughing in this lesson because, from what I could gather, my teacher was quite a shy person. I hadn't meant to highlight her crotch to the class, or to laugh about it.

This teacher sticks in my head too as she was one of two doctors I was taught by in my school. Although my grades at school were good, my general knowledge was pretty shocking. At seventeen, I had no idea there were doctors who weren't actually doctors. Like medical doctors. For the whole of my sixth form I was saying to friends, who maybe didn't know either because none of them had any family members with Ph.D.s either, or maybe thought I was making a rubbish joke or maybe were just being polite, *I just don't get why someone would train to be a doctor and then become an English teacher at this school.*

About halfway into the end of my final year, my friend Maddy really nicely told me that my teacher was a doctor *in English* and explained the system to me. I felt a bit stupid but was mainly just relieved that my teacher hadn't given up a lucrative career in medicine to watch groups of kids moaning about having to act out *The Tempest* or making uncomfortably disgusted squeals at the description of a vulva as 'a wet rose' in *The Color Purple*. Maddy knew everything, but never, ever did that thing where you look down on other people for not knowing.

My first memory of starting at Cambridge University was the opposite of this; a group of other students laughing at me in my first week because I didn't know what a Freudian slip was.

I was sitting with the group in a booth in the student bar, trying to make friends, and somebody said, 'Ooh, that was a bit of a Freudian slip,' about something I'd said, to which I replied, 'A what?' At that, the person next to me said, 'You are joking, right?' and everyone laughed a bit at me because of my stupidity in apparently not knowing who some man called Freud was. I remember wishing I could be back in the comfort of my school friends, who giggled and laughed, but wouldn't mock and chortle when I didn't know things.

In my first French translation class, we had to translate a piece of writing entitled 'Grand Cru'. I translated this as 'A Vast Belief'. I knew 'grand' in French meant large or big and 'cru' was the past tense of 'croire', which means to believe. I thought it was a fair guess.

After we'd handed in our best attempts, the French professor read mine out to the whole class, because he thought my translation of the title was *so* hilariously wrong. He and the whole class began to laugh – again, I'd call it chortling – at my lack of knowledge. Unlike the rest of the eighteen- to nineteen-year-olds in the first year of my Cambridge University Modern Languages class, I did not know that 'Grand Cru' is a classification for really good wine. I phoned up my friend Julie from school that night and told her about everyone taking the piss out of me.

'Who the fuck knows that?' she said.

It was all I wanted to hear.

I'm still angry about this being given as the first translation piece to new students because it wasn't just my French knowledge that was being tested. I can't believe that so many of my classmates, mostly still teenagers just out of school, knew this term. Maybe they didn't and just laughed out of nervousness. Maybe their teenage years *were* spent quaffing expensive wines rather than slugging from Archers and cider bottles in the local field.

That first week at university I was also asked, while watching *Blind Date*, my favourite show at the time, whether I was watching it 'ironically'. I was not.

I met some lovely people at university too (thanks here go especially to Lj, Helen, Tammy, Vim, Jo, Sarah, Simon, Amelia, Ajay, Graeme) and have great friends from that time to this day, but all of these incidents, plus the doctor–teacher in school, have made me very hateful of scoffers, mockers.

When Jade Goody was in *Big Brother* and said she hadn't realised

Bethlehem was a real place, I'm not a hundred per cent sure that I was a hundred per cent sure it was either. I mean, I think I definitely knew, I'm almost certain, and I'm not advocating for people being purposefully ignorant, but I wouldn't have bet my life on it. 'It's only easy if you know the answer' is perhaps my most beloved of game-show phrases.

It was when I was told off for my school skirt that I really started to question what was and wasn't naughty.

In the dictionary, there are two definitions of the word 'naughty':

1. (especially of children) behaving badly; not willing to obey
2. (informal / often humorous) slightly offensive and connect-ed with sex

As I hit puberty, the shift between these two meanings started to blur more and more. Increasingly I was told I was naughty or offen-sive or badly behaved for things I didn't consider to be 'wrong' at all. Like my thighs. Like my nipples showing underneath my clothes. Like the skin between my breasts. It all started to get very fucking confusing.

In addition, the idea of naughtiness itself, the word I mean, started to sound pretty pervy. This was highlighted most notably for me when looking for fancy dress outfits as a teenager.

Having dressed up as reindeers and pumpkins and two-headed vampires as a pre-pubescent kid, party clothes for teenage girls in particular consisted more and more of 'naughty' outfits: naughty nurses, naughty witches, naughty mermaids or naughty schoolgirl outfits. That last one confused me a lot the first time I saw one, whilst shopping after school wearing almost that same outfit. It wasn't so much the outfit, I guess, which I knew some people were attracted to – other school pupils, the twenty-year-old boys who hung outside the school gates waiting on us, the fifty-year-old men who shouted from cars as we walked home or bought me drinks at the local night-club. What I found weirder was the fact that the model who was wearing it was definitely older than school age. I wondered why on earth older people would want to wear school uniform again when I was so desperate to leave school and stop wearing it.

Julie was and still is my only female friend who ever goes to fancy dress parties dressed as anything other than a 'sexy' or 'naughty' something, which as I got older, I realised, often amounted to the same thing in our culture. I have always respected her immensely for this.

By the middle of my teenage years, I was fully aware that girls' school uniform was highly sexualised by the culture around me. I often found it sexy to wear. At the same time I understood that anything I, or the girlfriends I had, did that was actually owning our sexuality was often classed as immoral or disobedient or slutty. We were sexualised constantly in our culture whilst being simul-taneously demonised if we were sexually active or confident or knowledgeable, even about touching our own bodies. This is nothing new, of course.

Our knees were deemed controversial because other people in history had classed them as too sexy; make-up was regulated as if mascara would curb our ability to get good grades. At the same time, trousers, which were what all of us mainly wore outside school, were also deemed inappropriate in this setting. The contradictions and confusions based solely on our appearance, whilst we sat trying to study, were constant.

Entering my late twenties then thirties, just as I was getting used to these sorts of dilemmas and starting, I think, to understand my own body and desires a little better, a third definition of disobedi-ence and naughtiness emerged; a definition stuck midway between young children being told off for running around a swimming pool and adults role playing spanking whilst beautifully tied up in intri-cate knot work.

While I'm sure some people have no problem with it, it's the middle ground of adult 'naughty' I can't stand. The polite version I hear told to me at very dry adult parties where someone passes round a box of Ferrero Rocher and says, *Go on, be naughty, why not?* when I go to take a second chocolate.

This is perhaps the most annoying idea of disobedience for me; the type aimed at those of us not following a Gwyneth Paltrowesque diet regime; a naughtiness hijacked by chocolate and yoghurt and cream cheese companies trying to make a puritanical half sexy, half guilt-ridden idea of adult disobedience and naughtiness as being, at best, eating a piece of chocolate when on a diet, or sneaking downstairs at night-time to grapple past the 'fridge pickers wear big knickers' magnet to secretly spoon low-sugar yoghurt between our elated lips as if it is horny devil nectar.

That this form of diet naughtiness is marketed especially, but not solely, at women, is telling, and perhaps because of this, perhaps simply because it is so fucking annoying, it is this idea of naughtiness that makes me want to take the entire box of Ferrero Rochers and shove each of them one by one slowly up my arsehole.

It's a nonsense culture.

On one hand, I'm seeing increasing numbers of adverts telling me to stick jewels all over my vulva or slice it up to look 'neater' or cover it in perfume so that, I don't know, when my boyfriend – lucky man – gets his face close to that oyster of an ocean he will not be put off by the fact that I smell like skin. Instead I will smell like the chemical cross between flowers and laundry whilst very likely developing a rash or thrush or other complication as a consequence of messing with this area.

On the other hand, there are the adverts telling me that the naughtiest, sexiest thing I can do in the next twenty years is to eat an extra chocolate when I'm already apparently too fat. And we're not talking big chocolates here, no one's saying, *Ooooh go on, be naughty, eat the whole bar of Galaxy, Hollie.*

Now I come to think of it, I am *also* tired of hearing the term 'naughty' used to play down or add humour to what are actual serious sexual misdemeanours. My boss, who continually groped my arse at work, for example, was apparently a 'naughty man'. I disagree. He was a disrespectful arsehole. Yet another, who likes to stick metal clips on his nipples while someone consensually rubs his balls with coconut oil and pisses on his chest, is also often deemed 'naughty', in more of an immoral way by those outside of his safe spaces, while causing no (non-consensual) harm to anyone.

In fact, of all the people I've spoken to over the years about sex and relationships, it is a handful of people in the kink community, a community often belittled, stigmatised and stereotyped as consisting mainly of gimp mask-wearers and grown men in nappies, who have offered me some of the most sensible sexual and sensual advice; on consent and communication; on pleasure; on limits; and on which type of bread they should make sandwiches from to best keep up their energy between knife play and after-care blanket-wrapped chats about how they felt it all went.

What I'm saying, I guess, is that growing up is confusing enough anyway, and that while the UK loves to point the finger at more unequal societies, our ideas of sexuality and immorality and shame and disobedience are still confusing as hell. I really hope we continue to open up conversations, particularly in schools, rather than spend another hundred or so years measuring skirt lengths or shaming unexpected erections while ignoring all the more potentially dangerous sexual tendencies which dominate much of our mainstream culture.

Also, I'd really love it if we could stop pretending that a grown woman is likely to orgasm from eating a frozen yoghurt. It's getting really boring now.

And yes, I would like another chocolate, thank you.

Just pass me the whole fucking box.

arguing in the head's office

he said
my skirt
was distracting
the lads.

roll it down.
legal length.
below knees.
like a nun.

i said:
some of
the boys
have their
trousers
so tight
i can see
the outline
of their
dicks,
sir.

i still manage to get on with my work.

when i am dead, will you finally shut the fuck up?

when i was a teenage girl
the newspapers printed
stories about monsters
they called paedophiles

when i was a teenage girl
a special assembly was called
which told us all to watch out
for a man flashing his penis
in the park near the school

we all thought it was funny
walked there especially
looked out for the long coat
pointed with our friends

when i was a teenage girl
one newspaper printed
a list of home addresses
of people they called
'paedophiles', vigilante
justice and one count
of linguistic ignorance
graffiti-ing the walls of
a paediatrician's home

when i was a teenage girl
i bought a top ten record
by another teenage girl
dancing in school uniform
like mine,

she sang *hit me baby*
one more time i sang
hit me baby one more time
not wondering whether the
clever chorus line referred to
punching or being fucked hard
or replaying a record

when I was a teenage girl
my friend was called a slag
for owning a vibrator

when i was a teenage girl
my friend was called a prude
for not getting fingered

when i was a teenage girl
the front cover of this album
had britney spears in pigtails
looking up at a camera
as virgin as could be
i did not wonder who directed it

when i was a teenage girl
my friend told everyone
he had fingered me in the garden
at a house party that weekend
when really he was crying
about a problem in his family
he apologised at school
i agreed not to tell the truth
we stayed close friends

when i was a teenage girl
i opened the cd in my bedroom
a poster folded up inside
to put up on my wall
it had britney dressed in
a virgin white vest top
with virgin white teeth
sat astride a chair
legs parted for the camera
camera zoomed onto her
schoolgirl crotch

when i was a teenage girl
i was told not to use a tampon
when i was bleeding playing sport
because that would be like
losing my virginity to a tampon
before i'd had a dick in me

i was told not to put a dick in me

i was told the only sex that counted
was sex with a dick in me

when I was a teenage girl
two teenage girls in a
Russian pop video were
directed to snog each other
in school uniform like mine
looking sexy at the camera
singing *all the things she said*
all the things she said

running through my head
running through my head

when i was a teenage girl
i was told off for wearing
a skirt too short for school
i rolled it down each lesson
and rolled it up each break

when i was a teenage girl
i was told i could not play
in the tennis team
unless i wore the match kit
match kit was a short white skirt
i was on my period
i did not use a tampon yet
'cos that would be like
ruining my pussy
before i'd had a dick in me
sanitary towels leaked a lot
i learned how to check for bloodstains
between backhand lobs

when i was a teenage girl
i was told not to risk the short cut
i was told not to walk alone
i was told not to stay out late
i was told not to masturbate
i was told not to get pregnant
i was told not to get fingered
i was told not to be too sexy
i was told not to not be sexy

i was told to sing hit me baby
hit me baby hit me baby
one more time in a uniform
like hers, i was told
all the things she said
all the things she said
running through my head
running through my head
running through my head

when i was in my twenties
i fed my baby in the toilet
for fear of looking like
i was sort of trying to look sexy
i'm still not sure exactly
why i was embarrassed
to feed a baby with my breasts
but i was

when i was thirty
my friend organised a botox party
before we went on holiday
because apparently
when you are thirty
laughter is less attractive

when i was thirty-five
i was told not to wear a vest top
because women my age
do not show our arms now
for fear of bats apparently
landing on the skin below

when I was forty
i was told my sex drive
would dry up with my bleeding
but no one talks about the menopause

when i was fifty, i was told
when i was sixty, when i was seventy
when i was eighty, i was told
i am hoping this will stop

but my grandma is ninety-two
and she is on a diet, because
in our family, as i've been told
my entire life long, the women
in our family have 'bad' stomachs

(hold it in, hollie
hold it in, hollie
hold it in, hollie)

when i am dead
i am hoping i can stretch out
in my coffin;
silence in my bones

sex advice from my dad when i was fifteen

don't have sex till you're dead

vulgar

If I'd had children and had a girl, the first
words I would have taught her would have
been 'fuck off', because we weren't brought up
ever to say that to anyone, were we?

HELEN MIRREN

you called me vulgar after the gig
spoke it softly like a mother
as if it were advice

head weighted to the side
like one earring made of osmium
sympathising with something
missing in my life
which i am *obviously filling*
with these obscenities

you smile at me
the way my grandma did
softly tuck my hair behind my ears
to keep it off my face, whispering:

i just wish you'd make something of yourself
or *you look lovely with mascara on*
or *must you be so crude?*

you do not ask my reasons
just advise the lack of need
to swear inside a poem

as if a poem were a planet crust
unsuited to volcanoes

you suggest i channel
a little more virginia woolf

i think of stones in my pocket
i think of plath in my pocket
i think their beautiful poems
i think depression and solitude
i think how aidan moffat
was on stage just after me
spitting in the gutter, yet
you did not soap his mouth

i think about poets with penises
and how few of those i know
have been advised against swearing

i think rabelais' chicken
chaucer and broomsticks
robert burns's nine inch
dylan thomas boozing
i think lord byron fucking
i think sex work and heckling
in shakespearean theatres
i think how swearing
has been scientifically proven
to release oxytocin
so stop advising me please
not to swear in my poems
as if i do not love language
have not chosen those words

deliberately finding them
expressive and beautiful
homely or useful sometimes,
my taboos are not yours

i don't say that though
i don't like being rude

so i smile, like a good woman
smile, like a good girl
who does not use words
we have deemed less worthy
of other words, we have deemed
more worthy of other words

you check i have heard
nod
pre-empting agreement
like an ant you have saved
with a delicate leaf
drowning ignorant
in a literary puddle

then you go,
i wait for a second
say *fuck you* in my head

and feel immediately
better able to breathe again

things my grandmothers warned me to conceal

for your own sake, my darling

your legs, my love, they said
and your breasts, my love, they said
and your bra straps and your backbone
and your tiptoes, they said

and your tongue, my love, they said
and your womb, my love, they said
and your footprints and your blood spills
and your brain, my love, they said

and your arms, my love, they said
and your scars, my love, they said
and your screams and your daydreams
and your learning and your longing
and your lust and your hunger
and your anger and your thirst

and your death, my love, and your life
my love, and your birth

being a rock at cambridge university

for dad

first philosophy class
professor begs silence
issues a question:

if you stop in a forest
to sit on a rock
are you sat on that rock
or are you, in fact
the rock? – discuss

i scan the classroom:
frowns firmly tilted
to mimic intelligence

thirsty new students'
eyes gaze at the ceiling,
like *are we the rock?*
are we the rock?

i sit silent
in stunned disbelief
thinking *no, we are not*
no, we are not

we discuss it in depth
i feel for my neck
wonder if death
is as tediously slow

call my dad later
read him the question
he says: *you're no fucking rock, love*
i say: *i know dad, i know*

chatty

inspired by Jackie Kay's poem 'Fiere'

for a lifelong friend; for all friends –
there is no nobel prize for chatting,
but i'd like to think we'd have a chance if there were

it started in our mothers' skins
us rising loaves! us parasites!
prenatal class, us curled inside
besides ourselves with laughter

i can't prove this,
just a guess:

our mums chat, bellies bulging buns
we punch from the inside out
in telepathic unison; walkie-talkies
room to room. what i'm saying is
before we'd even left the wombs;

we chatted and we chatted and we chatted

one month apart, we're out, we bawl
roll around the village hall
cup our fists in pits of sand
shite our nappies, piss our pants
i steal your spade, you bite my hand
we cry into our mothers' laps
mimic sounds we've overheard
what i'm saying is, before we even
spoke one word

we chatted and we chatted and we chatted

you found love in teenage years
ran to mine with detailed sex
ten years on, down the aisle
i wore the bridesmaid dress you stitched
my grandad died; you called me up
we made perfume from forget-me-nots
found love lost love found love again
i gave birth first, you gave birth second
your twins slept in passing shifts
you called me up with pumps on tits;
we discussed how lonely this shit is

and we chatted and we chatted and we chatted

my phone buzzed; connection broke
phone buzzed again; you choked
no one spoke; silent hugs;
you, a widow much too young
played the boys their father's songs
each moonlit bedtime; laid them down
called me up when tears allowed

and we chatted and we chatted and we chatted

my gran wished her final breath
i bought a kettle for myself
found love found guilt found love
broke up broke down broke up
you called me up, called him darling
replanted roses in your garden
we came round to meet your newfound man

our kids now giggling in the sand
wiped our tears when tears ran free
another tea? we both get up
the sun comes out to warm us up

the way it always does
the way i know it always will
the way it always has

when we chat and we chat and we chat

TAMPON VIRGINITY

The powerless are so tempting.

MARGARET ATWOOD, *The Testaments*

The fact that, looking back, I was told not to put a tampon into my sacred virgin vagina until a boy's penis had been present and willing is gross, but unfortunately not rare. Surely my own fingers could come first. A dildo or vibrator if I wanted (I have never worked out why you have to be eighteen to buy this sex toy but only sixteen to have actual sex by law with an actual penis).

The phrase 'losing your virginity' in itself is such outdated and dangerous pish and I have been told particularly traumatic for those whose 'first time' was not consensual, as if this one moment of penetration is a marker between purity and, well, non-purity. Also, by that sexual definition of virginity loss, everybody in the world who does not have penetrative sex with a penis is officially still a virgin, no matter how much pleasure or how many orgasms they might have had.

It was my friend's beautiful eight-year-old son that pointed this out to me. After the school nativity play, he had asked his mum what was so special about the Virgin Mary. His mother replied that she had had a baby without having had sex with a winkie. He said *but loads of women do that, with that injection thingy.*

What? we both said.

The injection thingy. Women can have babies with the injection thingy, can't they?

I'd never thought about it. But yes. In our stupid sexual definitions of virginity, every woman who has had a baby without having had a penis inside her vagina is effectively a virgin mother. I'm not saying *Jesus's* virgin mother, but a virgin mother nonetheless.

I was not brought up as a Christian but was very much brought up in a Christian culture and our obsession with this sort of virginity loss, particularly female virginity loss, still permeated life from a very young age.

In primary school, we played out the nativity each year. I understand this is important in Christianity in that it is the story of Jesus's birth, but we never acted out the Good Samaritan or that bit when Jesus handed bread and fish out to lots of poor folk. If we'd have obsessed over that, I think I'd have grown up both sexually safer and a nicer, kinder person.

No, it was the birth story we acted out over and over, the bloodless child birth of a virgin girl who we then hear nothing of after she becomes a mum. I never played Mary. I was most often a grumpy shepherd, stood with a fluffy sheep in my hand and a tea towel wrapped around my head. I started calling Joseph 'Virgin Joseph' to my daughter just to try to balance things up during her years of nativity playing, but she told me off *because that's not his name.*

At the same time as I was being told not to lose my sacred vagina virginity to a tampon, I was also being taught in sex education class how to protect myself from carrots ejaculating inside me as if safe penetration was the only sexual possibility we had.

I understand the idea that having a classroom of teenagers practising how to massage a fake vulva or wank a fake penis seems very odd. It does to me. But really, is this more ludicrous than a classroom of students, which was my experience, sitting in rows learning how

117

to place a condom over a fake carrot penis? In that classroom, as we grappled with the rubbers, we were being taught 'safe sex'. Non-reproductive sex. Sex purely for sex's sake. Kantian sex. We had already crossed the immoral pleasure barrier but were only allowed to cross it if it still included penetration with a penis.

This annoys me for many reasons, one of those being that, of all the consensual sexual experiences I've had, it is penetrative sex with a condom which has been the least pleasurable. I don't like sex with condoms. This probably isn't a good thing to say for someone who did an advert for Durex, but it's true. Also, the advert I did was for clitoral stimulation gel. I can't say it did anything for me other than sting my vulva a lot, but maybe it is nice that condom companies are acknowledging that this body part exists.

I have heard some guys complain about condom use, mainly when trying to get out of wearing one, which is never OK. My favourite ever quote about this kind of pressure is a tweet by @danadonly:

when guys are like 'i'm not gonna be able to cum with a condom on' it's like ok. cool. sorry to hear that. i'm probably not gonna be able to cum at all, so i guess we'll get through it together.

I've used condoms of course because, as I was taught at school, they are the one form of protection against both STDs and pregnancy in p in v sex. For this reason, I am truly grateful that they exist. But of all the sexual experiences I've had, penetrative sex with a condom-clad penis has been the least lovely and, looking back, I'm really not sure who I was doing it for once I realised I wasn't getting much out of it. I don't hate it, but it definitely took more of a centre stage than I would have liked, had I known how to speak up a bit more about my own body.

Also, whilst I was taught how to place a condom awkwardly over a carrot, I was not taught how to gain the confidence to insist on this during a sexual moment or to communicate other things I might prefer. As a young person, there was an added nervousness or guilt in asking for this from a boy, which there shouldn't be, but there was for me.

If these hurdles were passed, once the condom was on, it then often seemed to imply that the sex we now had to have was fifteen minutes, or ten minutes or five minutes or two minutes (depending on the person and situation), of in-and-out penetration until he came.

It's tricky to do lots of different things with a condom on. It's hard to have a little bit of this and then a little bit of that and then a little bit of this again and so on. All that chopping and changing, which is one of the things I love in sex, is not easy with a condom on. Condoms are designed mainly for safely cumming into.

I've had a condom slip off. I've chickened out of buying them for fear of what the person at the pharmacy would think or say about my morality. I've thought I had one 'lost' inside me (before I knew that your vagina has an end point and that condoms and tampons cannot physically get past the cervix and get lost inside your body as I panicked for many years could happen).

So pleasure was a condom carrot for us to grapple with in front of all the boys, learning how to make their penises safer to put inside us or each other, though the latter was of course also not mentioned.

Not once did the boys have to sit in front of a classroom of us girls learning how to stroke us by fingering a fig, which would also, I'm sure, have helped many of the girls. I would have appreciated that. Especially because this obsession with penetration also extended to fingering, which, for most teenage boys, appeared to translate into finger banging and finger banging only, a mimickry of continuous poking but with a much smaller tool. It didn't count unless you got inside. Home run.

Our continual cultural focus on penetrative sex as both the sexual norm and the marker of a loss of some sort of invisible innocence seems both confused and dangerous, especially for young, inexperienced or less confident people. It makes penetration *the thing* that

119

counts, *the thing* we should focus on sexually and *the thing* which has, for thousands of years, become a sought-after commodity, still putting children and young people at risk worldwide.

Many parents around me still baulk at the idea of saying anything other than 'Mummy and Daddy have sex to make babies' to their children, as if sex for closeness and pleasure and love is *still* something not to admit to, even in long-term holy blessed marriages. But if fingering, for example, was discussed more openly from an early age, I think it'd dramatically lower future stress levels, unwanted pregnancies, STDs, the orgasm gap, the pay gap, electricity consumption and possibly save the planet. OK, not that much, but it would sure as hell help.

Sex education in the UK has undoubtedly moved on, but many traditions around me still cling to these ideas of purity. In my adult life, weddings have been the biggest example of this. The wedding dress in particular.

Most people I have known, despite having been sexually active with their partners for years before marriage, still opted for white. Understandable. It is their tradition and the dresses look amazing and it is the epitome of the beautiful (Christian) bride. Beautiful, in its historic sense, meaning untouched, virginal; as bleached clean as the Holiday Inn towels which I frequently have to stain with period blood after showers and feel terrible leaving in the bathroom. The history behind the white wedding dress is not something I knew about until a friend opted out of it for her wedding and explained why.

There are of course many situations worldwide in which the virginity of a bride is still brutally checked pre- and post-wedding, where girls are chosen young to ensure this virginity is still intact, where women have surgery to sew their genitals back up to a supposed virgin state pre-marriage, where child sex workers take a higher price because of a belief that their purity and youth will rub off on those who have sex with them.

Wearing a white dress to consensually marry someone you love is of course not this. It is a tradition, but one which I do sometimes wish we'd stop promoting quite so much as the ideal of women's beauty if we ourselves are aware of its meaning and do not consent to the mindset it promotes. The other side of this, I guess, is that the idea of telling someone that they shouldn't wear a white dress because they've had penetrative sex as if they are no longer pure enough to wear the gown is maybe worse.

Virgin fixation aside, white dresses are really impractical, especially as, according to weddingstats.org, they cost, on average, $1,259, roughly £1000. But there's still undoubtedly also a stigma to not wearing white as a bride in my culture. A shock. A scorn of traditions, as if you're advertising yourself as a broken slag for all the world to see as you walk into a promise of lifelong compassion.

I was talking to my gran about it all, as per usual, and she said she believed in pre-wedding celibacy, by which she meant all sexual acts, which made my pregnant unwed body slightly unbearable for her to look at. She said she thought it was right not to have any sex before marriage. By the sound of it, she also seemed to be including kissing with tongues within this abstinence, though I can't be sure. She then said, *But you kids are doing it more sensibly these days and living with partners before marriage because it was a really stupid idea in my day to marry someone you've never lived with.* Then she said she thought it was also good that we were often getting married later in life, not as a teenager, like she was.

So, don't marry until later, live together for years, but don't have sex until marriage. It's a tricky ask, Gran! I laughed. She scolded me for being obsessed with penises and asked if I wanted another cup of tea.

In the end, my friend Hanna convinced me not to listen to that tampon teacher, and helped me work out how to use one. Thank the Lord for friends. I managed it after a few attempts and tennis matches became a lot less stressful. I used a tampon before I ever had p in v sex and am one hundred per cent sure the boy did not notice that he was not in fact my first true love, as we lay together kissing and hugging and watching the sunrise afterwards.

There is a poem by William Letford called 'The songs we have'. I flick to it sometimes when I find myself batting my eyelashes in that apparently attractive frightened child-model pose, speaking in a voice which is much more high-pitched than my own actual adult voice and looking to the floor as if my head was born with a downward tilt, embarassed by its own brain.

This poem is the first love poem I ever read written by a man for a woman, in which the woman's previous sex life is held up as beautiful. Not beautiful as in 'she'll be a good ride' sort of a way. Just OK. Interesting. It begins: *I don't know how many people she'd slept with / it's not often that you do. I had an idea she'd / travelled with bands.* After admitting occasional jealousy, it ends: *But you know, I had the feeling she'd lived / I liked that too. She reminded me of vinyl, and she loved vinyl . . . Listening intently to the versions of herself still alive in the music.*

summits

for the other beautiful first times in my life that no one has ever asked about

first
first time i
first time i came
first time i snogged
first time i slow-danced
first time i slept on sand
first time i had an orgasm
first time i tried to orgasm
first time i dived into the sea
first time i saw shooting stars
first time i ate above the clouds
first time i heard my child laugh
first time i got a train on my own
first time i got fingered on a train
first time i got given a pay cheque
first time i rode without stabilisers
first time i went to see a live band
first time i used a dildo exquisitely
first time i popped a sweet pea pod
first time i sat with someone dying
first time i managed to do the splits
first time i held a penis in my hand
first time i gave someone an orgasm
first time i made a chair out of snow
first time i enjoyed giving a blowjob
first time i saw other people have sex
first time i really enjoyed cunnilingus
first time i kissed in a lightning storm
first time i dreamt in another language
first time i came onto someone's palm
first time i came onto someone's tongue
first time my child wrote me a sorry note
first time i had penetrative sex in a forest
first time i orgasmed at a lego conference
first time i had an orgasm during p in v sex
first time i let someone touch me on the anus
first time i was fingered by someone on mdma
first time i saw gok wan walking down the street
first time i managed to do a front flip on a trampoline
first time i stepped off an aeroplane in a really hot country
first time i read the ending of the lion, the witch and the wardrobe
first time i walked to the local shop on my own (as mum followed me in the car)

the morning after

i stared into the mirror, searching for the change
counted all my freckles, every one of them in place
counted every hair, every eyelash, every brow
five knuckles on each hand still, thirty-one teeth in my mouth

i cut open my flesh, counted seven layers deep
for a minute, held my heart, counted eighty solid beats
lips still as pure as blood, i spat into the sink
walked into the world again

i hadn't lost a thing

the holy lesbian

according to our traditional definition of sex
a lesbian never loses virginity

an unrivalled purity
a sexual deity

i'm thinking mary.
maybe?

shoe shopping in the girls' toilets

for hanna, and your help
for the pride in those first school shoes

like catwalking the shop floor
to test how well they fit

the heady smell of patent bows
the smile of the assistant

mum thumbing at the universe
between your big toes and the leather

          have you managed yet? she whispers
          tiptoeing next door's toilet lid

          her nose and forehead haloed
          in the glaring uv lights

          a few more clenching wiggles
          a few more squats for size

one last circuit of the shop floor
buckles buckled tight

shoes gift wrapped into tissue; box appearing
out of nowhere; magician at the till

try to touch your toes
you shouldn't feel it when it's in

you bend and touch your toes one time
you bend and touch again

leave the cubicle at last
catwalk slowly to the sinks

you carry that big bag yourself
like someone fully grown

wonder, when you step outside
if everyone will know

safe sex (poem to my younger self)

dear hollie
there are other things safer
than a condom on a carrot
despite what mr clark says
as you grapple with the package
and kathryn says *they smell weird*
and peter says his ripped
and chris's slips away
flicking thurston in the face
which doesn't seem too safe

dear hollie
there are other things safer
than a condom on a carrot
despite what tv tells you
like, fingering yourself
like being fingered in your bedroom
like being fingered on the bus
like being fingered on the big wheel
at the annual newbury fair
on half price wednesday
when all the rides are one pound
instead of three pounds
which i still agree makes
a really *massive* difference
to how many rides you
can get fingered on
make sure hands are washed
if candyfloss is stuck to skin
    – the big wheel gives the most time

– romantic as the sun sets
– do not rock the carriage

like sitting on a lover's lap
in leggings or those spiffy jeans
you thought were really cool
because rowena had them first
pretending he's a rocking horse
denim denim crotch to crotch
it's called dry humping, it's lovely
don't tell queen victoria

like being licked out on the sofa
while eating a bag of
pickled onion monster munch
(they are still your favourite crisps)
try to tell him what feels nice
you do not have to scream

like trying out a sixty-niner
which can feel a little clumsy
and which, by the way
that song by bryan adams
which you dance to every week
in the second room in liquid
is actually about
which you know now
because if you look at the date
bryan adams was only ten
in the summer of 1969
also, you watched an interview with him
and he said it was about sixty-niners

like wanking a guy
onto any of your skin
other than your vulva or vagina
(curled up hands work well
/ inner thighs work too
/ boobs, if not as small as yours
although you can shoogle them together
if you really want to try it
but sometimes it feels desperate
and you have no side boob left
'cos you need it all for the wanking bit
and it's like your boobs are being
humiliated, but sometimes it's ok,
it all depends on how comfortable
you are with the person
this will always be the case
   – armpits work well too
    rhiannon tells me that's called bagpiping –

like cuddling in bed
like hugging naked for a long time
licking one another's heads

like role play, if you're into that
wearing flippers and a scuba mask
shouting *aarhhhhh arrhhhh arhhhhh*
whilst you stroke each other's arseholes
making noises like the noises
of whales you will see one day
off the coast of kaikoura in new zealand
where you will vomit on the boat
but still have so much fun

is still safer
than the safe sex
anyone will teach you
on the safe sex school curriculum

updating shame

if we're going to save the planet
perhaps we need to ask:
is the virgin sipping bottled water
still more holy than the whore
who fills a flask?

conversation with kids

when did you first have sex?

i said:

thirteen – by myself
fifteen – sharing hands
seventeen – with mouths
twenty – when I did
the only type of sex
they'll teach you all to count

DRESS UP

I didn't think clothing rules would start so young when I had a baby, but from Babygro get go, they did. Pink or blue, love hearts or tractors, bunnies or sharks. The animal world, my editor Helen Mort pointed out to me, has been divided into our binary human clothing categories: predator animals for little people with penises, prey for the little people with vulvas.

Now, there are new issues: like letting my daughter coat her face in kid's make-up, or not. Like letting her wear belly tops, or not. I don't *like* the fact that we promote hot pants and belly tops for young girls, but I also don't like the idea that, from the age of five, I'm meant to police how much of a particular body part my child shows.

There's a great photograph by artist Rosea Posey, which shows the varying labels attached to a woman's personality as she wears varying lengths of skirt. From just below crotch to ankle, the labelling goes:

(crotch)
> whore
> slut
> asking for it
> provocative
> cheeky
> flirty
> proper
> old-fashioned
> prudish
> matronly

(ankle)

As my child grew up, I increasingly heard the word 'over-sexualised' used in relation to clothes sold for young girls. And I agree.

When you shop in the boys' section, there are no hot pants designed for toddler arses to hang out. His chest and nipples are not so sexualised or censored and therefore allowed free rein to the elements when he gets too hot whereas little girls are sold bikinis and crop tops to cover their illegal girl nipples from the age of about one. But, when little girls *wear* those bikinis or belly tops or anything else designed to cover their offending nipples, these outfits themselves are often also deemed over-sexualising. It's a fucking lose–lose scenario and it has started to piss me off every day of my life as a parent. I never thought I'd have to grapple with what swimwear was or was not 'appropriate' before my daughter even learned how to fucking swim. It's bullshit.

As she got older and more interested in dressing herself, every time she asked to wear anything which could be interpreted as 'dressing as an adult' – like wanting to wear a bikini like mine or trying on my make-up or belly tops – it was frowned upon. If not directly, then by other girls letting my daughter know that *they* weren't allowed to wear *those things*. Hearing two six-year-old girls discussing why one of their T-shirts was inappropriate was challenging.

I guess wearing make-up is an easy example. My daughter often watched me put on make-up when I was going out for the night and then wanted to 'dress up' in it too. I let her. She coated her eyes in all the colours of the rainbow and painted lipstick on her lips (and half her face). But when she did this when we were going to leave the house, I froze because I knew that if other people saw her there'd be a whole heap of judgement. On me.

There are arguments about people wearing make-up in general, and I agree with both. I can't stand the insecurities deliberately fuelled by the beauty industry but I love the fun of dressing up. I think there's a huge difference between being made to feel like I *have* to wear make-up to achieve what is pushed by this industry as a good enough face or good enough skin or individually curled eyelashes and so on, and then there's wearing make-up in the way most kids do – because it's colourful and fun and can give you a whole new character. Like face paint.

I was 'talked to' on quite a few occasions for allowing my kid to go to a friend's party in eyeshadow, or wear a sporty crop top in the park to play football with a bunch of topless boys. It started to seem like anything my daughter wore that emulated adult women or showed the area of flesh that would one day possibly contain more fatty tissue than its male counterpart was deemed 'sexualising'.

The same did not seem to happen to little boys. Their nipples, for a start, were fine. When they gelled their hair like their favourite pop star; even when, on the primary school dress-up day, half of them turned up in superhero costumes which consisted of thick padded nylon suits, producing comically over-muscled-torso male adult bodies, nobody batted an eyelid. Instead everybody found it funny to see these mini men puffed up with six packs.

Don't get me wrong, I don't think the over-muscled over-gendered superhero complex is doing anyone any favours either. Campaigns surrounding toxic masculinity increasingly highlight and debate this.

Perhaps it's because little girls *are* more at risk from predatory men if they look more like adult women. Perhaps it's because women's bodies are just seen as intrinsically sexual because they have been presented that way for years, and therefore anything that makes a little girl look more adult is viewed as over-sexualised. Perhaps it's a mix of all that. Either way, it's a horrible thing to watch develop.

On that school dress-up day, I tried to imagine what would have happened if I'd allowed my daughter to go to school in a costume comparable to those boys' muscled superhero costumes; if I'd let her stuff socks into a bra and wear it under a female superhero costume, fake tits and hips bulging through the nylon. Probably the same thing that would have happened if a little boy was put in the belly top and short shorts that most young girls are sold.

It pisses me off daily that I'm so torn between policing everything my child wears and being seen as a totally shit and even dangerous unprotective parent if I don't. I am sick of explaining to her why her friends are not allowed to wear belly tops like hers. I'm sick of her having to even think about her belly the way I was made to think about my thighs and knees during all my school years.

The same week I was grappling with the 'But what's wrong with showing our bellies, Mum?' question, I read an article in the *Guardian* magazine entitled 'The wardrobe remix: show just the right amount of skin in a portrait neckline'. The model 'showing just the right amount of skin' was the standard smiling white middle-class cis woman looking like she'd just baked a new round of cupcakes just because she wanted to. 'The right amount of skin for what?' I yelled at the page. 'For being allowed to join the local tennis club? For not being called a slag by the other mums on the school run? For not being seen as a woman who likes to have her fanny licked now and then? For what, motherfuckers, the right amount of flesh for what?'

It never stops. It is this sort of polite, subtle reminder still permeating society even for fully grown adult women to show just the 'right amount' of flesh that makes me want to either wrap my daughter's body up in protective-parent packaging and hide her in a lightless cave, or run through town with my tits out screaming 'Fuck this shit'.

For the little boys, there are equal controls to deal with. Different rules, different reasonings, but just as strict. Put bluntly, as far as I can see, in order for our little boys to be accepted within a still largely homophobic and transphobic society, they must keep their hair short, enjoy football and dress either as Batman, or in the dullest fucking colours we can force them into.

dress-up day

the little boys giggle to school
superhero costumes fast-forward
protein shaken skin
for fundraising dress-up day

six packs stuffed like puppeteers
chests puff big man muscles
red knickers over lycra

i imagine the uproar
if my daughter did the same;

superwoman body
cleavage sewn in place
grapefruits stuffed in corset
for childish-bosomed chest;

they'd say *inappropriate*
they'd say *over-sexed*
girls giggling cartoon women skins
as boys giggle cartoon men's

the boy in the pearl earrings

you'd have thought
another comet struck
the day we caught
their only son
clipping on his mother's bra
toddling stiletto stilts
gaping gap from skin to heel
the way i used to wobble
spiralling my mum's fake pearls
before scavenging my father's clothes
shirts skimming skinny knees
jacket tents and tartan ties
as everybody laughed with me
and no one seemed to mind
as i transitioned girl to boy
to girl to boy and mum
mascaraed me a moustache
above my grinning lips
and my uncle took a photograph
and someone shouted
just a minute, man . . .
placed a beer can in left hand
cigarette into my mouth

testicles

unless, of course, there is fear of attack, Hollie,
never, ever kick a boy in the nut sack again

of all the words my dad spoke
these still echo off each crotch i see

i watched him, from that day on,
differently,

the boy, releasing mother's hand at gates
the boy, bundling playground friends
the boy, tensing molehill biceps
the boy, sweating sudden stiffness
the boy, plucking at our bra straps
the boy, plucking at guitar chords
the boy, plucking at his moustache sperms
bum fluff growth inversely graphed
with how many times we would ever
see him weep out loud again

in crowds, i still picture them, pinned to the outside
those soft hearts hid in cotton, slapping thigh to thigh
open to the elements; waterbombs of effervescence

vulnerable as virgin boys, whistled over trenches
dreaming of their womb

not fucking teenage boys in france

after claims that the schoolgirl the teacher ran away with
'actually came on to him first though'

at twenty-two years old
i was handed the basketball team to teach;

eighteen years
each one of them

their flesh, a surgeon's textbook wank
vital organs fresh as bleeding steak
muscles just a flick of heat
sirloin at its tend'rest;
french accents melting in my mouth

as legal as raping wives
in the eighties

at least a couple boys each lesson
lingered after class; flirting pre-ejaculate
as if already inside me; smiled cheeky
as they left, winked, let me let me
let them

so what i did
was *not* fuck them

i'm not saying this for medals
just right now some folk are claiming
this shit's trickier than it is

141

ROUGH HISTORY OF SKIRTS, PANTS
AND OTHER APPARENT OBSCENITIES

When I started secondary school, we had no option to wear trousers until I was in sixth form. The only reason the school rules were changed was because the entire sixth form refused to go to lessons until the powers that be changed them. Obviously, sitting chatting with mates in the school canteen rather than being in class was a bonus. I had nothing to do with organising this. I was forcefully unpolitical in my teenage years. But it worked. The rules changed for everyone.

I didn't know anything about the history behind my newfound freedom to wear trousers in public institutions as I sat chatting to friends in the canteen that day. I didn't know that it was part of a timeline which, picking and choosing random facts about trousers and other aspects of our incredible human fear of letting people wear what they like, went something like this:

3,500 BC: Archaeological evidence suggests that nomadic steppe people all wear trousers, whatever bodies they own.

2,500 BC: Sumerian and Akkadian texts document transgender priests.

3,500 BC – present: All around the world, it becomes the case that people who are identified as female are banned from wearing trousers and then start wanting to wear trousers but are routinely arrested for wearing said trousers under indecency or morality laws, either because wearing trousers goes against a religious dress code or because these people are deemed as cross-dressers if they wear trousers and this goes against morality or obscenity laws. Like people identified as male wanting to wear stereotypically 'feminine' clothing, whose rights have been much, much slower to change in this respect.

1841: As part of an investigation into working conditions in British mines, commissioner Samuel Scriven describes as 'something truly hideous and Satanic' the sight of men and women working side by side, all stripped to the waist in the heat, the women wearing trousers and bare-breasted. The young women miners were condemned in the Victorian papers as 'unsuitable for marriage and unfit to be mothers' and the *Manchester Guardian* described trousers as 'the article of clothing which women ought only to wear in a figure of speech'. The miners' union declared the findings of the report – the part about women in trousers (not the other parts about sickness and injury and squalid working conditions for all the miners) as 'a sickening sight'. In 1842 in a speech to Parliament, Lord Ashley described how this work sometimes led to holes in the women and girls' trousers, stating, 'Any sight more disgustingly indecent or revolting can scarcely be imagined than these girls at work. No brothel can beat it.' Nice.

1908: Fashion designer Paul Poiret popularises the 'hobble skirt', a skirt which caused a scandal for being worn without heavy petticoats below, but which also wrapped the ankles so that women could only move in tiny steps. Some entrances to street cars and trains were redesigned to be lower so women in these skirts could still board them. When talking about the skirt, Poiret, who is often hailed as having helped rid women of the corset, stated, 'Yes, I freed the bust

143

but I shackled the legs.' The fashion becomes even more impractical with the outbreak of the First World War and fades, taking with it the heavy petticoats previously 'essential' for women.

1910: Magnus Hirschfeld coins the term 'transvestite' to mean someone with a sexual interest in cross-dressing, applied to people who are seen to habitually and voluntarily wear clothes 'of the opposite sex'. He aids Baer, Richter and Elbe with work at the Institut für Sexualwissenschaft for trans medicine and rights, which is then destroyed by the Nazis in 1933.

1917: Shortly after the United States' entry into the First World War, the US War Industries Board asks women to stop buying corsets to free up metal for war production. This step liberates some 28,000 tons of metal, enough to build two battleships.

1919: Labour leader Luisa Capetillo is declared the first woman in Puerto Rico to wear trousers in public. Capetillo is sent to jail for what is then considered to be a crime in her country, although the judge later drops the charges against her.

1939: *Vogue* features a woman in trousers for the first time.

1969: Barbra Streisand is the first woman to attend the Oscars in trousers. The media world loses its shit, though it is unclear whether this is because of the trousers or the sheer fabric they are made from. Likely both.

1998: David Beckham wears a 'skirt-like' sarong in public. The media world loses its shit again, despite this style of clothing being worn by men in many other cultures.

2000: My secondary school adds trousers to the girls' uniform policy.

2013: I buy more plasters to cover my feet because we are going club-bing again and my stiletto heels are fucking painful to dance in and I already have a cut on the back of my foot from the shoes rubbing last week as well as blisters on my soles and a cut on my toe from the pavement while walking home barefoot after the kebab van closed.

2014: The *Daily Mail* are still writing articles about David Beckham having worn a skirt-like sarong almost sixteen years ago. Headline reads, 'Sarong, so right! David Beckham says he doesn't regret wear-ing that skirt'.

2015: After complaints about regulations forcing women to wear high heels to work, the Israeli airline El Al establishes a rule* that all female cabin crew have to wear high heels until all passengers are seated and then they can change into flats.

2016: Nicola Thorp, a twenty-seven-year old employee of auditing firm PWC, starts a national petition against women being forced to wear high heels to work.

2016: In the first week of primary school my daughter wears leg-gings. When she sees the other girls in the uniform skirts, she starts refusing to wear leggings. The second week of school, in a skirt, just above her knees, she leapfrogs over the bollards she always leapfrogs over when wearing leggings. The middle of the skirt catches on the concrete bollard and she falls head first onto the pavement. The next day, she starts hanging upside down from the climbing frame as she'd always done at pre-school, only now you can see her knickers. Parents recommend she wears shorts underneath her skirt so as not to flash her knickers. I don't know how to tell my daughter that it is no longer

* jpost.com/Israel-News/El-Al-slammed-for-new-high-heels-rule-for-flight-attendants-406065

considered acceptable for her to hang from the climbing frame without wearing shorts underneath her skirt whilst also explaining why she can't just wear the shorts to school without the skirt, because I don't know the answers to this myself.

2016: A primary school in England bans any girl who is wearing a skirt or dress without shorts underneath from doing cartwheels or climbing on the climbing frame. There are no girls' shorts in the school uniform policy though so they still have to wear the dress or skirt over the shorts.

2017: *Guardian* headline relating to another UK school reads, 'Teenage boys wear skirts to school to protest against "no shorts" policy'. This is a school where boys are not allowed to wear shorts, even during the summer term.

2018: *Esquire* releases another article about how David Beckham feels twenty years after wearing 'that sarong'.

2019: My kid's teacher at primary school tells the class of eight- to nine-year-olds that none of the girls are allowed to wear 'two-pieces' for swimming lessons, not even tankinis, and reiterates this the day before their lessons with the words, 'and, girls, I do not want to see any belly on show'. My daughter complains about this after school. I ask my daughter if seeing boys' bellies in swimming is OK. She says yes, the boys show their bellies but some of them don't want to. I ask her if boys can wear swimming costumes to cover their bellies. She says no. We discuss why boys have to show their bellies and girls have to not show their bellies. One of my friends points out how lots of the boys are actually wearing shorts and rash vests for swimming and *are* therefore wearing 'two-pieces' and we wonder if this will be banned as well. At home that night, my daughter and I play illegal belly Barbies for two hours and she laughs a lot as all the Barbies are arrested for having their bellies on display in bikinis or their nipples out at the swimming pool (although Barbie's boobs of course don't actually have nipples because that would corrupt the minds of all children who play with them). I go to sleep that night crying because my daughter now thinks that her belly and nipples and bikini tops are somehow going to get her in trouble at school and are therefore 'wrong'.

2019: My daughter is called a tomboy while wearing a tracksuit in the park.

2019: My daughter is called a girly girl while wearing a sequined dress in the park.

2019: Facebook agrees to rethink its policy on nudity, which currently allows male nipples but not female nipples to be displayed; female nipples still being deemed more obscene by legal standards because . . . they might be able to feed a baby? Have more fatty tissue inside them? The move comes after protests from photographers and breastfeeding mothers about their accounts being closed. Examples of these online protesters include artist Micol Hebron, who invents the 'male nipple cut-out', an image of a single male nipple that photographers begin pasting over female nipples to allow photographs to be left uncensored online. If these male nipple cut-outs are held up by models to just cover their females nipples, they are not censored online. Another example is @genderless_nipples, which consists of close-up photographs of nipples which do not allow their owners' gender to be seen, again highlighting the absurdity of this disparity in social media regulations.

2019: Singer Sam Smith makes headlines after wearing high heels to a public award ceremony. They are quoted as saying, 'There was a time I thought I'd never ever ever be able to be myself like this in front of the industry or anyone. It feels so good.'

2019: Mattel launches range of gender-neutral dolls.

2019: Merriam-Webster adds non-binary 'they' pronoun to the dictionary.

2019: *BBC News* article headline reads, 'Transgender hate crimes recorded by police go up 81 per cent'.

pink or blue

pink
or
blue

pink
or
blue

pink
or blue

go!

babygros for blue with robots on
babygros for pink – no robots on
babygros for pink with flowers on
babygros for blue – no flowers on

little pink picks a daisy chain – great!
little blue picks a daisy chain – gay
little blue climbs a tree – strong boy
little pink climbs a tree – tomboy

pink falls down
pink is given more hugs
pink tears allowed
blue tears must man up
grow some bollocks, toughen up
don't be such a girl, blue!

now blue hair is cut short
pink hair is grown long
pink is given toy dolls
blue is given toy guns
pink is told to be cute
blue is told to be bigger
pink shoes – no grip
blue shoes – no glitter

now
blue legs start growing hairs
and pink legs start growing hairs
blue told this is manly
pink is told to shave theirs

blue is shown as blood
action film, fight, pride
pink starts bleeding every month
blood *shh!* shame hide

pink discovers lust – wrong
blue discovers lust – right

now
blue is called a player
pink is called a sket
pink is told they glow
blue is told they sweat
blue is told they wank
pink is told they sin
or
blue is called a pussy
pink is called a bitch

now
pink is told to be a lady
do not spit – swear – smell
blue is told to be a man
do not cry or ask for help
blue is told to man up
pink is told to make up
blue is told to stay strong
pink is told to stay young
blue is told to get rich
pink is told to want kids
blue is told they mansplain
pink is told they gossip
blue is told they're bosses
pink is told they're bossy
blue is having breakdowns
pink is having botox

cunnilingus is censored
more than rape scenes
or blowjobs

blue is told: this makes a man
pink is told: this makes a girl

babies born in naked flesh
welcome to the world

taking a compliment

for that moment in every teenage romance film I ever watched
when the boy declares his love for the girl by insulting every
other girl on the planet and she smiles as if her life is now
worth living and lets him kiss her and i wish she would say this
instead (and then kiss him still if she wants to) but she doesn't
say this, she just smiles because she either didn't get to write
the script or, after watching so many similar films in her own
upbringing, she also believes that she is only attractive to this
boy because she's different to the other stupid, boring bitches
around her

he calls her clever
he calls her curious
he calls her witty
he calls her fun

he says
she isn't like the other girls

she says
yes

yes
i am

taking a compliment

because it works the other way too

she calls him sweet
she calls him caring
she calls him timid
she calls him soft

she says
he's different from the other guys

he says
no

no
i'm not

A NOTE ON 'PINK OR BLUE': CHAUCER AND KHIA

There's a video for the poem 'pink or blue' online, directed by Jake Dypka. He's a brilliant director. He is also one of my good friends from school and I didn't know he worked in film till he offered to do a video for another poem I wrote about breastfeeding on toilet seats, which he did unpaid, as did all the film crew. He's the only person I've tried to smoke banana skins with. It didn't work. We played laser quest instead.

I get asked to do readings in schools quite a lot. Annoyingly, but understandably, a lot of schoolteachers have emailed me to say they'd love to play the video of this poem to their students but *do I have a version without reference to cunnilingus* (a man looks up and winks, smiling, from between a woman's legs – no nudity shown) *or without the picture of a vibrator in it?* These are the only two parts of the video that schoolteachers have ever said would stop them from being sure they could show it to their class. Not the mention of guns. Of course not. Just the mention of cunnilingus and vibrators.

I find it quite ironic, if I am understanding the meaning of irony correctly. (I loved Alanis Morissette's album *Jagged Little Pill* and I always felt bad for her when she was dissed so much for getting the meaning of irony wrong because even after studying irony at school for a long time I'm still not quite sure I get it. Maybe that's ironic, is it? I just don't know.)

Anyway, teachers don't feel comfortable showing a poem which mentions cunnilingus. The ironic (maybe) thing is that the line in this poem about cunnilingus is specifically referring to the censorship of cunnilingus: 'cunnilingus is censored more than rape scenes or blowjobs'. I added it to the poem after reading about a film that came out called *Charlie Countryman*. The lead actress, Evan Rachel Wood, objected to the editing out of a scene in which she receives oral sex. She didn't know it had been cut until the premiere and made a series of protests on Twitter:

> After seeing the new cut of #CharlieCountryman I would like 2 share my disappointment with the MPAA, who thought it was necessary to censor a woman's sexuality once again. The scene where the two main characters make 'love' was altered because someone felt that seeing a man give a woman oral sex made people 'uncomfortable' but the scenes in which people are murdered by having their heads blown off remain intact and unaltered.
>
> This is a symptom of a society that wants to shame women and put them down for enjoying sex, especially when (gasp) the man isn't getting off as well! It's hard for me to believe that had the roles been reversed it still would have been cut. OR had the female character been raped it would have been cut. It's time for people to GROW UP.
>
> Accept that women are sexual beings ... Accept that some men like pleasuring women. Accept that women don't have to just be fucked and say thank you. We are allowed and entitled to enjoy ourselves. It's time we put our foot down ...

This incident started a lot of online discussion about how oral sex in particular is censored in the media, censored least of course if it's a straight guy receiving it from a woman.

It also opened discussion about how rape can be implied more easily on TV and film because it comes under the 'violent' category and not the 'sexually stimulating / pornographic' category of censorship laws. This means that an implied rape scene may be shown with a lower censorship rating than a scene depicting consensual sexual pleasure, particularly if that sexual pleasure is not shown in the form of heterosexual p in v sex.

If this is still the case, it is royally fucked up. We can imply violence and pain on screen, including sexual violence, before we can imply many forms of consensual sexual pleasure, particularly when that pleasure is female-led, queer, kink.

The team behind *Basic Instinct*, hailed during my teen years as the height of sexiness in film mainly because of the scene where a white woman opens her legs without pants on in front of a group of men, cut a cunnilingus scene too. This is a film which starts with a man being murdered during sex and goes on to recount a series of murders after that. Murder, no problem. Murder during sex, no problem. Cunnilingus, too much. When another film, *Blue Valentine*, refused to cut a scene depicting cunnilingus, it was subjected to a higher rating.

Programmes such as *Fleabag*, *Chewing Gum* and *Sex Education* have undoubtedly been fast-forwarding many sexual conversations, and the joy and shock that these programmes have been met with within my friendship groups has been illuminating, messages like 'Fuck me, they showed a tampon, did you see they actually showed a tampon!' or 'Oh my god, he sent her away to masturbate, hallelujah!' filling my phone. Periods and masturbation, two very normal parts of many people's lives.

One of my favourite modern film scenes in this respect is in *Marriage Story* when the lead character, a woman, tells a man she is getting together with for a fumble in a car during a drunken night, 'I want you to finger me, that's all we're going to do, I'm changing my whole fucking life here.' The film was hailed as a masterpiece in general. Personally, I hated it but I cried at this scene. This sort of heterosexual sex, the quick party one-night-stand variety, I have never seen portrayed as anything but a quick bit of p in v. Scarlett Johansson saying the word 'fingering' will turn me on for ever, as the queer community around me once again laughs: 'Have you straight women still not worked this shit out?'

The relationships and sex education curriculum finally changed in September 2019 in the UK after ten years of stagnation but, from the limited insight I have as a poet going into schools to read poems, it is still the poetry I write about anything sexual which I have been made extremely nervous about reading.

I rarely work with pupils under fifteen years of age. Many of the pupils I do read to are knee-deep in war poetry syllabuses relating graphic violence and suffering in war. Many, I assume, though I have no specific evidence other than a handful of pregnant students I've taught, are sexually active in some way or another.

This is no criticism of teachers. I have friends who now have to teach a PSHE education syllabus sometimes with no specialist training to do so and who are constantly petrified of crossing lines of conversation with pupils they're unsure of, to the extent of even fearing their jobs are at stake if they do so.

They are tiptoeing into a new era of sex and relationship education within the parameters of our still largely sexually repressive and prejudiced society. I imagine that's a very tricky thing and it's understandable within this context why the concern is still about the vibrator and the licking and not about the image of a gun.

Not only what we censor in schools and the media but also who we censor seems fairly dubious. In sixth form, I studied Geoffrey Chaucer's *Canterbury Tales*. Chaucer died on 25 October 1400. He was considered by many to be the greatest English poet of the Middle Ages and was the first poet to be interred in Westminster Abbey. The section where he was buried is now given the name 'Poets' Corner' because of the number of poets, playwrights and artists buried there since.

I liked studying Chaucer's poems. There are two main reasons for this. The first was that he wrote in English. At the time, this was rare, as Latin was considered the language to write in and most upper-class English people spoke in French. He chose 'to use the language of the lower-class Saxons rather than Norman nobility' and is considered the first English Author, or rather Author in English, for this reason.

The second reason Chaucer struck me, I won't lie, was because his poems were often 'filthy'. I clearly remember reading *The Miller's Tale* for the first time. In this poem, the character Alisoun sticks her arse out a window and tricks a guy into thinking it's her mouth, so that he snogs it. It works, until he feels the hair around her arsehole and realises it's not her mouth at all. Here it is in Middle English:

> And at the wyndow out she putte hir hole
> And Absolon hym fil no bet ne wers
> But with his mouth he kiste hir naked ers

There was another scene with a broom handle I can't remember exactly but I'm pretty sure someone had it pushed into their vagina for a while.

About six hundred years later, at around the same time I was studying Chaucer in college, a rapper called Khia released 'My Neck, My Back (Lick it)'; a rap song with the chorus, 'My neck, my back, lick my pussy and my crack' and everyone around me thought it was the 'filthiest' thing they'd ever heard.

These are the only two poems or lyrics I've come across which reference a literal arse-licking. Granted, Khia wasn't suggesting women trick men into doing it like Chaucer described, and there were no hot irons skelping anyone's arse as a retaliation. But I do find it fascinating that there are six hundred years, six hundred whole, entire years, between these two references and that we (my research pool here is one classroom-sized) are still so shocked by both of them.

The Miller's Tale is an example of a fabliau, a short, usually comic, coarse and often cynical tale in verse, popular especially in the twelfth and thirteenth centuries. I would love to know how society responded in Chaucer's day. I would love to know if six hundred years made any difference to our shock at people discussing these very intimate parts of our bodies. Perhaps there is even *more* controversy now over these arse-licking references, though perhaps that's because Khia is a young, black female talking about it openly, confidently and positively, and actually asking for it to be done to her, not a white male speaking fictionally in the third person. Not sure.

Either way, I am looking forward to the day when implied murder and/or rape is seen as far, far more controversial than an implied consensual, pleasurable and requested arse- or fanny-licking. I wonder if that will happen in another six hundred years or if future humans, if we're still knocking about, will once again lose their shit over arseholes.

I was asked to do a reading at an anti-porn event once. I turned it down, telling the organisers I was not anti-porn. I got a pretty annoyed response back.

There is a lot about the porn industry I *am* against. Trafficking, rape, slave labour, human rights violations, breaches of labour laws, non-consensual humiliation, paedophilia. I think these things go without saying.

The actual desire to watch other people having consensual sex, however, I am not against. I find, for example, the idea of getting off by watching couples shagging in a car in a forest at night much less strange theoretically than our fascination with listening to an account on a true crime podcast of another young female murdered, or our sipping tea and scoffing scones as we watch *Midsomer Murders* with our grandparents, or our fawning over war reenacted by new hot film stars covered in fake blood as we stuff popcorn in our mouths wondering which poor, less attractive or non-white soldier will be blown up first. I'm not saying watching *The Texas Chainsaw Massacre* is wrong, I'm just saying I'd rather go dogging than ever watch it again.

porn versus the world

i spent last night buying porn
downloaded on my phone
titles like: the massage bed
watch the way my clients moan

infrequent treat i tend to hide
but lord!
to glimpse some actual joy
in the midst of all this dismal shite

and the client's flesh is stirring
as they warm her slow as home-made stew
their oiled-up hands swimming
lengths of breaststroke on her rising boobs

hands turn to fingers
fingers turn to tongues
the sheen across her skin shines
like seal cubs on a fresh sea jump

her bum is buttered crumpets now
she turns around to bite the bread
you drift into my head again
licking till your dimples sweat

your cock, sure as evergreen
me, moist as forest moss
i close my eyes; concentrate
pelvic thrust a ghost above

one deep breathe in to hold the tide
one deep breathe out to float
i do not meditate, i masturbate
i simply don't have time for both

one final stroke for humankind
come serotonin soak these veins

i flick back to the news;
and the world is dismal once again

i want to spoon you and watch star wars tonight

today has been a long day
that's how the saying goes

i do not want to talk
i do not want us wearing clothes

i want to be the front spoon
lamp off; duvet up

yoda and a spaceship race
some kisses on the nubbin
at the bottom of your neck

your crotch nudging my buttocks
with a hint of maybe sex

warm semi on my backbone
arm loped across my chest

a second chance for anakin
that mask still makes me weep

a fondle of at least one breast
then, silently, to sleep

SHORT STORY: IN MY HEAD,
I SHOT THE WOMAN

It was the same journey we always did.
Great-gran's house to Glasgow Queen Street train station.
Queen Street station to Edinburgh Waverley.
Edinburgh Waverley to London King's Cross.
London King's Cross to London Paddington.
London Paddington to home.

It was difficult with a one-month-old.
Then a one-year-old.
Then a toddler.
This time a three-year-old:

> *How long left, Mummy?*
> *Only six hours now.*
> *Can we play I spy?*
> *Of course.*

So we do. We play I spy. I say:

> *I spy something with my little eye beginning with 'b'.*

She stares out of the train window until inspiration strikes.

No, not a sheep. Sheep begins with 's'. My word begins with a 'b'. Buh. B.
No, not an elephant. That begins with an 'e' and there are no elephants I can see.

She giggles. Plays up to it.

Tiger? No. Gorilla? No. Tractor? No. Bird? No, but that does begin with a 'b'. Good guess, honey. But it's not bird.

We carry on till she guesses.
Bushes.
Her turn.
She spies something with her little eye beginning with. She thinks.

Beginning with . . . cloud.
Is it a cloud?
Yes!

She is overjoyed. Thinks I am a genius. Wants another go.
She spies something with her little eye beginning with . . . cloud.

Is it a sheep? I say.
No, she laughs.
This is difficult, I say.
She claps her hands.
Is it a field? I say.
No, Mummy. She looks up out of the window, hinting.
I look up. She watches my eyes scan the sky. Fiddles on her seat.
Is it a plane? I say.
No! She bursts out laughing again.
Is it . . . a cloud? I say.
Yes! She hugs me. Wants to go again. She starts again:

I spy with my little eye something beginning with . . .
cloud.

I look around, thinking what it could be.

The first journey lasts almost one hour. I spot thirty clouds beginning with cloud. The change of trains is easy. Twenty minutes. No stairs.

The second journey lasts four and a half hours. My bag is loaded with hard-to-peel fruit and bits of bread and cheese for her to build sandwiches from. I hope there's a tea trolley soon.

After an hour, we spot the sea. We spot the caravans on top of the cliffs. We talk about going to one of them. We spot an elephant swimming further out in the waves. We spot a whole family of elephants diving under the water. She giggles.

By Newcastle, she's hungry. I pass her one lychee. She takes two minutes to peel and eat it and I close my eyes to ease the sting of tiredness, holding her hand as I do, just to be sure. She asks for another. I pass her one. Close my eyes again. I ask if she wants to put the peelings in the bin. She does. We go to the bin together and she jumps around in the vestibule for a few minutes and enjoys the challenge of not falling over.

We go back to the seats. We play snap. *Quietly*, I say. I show her how not to bang her hands so loudly on the table. Not to get too excited. The man opposite looks up again without smiling. I change the game. She is annoyed at me for this.

We play I spy again.

I try to remember the names of clouds. I can only remember cirrus. I tell her that the clouds outside are cirrus clouds. I think they are. She's uninterested in this knowledge. She asks me if she can count the sheep instead. I thank the lord. *Yes, good idea, count the sheep, honey,* I say. She stares out of the window and reaches thirty-seven before the fields become barer again.

She smiles at the man opposite. His response is so forced I think his lips must be constipated. The thought of this makes me laugh a little. I'd like to share the joke but I don't have anyone to share it with.

I never ask her if she's hungry. It's a waste. I just wait. By York, she's hungry again.

I lay a tea towel out with slices of bread and cheese and she makes us both a picnic. She says she's tired and sits on my lap and I read her four books and feel a bit queasy reading on the train. She asks for the chocolate. I remind her that the pudding is for the last train. This one, then the underground, then the last train.

> *How long will it be till the last train?*
> *Just three hours left, poppet.*
> *And then we share the chocolate?*
> *Yes*, I say.
> *Yes*, she says, smiling.

She starts to fidget. I apologise to the new couple opposite us when she sings gently. They say it's fine and I love them. She starts to fidget a bit more. We walk up and down the corridor ten times. I take my bag with me just in case.

She needs a wee. I carry her over the drips on the floor of the toilet cubicle, balance her on my hip while I wipe the seat clean of the previous person's piss, make *ugh* noises to mimic her and turn her disgust into a game not a struggle. She likes the voiceover about not putting jumpers and fish into the bin. The soap dispenser is fun so we press it a few times and she wiggles the soap between her fingers and I wash it off for her with the water, thankful there is water working, balancing her on my thighs now. I am a chair.

We sit back at the table again. I draw fifty dots on a piece of plain paper and she draws lines between them and writes the first initial of her name in the boxes. We fill five pages of paper. We share some carrot sticks and pretend they are people's legs walking into our mouths. She giggles and eats.

We change trains.

The lift is hard to find at Paddington. I have to put her in the buggy because I can't carry it and carry her and carry the bags. I balance the buggy on the escalators with her in it and imagine us tumbling to the bottom, both dead, me to blame. She falls asleep in the buggy. She's due a nap and I breathe in slowly at the possibility of peace on a little of the next step of the journey. We get to the next train and I have to fold the buggy down because there is no space for it on the train. I cry inside my skin. I wake her and grapple with the buggy folding while she stands sobbing *Mummy, I'm tired* into my leg but I can't lift her and do the pram folding down at the same time and I just woke her up which pisses even the calmest of adults off.

I apologise to everyone trying to get on as I grapple with the buggy. It's nearly evening now. We find our seat. I soothe her crankiness with head strokes and a story about moon cheese and ask if she wants to nap on my lap. She points to the pictures and looks at me. She is not going back to sleep now. I wonder if bedtime will be better or worse because of her missed nap.

She asks if this is the chocolate train. I say it is. She cheers up. She waits until the train starts moving. I pretend I can't wait for the train to start moving to eat the chocolates. She scolds me to be patient. Says it's *our rules, remember.* She feels the first jolt. I break the bar in half and hand her the slightly larger half and we eat slowly and silently. She is always silent when eating things she loves.

I stare out of the window. Soak it up. I breathe the view through the window into my chest and out of my nose. I have almost made it. I close my eyes for at least a minute as she eats the chocolate. Tastes it.

The woman opposite us looks up from her book. She smiles at me, head tilted a touch. I smile back. She looks at my daughter, mouth painted with chocolate, and smiles again. My daughter smiles back.

The woman comments on the time. *This is late to be up, isn't it!* She says it to me through my daughter. She asks my daughter if the chocolate is yummy. She tells my daughter that they didn't have snacks in her day. Advises me of the health effects of giving children too much sugar. Says it's a shame for the kids is all. Smiles again, exhales a saddened sigh.

Goes back to her book.

PARENTING

Is it Gin O'Clock Yet?

You will be the most loved, but also at times the most hated

PAM MCNISH

bartering with a seven-year-old

'i shared my body with you
for months before birth
the least you can do
is offer me one of your crisps'

sweet separation

how strange it is this feeling; swaddling you in love
just to help you leave me

first, you did not need my body any more
tombstone of a star; stormed out blind and screaming
then, you did not need my heartbeat any more;
cord cut and pegged till currents stopped; till tide dried up,
till shrivelled skin; our bitter carnal closeness
dashed into a dustbin;
then, you did not need me; breasts hardening, redundant
cabbage leaf companions to ease the swell of loss;
then you did not need me to hold your head as you sat up;
to hold your hand as you walked; to hold the spoon as you ate;
to jog beside your bicycle; to catch a falling rollerskater;
to run beside your scooter; to sit beside your bed;
to read a story till you sleep;
to run my finger under every letter;
to mouth each word you read

sometimes i worship you

i spied an angel yesterday
it skipped towards my legs
threw school bags at my altar
prayed to play with friends

when rain fell, i took it home
filled its belly, kissed its head
poured warmth into a bottle
put the bottle in its bed

i watched the angel drift
tucked its wings into its back
laid its halo on the table
switched off the beside lamp

ON CHILDREN ASKING YOU TO WALK
THREE METRES AHEAD OF THEM

I read somewhere that having a child is like being in an abusive relationship. I don't agree. That idea surely undermines how awful abusive relationships are. I do, however, think that the shit you take from these small people is bloody difficult sometimes.

I still remember the time I made my mum cry. I'm sure there were many, but I remember the time I actually *saw* that I'd made her cry. I was sat doing homework, fourteen years old. I was meant to be drawing the view out of my bedroom window: another house facing our house and a forty-mile-an-hour speed limit sign around which a lifetime of friendships was being built. I was drawing the view, moody because the drawing wasn't very good and because at some point in my life I wanted to do something other than go to school then do homework all night. I always did my homework, it took up a massive amount of my teenage life. I remember being up till midnight most nights.

That evening, as I was sketching and rubbing out and cussing and re-sketching a very average set of bricks, my mum arrived home from work. She immediately came upstairs and into my bedroom to see how my day had been. I took this for granted as a kid. For some reason I still can't understand, I said 'Go away' to my mum. Didn't even look up. Just said 'Go away'. She burst into tears and scampered out of my bedroom.

I felt sick, ran after her, telling her how sorry I was. I remember her saying, 'Oh, it's OK, I've just had a hard day,' in exactly the way I guiltily now say to my kid, 'Oh, it's OK, I've just had a hard day,' when it's all a bit too much.

The big difference between my mum and me here perhaps is that my mum was a nurse. All day long she dealt with people's problems and traumas and injuries and, often, deaths. I imagine she was an excellent nurse. Firstly, because she is an excellent and patient and exceptionally kind mum. Secondly, because very often she would come home with presents from patients: Ferrero Rochers on a Monday; a bag of allotment vegetables during summer from the ninety-year-old brothers who lived together; sporadic Terry's chocolate oranges; DVDs to borrow from the lovely woman with diabetes. I associated her patients with these gifts and, as a child, selfishly lamented the death of some of them through the ceasing of these treats.

I, on the other hand, have never been and am in no way an 'essential worker', as the corona-crisis vocabulary aptly highlighted. My mum very much was. After a day of this sort of underpaid, undervalued, highly stressful work, she gets home and immediately comes to see her daughter and her daughter pretty much tells her to fuck off.

If I could change one day in my younger years, it would be that day. Not the day I stuck my finger in cement. Not the day I shit my pants before going to the park and my parents told my friends' parents and their parents told my friends. Not the day my mum forced me to wear the red velvet pinafore my gran had sent me because we had a school trip to the theatre and would need something nice to wear and I locked myself in the bathroom screaming *I will not wear that dress I will not wear that dress* but was still forced to wear it, plus big frilly blouse beneath, and we got to the theatre and all my friends were in tracksuits laughing at me. It wouldn't even be the time, in later years, I all but ended a lovely relationship with a first boyfriend because, instead of simply saying, 'I don't really know how to wank you off but I'd like to do it well if you'd help,' as my awkwardly positioned wrist began to cramp around his penis shaft, I told him, 'This is really boring, do it yourself,' and left. None of those come close to the day I made my mum cry.

Nowadays, I stand at the school gates, watching children walk up to their mums – mainly mums, some dads and grandparents and carers, but mainly mums. I watch them: mums who I know have just rushed from another prolapse examination; mums who have spent the morning belittled by bosses for being part-timers; mums plucking up the courage to ask for flexitime shifts; mums who have given up career prospects and financial independence and bodies that worked much better than they do now; mums who in some cases seem to have forgotten they are actually allowed to leave their children sometimes to go out; mums who no longer seem to have a first name.

I watch these mums' daily smiles thrown back at them in the shape of disgust and complaints and frowns, school bags dumped at their feet like piles of horse shit, meals criticised and rubbished before one morsel has passed through the kid's lips; insults hurled; scowls spat.

I cannot take this. As a parent, I have slowly morphed into my gran, banging on about being grateful and respecting those who respect you, and eating what the fuck is put in front of you at dinnertime, whether you 'fancy it' or not. *If I was able to eat turnip mash all those years, so can you.* (Sorry, Mum.) Allergies excepted of course.

Recently, I made my daughter applaud me for hanging out the washing. If her friends don't say thanks as I put food on the table, I just pick up the plate and walk away until they clock what's happening. I am becoming an embarrassing and ridiculous mother and I'm sure it's only going to get worse from here.

jekyll and hyde

at bedtime, in the gloaming light
you hug me tight as nightmare
play-doh in my lap
arms wrap my back like re-ribboned gifts
you beg another story
cheek upon my chest
beg me not to die
start crying at the thought of this

i plump your pillow
tuck you in

nearing school gates the next morning
you walk two paces wide of me
like crossing roads from threat
in the playground, dump your bag and coat
my ankles turned to carthorse hooves
eyes roll at any word i speak
side glances to your friends
the heaviness of playing cool
bending you in sharper shapes
till even my shadow
        overlapping your shadow
embarrasses your space

home again, clear dinner plates
pyjamas radiator placed
i tuck you into bedtime warmth
tell you that i love you
you tell me that you love me more
beg another cuddle

my arms unfurl again, of course
my arms unfurl again

reasons i might be late for the school pick-up

a late train
bastard boss
quick wank that took too long

a clock that didn't stop a nap
train delay
traffic jam

a snowstorm
a desperate shit
forgetting that i have a kid

i understand now mum, sorry

she would stand at the sink
having laid down all the plates
on the table in the kitchen
for her children, and her
children's friends; whoever
came to play; and we would
thank her in muffles, spoons
already filling mouths and she
would stand up eating hers from
the saucepan at the cooker and
it annoyed me that she did this
and we would pass our plates
to her, her already at the relay line
hands submerged in bubbles
us, dashed back out to play

and she would fall asleep to movies
just before the end, and it
annoyed me that she did this
and i would nudge her, and explain
that *a film night is for both of us*
and she would prop the cushion up
again, and smile at me and nod

and snuggled up in bed
a child tucked in each bend of arm
like stolen sacks of love, she would
start to slur the stories, and it
annoyed me that she did this and
we would pull on both her arms
again to shake her from the snores

and she would jolt
and she would smile
and read some more

mother karma

*Before I got married I had six theories about
raising children; now, I have six children and
no theories.*

JOHN WILMOT

when my friend (who does not have a child
and has never had to care for one, not even for one day)
said to me,
as we stepped into london's underbelly rush hour legs
jumping tube to tube between a thousand child-height knees
and i hooked reins onto my toddler because i'd dreamt each
night that week of loosing her in crowds of crows
flocking crumbs in london caves
my child, on the platform, me, banging fists on moving glass
screaming frantic orders to *stay exactly where you are my love
stay exactly where you are*
as her sobbing tears turned flame hot
her body melting out of sight
as the carriage took a tunnelled bend

when my friend (who does not have a child
and has never had to care for one, not even for one day)
said to me that day

*if i had a child
i would never use reins
treating children like dogs
don't you think?*

184

i listened. i nodded. i breathed in.

when my friend (who does not have a child
and has never had to care for one, not even for one day)
said to me, as we ordered lunch in the café and my daughter
from her backpack, revealed three favourite barbie dolls
curls that matched her own, skin colour just like hers
which was very hard to find and more expensive
than the blonde ones and she sat them on the table
made a castle forged of sugar sachets, took them on
a thousand trips as we got our food and ate

when my friend (who does not have a child
and has never had to care for one, not even for one day)
said to me that day

if barbie was a woman she wouldn't even bleed
an anorexic's breeding ground
if i had a child i would never give her barbies
not a way to raise a woman
don't you think?

i listened. i nodded. i breathed in.

when my friend (who does not have a child
and has never had to care for one, not even for one day)
said to me that day

she would never bribe her child with sweets
she would never let her play online
on her phone during a sit-down meal
she would never lock herself in the bathroom in the evening
pretending she had chronic diarrhoea

just to get ten minutes' peace
she would never wish upon a star to break a leg or maybe two
just enough to go to hospital
for the free food and a few days rest

when my friend (who does not have a child
and has never had to care for one, not even for one day)

when my friend (who does not have a child
and has never had to care for one,
not even for one fucking day)

when my fucking friend (who does not have a fucking child
and has never had to fucking care for one,
not even for one fucking day)

said to me that day: she would *never* she would *never*
she would *never never never*

when my friend, who does not have a child
told me she was pregnant

i grinned and said *that's great,*
congratulations

tonight,

i'll prepare crisp sandwiches for dinner;
flying saucers on the side

sometimes i'm just desperate to be liked

gin o'clock

After reading the following cards for Mother's Day

- *Happy Mother's Day. It must be ginetic!*
- *Happy Mother's Day from your favourite (not gin, your other favourite) child!*
- *Mum, thanks for being there, through thick and gin*
- *Mum, you are one ginspirational woman!*
- *Mum, thanks for teaching me how to deal with life's problems* (picture of a bottle of wine)

is it gin o'clock yet?
is it wine o'clock yet?
is it prosecco o'clock yet?

is it time to buy a card which reads:
instant happy woman: just add wine
and laugh about it then cry a bit?

is it time? is it wine o'clock yet?
is the baby sleeping? has the baby ever slept?
is the baby in the pram?
is the toddler wriggling out again?

is the bus late again?
is there a wheelchair user on the bus?
is it time to fold the buggy up?
is it time to wake a sleeping baby up
because i have to fold the buggy up?
is it time to work out if standing in the rain with two kids
is better than waking

up the baby in the middle of a busy bus
knowing all the awful looks i'll get?
is it time to invent buses with spaces for buggies
and wheelchair users yet?

is it time?
shall i get the train instead?
do i have to sit on the floor again?
is there space for a buggy in the vestibule?
is the drinks trolley coming?
is there wine on the trolley?
is my baby too noisy?
is it time to invent trains with quiet *and* loud coaches?

is it time to pluck up the courage to ask my bosses
if i could maybe breastfeed in the back room of the office
next to the boxes of toilet paper
just for five minutes once a year if that was at all possible
and then apologise for asking?
is it time to realise it's impossible to breastfeed
on zero hour contracts?
is the heaviness a prolapse? are all my stitches healed?
is it time for a medical professional to actually check
you are doing your kegels the correct way?

is it time to beg for flexible working days
to possibly maybe start at 5am each morning
so you can rush to the school run
twice a week pretty, pretty please?
is it time to grovel on our knees?
is it time to talk policy?
is it time to make childcare fully tax deductible?
is it time to bake more cupcakes sold for twenty fucking pence

when the ingredients cost me twice as much
because of underfunded governments?
is it time to admit parenting is political
and most politicians do not give a fuck?

is it?

or is it gin o'clock again?
is it wine o'clock again?
am i gintastic yet?

parent bench

for everyone else who has been both of these people

sitting on the bench, as the children take turns
floating on the zip wire, legs thrashing at the sky

you ask me if i know *there's a new tesco*
opening up on the andover road

no, i say, *i don't. yes,* you continue
bigger than the tesco's on the high street
but not as big as the tesco's in the retail park, of course
you laugh. i laugh. *of course*

sitting on the bench, as the children make their way
from the zip wire to the roundabout
from the roundabout to the seesaw
from the seesaw to the swings
from the swings to the treetops
from the treetops to the clouds
from the clouds and back down
into a frantic game of hide and seek

you tell me that the new tesco
is on the site where staples used to be
i say *oh really* you say *yes*
you ask *if i ever used to shop in that staples*

i say *i did* because i did
i bought my printer paper there
you say, *that's lucky*
tesco's sells printer paper

fun

has become something i have to clean up after

pudding treats in bowls – to wash up
paintbrush stains – to scrub from carpets
extra clothes – to spin; to hang up
biscuit crumbs – to wipe up
sweets stuck to tabletops and bedroom rugs

fun has become something i plan for other people
tidy once they're gone

THE TURNING POINT
OF PARENTHOOD

There is a bifurcation in the weekend role of parent that happens, depending on your friends and where you live and how guilty you feel, when your child is around the age of four.

Birthday parties.

Number one rule before this age is: if your kid goes to a birthday party, you stay at the birthday party. After this age, the rule is: if your kid goes to a birthday party, you do not stay at the birthday party.

The realisation of this turning point was a parenting moment I will never forget.

I arrive, ready to sit for three hours, second weekend in a row, at Funky fucking Fun House, drinking shit tea and trying to find a spot on the floor for my bag that's not got either squashed baked beans, chips or vomit on, oblivious to the sunshine or storms of the outside world, because, like so many children's funtime warehouse conversions, there are no windows here for adults to crave the outside world through.

I walk in. Something's wrong. There are no other parents hanging around with sour 'it's your turn to go to the fucking birthday party' expressions on their faces. There is only one set of parents; the set greeting us and collecting the presents their child will later open whilst complaining about something that went wrong at the party, despite the fact the parents have been meticulously planning it for the last three years.

I smile and hand over the present, having been extra careful that this is not the present they gave my child which I'm giving back, but one from the parent of a different friendship group. Perhaps, I think, this pin-art-making kit will simply spend eternity wrapped and opened and hidden and rewrapped until finally the cardboard disintegrates so much that the final set of parents says, 'Oh, this is a bit tatty to give as a gift, isn't it?' or, 'Are you sure this wasn't the one we gave him?' and actually make their kid do the pin-art picture of a boat.

I check again. *Are you sure you don't want me to stay and help? No? No? Cool.*

Run.

Before this point in my parenting life, I almost *wanted* my daughter to be disliked, because the more friends a child has at this age, the more Saturdays and Sundays are taken up with children's birthday parties. It's a dilemma.

Obviously, it's great if your child (or children) has friends. You want your child to have friends. You also want them to be kind and caring and fun and interesting and being kind and caring and fun and interesting, you imagine, might result in more friends.

Only thing is, when they *do* have lots of friends, you slowly begin losing weekend after weekend to Marven the Magician or farm animal petting or princess makeovers or men dressed in pigsuits or pass the parcel passed in cross-legged circles slowly unwrapping layer after layer of your previous weekend afternoons until you realise that the person crying in the corner is not the child who the music never stopped on but in fact you, as you watch that same mangy-looking rabbit pulled from a hat as one of the more obnoxious kids shouts 'I want cake now'.

At this moment in reminiscing, I would like to thank my neighbours in particular for the birthday party they had 'for' their one-year-old, which consisted of a ringed-in bouncy castle jail for all the children and a bar for the adults.

Anyway, for a few years, there's this dilemma. Then, a turning point, after which birthday parties take on an opposite meaning. A direct reversal. Now, the more parties your kid goes to, the more free afternoon-childcare there is. Even better, because you know they are absolutely loving their time and therefore you are free of both responsibility and guilt. It is the perfect situation. At this point, you must train your child to reignite the friendships you forced them to give up because, fuck, you didn't want to see that fucking magician again. Even with the obnoxious little shits, just bite your tongue, love, and go enjoy the bowling.

I feel bad badmouthing the magician here. He is a real person who is very, very skilled at his job and a very good person to hire for children's parties because he somehow manages to entertain for a good two hours. I just saw him too many times for a few years and too frequently imagined him having naked orgies with the other parents when I needed something other than refilling crisp bowls to think about.

magic show

*after seeing the same magician in the same village hall at a few
too many children's birthday parties*

i've begun craving absinthe shots
licked bare from bar tops more and more

because i'm just so fucking bored
at children's parties

smiling from our fold-up chairs
us adults round the edge

making conversation suitable
for parents we don't know well

  *yes, my child is that one
  yes, we're very blessed*

the more orange squash i pour
the more pissed i long to get

little jamie says he *hates orange*
tells me
it's summer fruits, or nothing else

little jamie can fuck off, i think.
i lie: say *there's just orange left*

i help to hand the party food out
rapid fists pile crisps on plates

parents hover, panicking –
trying desperately to sell some grapes

jake's dad adds three carrot sticks
jake looks at his dad like *cunt*

someone tells me that the waiting list
for cubs *is almost one year long*

and i nod
and i panic
unsure how to respond
because i just don't fucking care

i have my tits out in an absinthe bar
liquor lapping down my front
calling to the bartender
to pour me out another one

my daughter runs to me and smiles
climbs on my lap. we sit. we hug.

we watch the magic show again together.
i'm glad she's having fun.

mother (fucker)

You can be a businesswoman, a mother, an
artist, and a feminist – whatever you want
to be – and still be a sexual being. It's not
mutually exclusive.

BEYONCÉ

inspired by a book called Little Deaths *by Emma Flint, a*
poetry collection How You Might Know Me *by Sabrina*
Mahfouz, the huge disparity in the popularity of pregnancy
compared to post-partum photoshoots and the fact I've still
never seen any birthing marks or scars in any sex scene in any
film I've ever watched, as if mothers don't have sex, or at least
not if they have the marks of being a mother visible on their
skin (the only exception to this is in porn, where 'milf' is in fact
a very popular search)

if, every time i went away
distant from my children's side
stripped out of this mother's suit
zipped up in a new disguise

if, every time i went away
child safely in another's keep
i lapped the sweat of twenty lovers
licked them of their body heat
cotton dripping backbone sap
vulva pulsing, veins unleashed

if, every time i went away
i feasted forty lovers' tongues
crawled into their open mouths
sucked their tonsils tea bag clean

kneeling under tablecloths
full-face dive in broths of balls
translucent soups of semen
till my stomach split its seams

orgy for my pudding
orgy in my dreams
orgy on my breakfast plate
orgy for my lunch

if, every time i left
i loved and sucked and swallowed

i would still be just as good a mum
when i returned tomorrow

post-partum

they told me i was beautiful
they told me i was glowing
they told me i was blooming
belly slowly growing life

i gave birth to a baby
took the baby home with me

they told me she was beautiful
they told me. i agreed

my body bound in silence now
to feed and weep and bleed

an apology to my daughter in advance

for my mum, who said her fifties were the best years so far
and i realised later that that was when i'd left home

for my daughter

i'm waiting for my forties for my twenties to begin
so please forgive me, my love, if i embarrass you then
but in my twenties i was swelling and i was feeding and i was up
and though i love you with my life it was not the type of fun

that twenties are renowned for. still, on all our nights awake
if i had the chance to plan, there is nothing i would change
but there's a missing time inside
and there's adventures unfulfilled
constellation cocktail glasses waiting to be spilled

while friends were sweating dancefloors, i was leaking milk
bathing on your sleeping cheeks in midnight moonlit drool
so please forgive me, my love, as my forties come around
and i slowly spend more time away, begin to venture out

creeping back in morning light,
mascara panda-smudged again
and when strangers deem my dress sense
inappropriate for my age
i will not give a shit, because i'm twenty years more confident
and i'll have earned this fucking time
what a good idea! i'll cry *to be twenty when i'm forty!*

so please forgive me, my love, roll your eyes all you need
as the twenties of my forties are unleashed

WHITE PARENT

If I'm in a bad mood, I often go and stand in a card shop and read the greetings cards. I have a massive respect for anyone who can design something which can have another person pissing their pants laughing by just reading a couple of lines or looking at a picture.

In a small shop in Ely with my daughter, I stood reading one after another joke on the cards of one of my favourite greetings card companies. I bought a few of the cards and when I got home, I sent them to people I love and then wrote to the company, because, so far as I could see, of all their cards' cartoon characters, there were none with anything but light pink skin. Same light shade of pink clicked on a computer to fill in all the faces and hands. Must take a few seconds to 'fill' on a computer programme.

I was very polite in the email. I asked if they had any cards with cartoon characters painted various shades of brown, because I would like to buy some. I received this reply:

Thanks for your email.

I'm afraid we only feature a few characters on our cards at the moment and yes, all of them are white. This is something we get asked a lot and the simple truth is we haven't ventured from the same skin tone as we feel it might make the cards a little specific. Maybe we need to add a bit of ethnic diversity and see how it goes. Watch this space . . .

'Specific'.

It's this word that I think is really important for any white person who thinks their skin colour is meaningless these days. As a white person, my skin is not specific, it is the norm, neutral. I can be on a greetings card about women drinking gin or a card about work meetings or a card about tractors or football or ballet or dinosaurs or a card where two women in long dresses tell each other how fabulous they are.

'Specific'.

I replied that this was a fairly sad reasoning, especially if this was something they got asked a lot and therefore was in demand from a sales point of view (I don't know if this was true or not, but if not, it is all the more reason to request this from companies). I got a reply that the word 'specific' was probably the wrong word and that it was just because they only had a few characters and were really busy. Not calculated. And they were adding more characters soon.

Perhaps, yes, as they said, it wasn't calculated. But I think the word 'specific' *is* the word they meant to use.

Unless it is Doc McStuffins or Moana, I don't think I've ever seen any white kids at birthday parties open cards with brown skin on them. Not that I stand and gape at each opened card. But unless there is a group of kids in the picture, and one or – *faint* – two, might not be the generic pink, the birthday cards I see depict white children. I'd say that many white parents would feel uncomfortable or awkward giving a card featuring a character with brown skin to a child with pink skin, though the other way round is unavoidable. The effect of systemic racism on children is very well documented. A few books immediately spring to mind: *Natives: Race & Class in the Ruins of Empire* by Akala, *My Name is Why* by Lemn Sissay and *Bringing Up Race: How to Raise a Kind Child in a Prejudiced World* by Uju Asika.

I hear many white parents answering conversations about racism with 'surely not' – as in, surely not here, surely not in the UK, surely not now, surely not in our school or village or town or neighbourhood. There's no racism at my daughter's school, I've been told. None. Zilch. *Nul Points*.

Surely that boy who got beaten up outside the village shop wasn't beaten up *because* he was black? Surely the kids in the class didn't actually say that the little girl was *too dark* to play with them? Surely the teacher didn't *actually* separate the kids based on 'white' and 'not white' skin colour in pre-school – four kids on one side, thirty white kids on the other – and then get them all to sing the song 'Some People Are Black, Some People Are White' when they were only four years old? Surely the police didn't handcuff him for no reason at all? Surely not here? Surely not now?

I'm not saying that if your kid goes to a birthday party you have to match the skin colour or features of any character on the card you buy to that of the kid that receives it. I'm just saying little things add up. And big things happen. And we need to think about both a lot more.

In the same week that Laurence Fox claimed that pointing out white privilege was racist, whilst hailing the UK as one of the least racist countries in Europe (as if he would definitely know from all the experience of racism he must have had in those various countries), I found myself having an argument on the school run about ballet outfits.

It wasn't a long argument, because the person I was talking to refused point blank to admit that most ballet slippers and tights, as well as a lot of leotards, were, and had been for a long time, pink. We'd been talking about prejudices and, from her point of view, how there was no difference at all any more in a child's experience, based on skin colour, at our kids' school. There was no racial bias in our school and certainly none in her family. Any white person who tells me they have no racist family members I believe must be either an orphan or a liar or unaware of the meaning of this word.

I said that even little things, like ballet slippers, affected kids differently.

I mentioned an instagram post I'd seen by dancer Chyrstyn Fentroy. In the photograph she is in the process of painting a pair of 'nude' ballet slippers brown, to match her skin tone. Another article focused on the 'nude' ballet tights.

In a blog post for Brown Girls Do Ballet,[*] ballerina Selena Robinson weighed her options between the brown tights that match her skin tone or the pink ones most other ballerinas don. Wearing the pink, many dancers point out, is a part of maintaining uniformity among the corps de ballet dancers meant to perform in sync.

> 'Whether I stick to tradition and wear pink or channel Dance Theatre of Harlem and wear brown,' she wrote[†], 'I just want to be comfortable in my beautiful brown skin and dance for myself.'

The person's response was the solid standard refusal I hear all the time and have, I'm sure, given myself about things. No. Ballet slippers and ballet tights came in all colours, always had done; pink or 'nude' shades had never been any more standard than brown and if they were, it was nothing to do with skin colour. End of.

When people are so adamant about their opinions I tend to find it hard believing they aren't right. I went home and googled ballet slippers again.

[*] https://www.huffingtonpost.co.uk/entry/brown-girls-do-ballet-book_n_5714ea72e4b0060ccda3ad2a?ri18n=true&guccounter=1&guce_referrer=aHR0cHM6Ly9jb25zZW50LnlhaG9vLmNvbS8&guce_referrer_sig=AQAAAAI3N_8VZyLfDpdd3xRhcFt0qkNS65vsJQuELSk432JmzG1Rly_Pom8uRQ5IrHY06qlsNygNRiqoLEaRk0XhgUboaKF42uqRI_SDGAfH0xcWq5E4-VXDLz34T0ETZOr4dlFDzXWwKpIpUq-_wBmVno0hlITj5Hec6a12-vvhlfcJ

[†] https://www.browngirlsdoballet.com/blog2/2014/06/03/ask-a-ballerina-from-flat-shoes-to-tutus-dying-your-costumes-nude

Another trait I notice amongst us hopefully well-meaning white parents is to try to tackle or address racism by highlighting it to our children, talking about how bad racism is, whilst continuing to surround our white children with white-centred toys, books, films and so on.

Similarly, when I have asked white library staff or bookshop assistants if they had any *less white* books for children or books where the main character was not a white child, they have often recommended books *about* racism itself. Like the cartoon series featuring Rosa Parks, or *Bedtime Stories for Rebel Girls*. Don't get me wrong, I think these are excellent books, but they aren't *normal stories*, they are stories that focus on racism or diversity.

My daughter didn't want to read a book about how someone with her skin colour might have to fight a lot of prejudice, she wanted a story about someone with her skin colour flying into space with a teddy bear or going shopping for dinosaurs or eating baked beans. Anything. Just stories that were funny and silly or loving or magical or sad, in which some or all of the people looked like her and her family. And she wanted her friends to be reading those stories too. Ditto toys. Ditto birthday cards. Ditto films.

The fact that hugely popular books like David Walliams' *The Midnight Gang* can still pass through god knows how many publishing meetings and come out with front covers consisting of five white kids is fairly shocking, and also not at all.

In 2020 the card company finally created some designs featuring different shades of skin colour. But whilst the majority of their designs feature one white character, sometimes two characters, the 'diverse' designs consisted of six characters, four of which were white, or four characters, three of which were white or, finally, two, one of which was white. In order to include characters which were not white, it seemed the company felt it necessary to create cards with big groups of people on them to appease the white customer base.

This is not just down to the card company, it's down to supply and demand economics, racism and us white people apparently being incapable of relating to, connecting with or associating ourselves with characters who do not have our skin colour; as if buying a card for a white kid which features, for example, a black girl ballerina or watching a film or reading a book which does not focus on a white person's life or thoughts or dreams will somehow be awkward, or too different or simply unimportant. Ironically, because our skin colour allows us the privilege to do so, we are also then the only people on this planet who ever claim not to see colour, whilst gaping at every rainbow that floods the sky.

white children's birthday cards have white children on them
black children's birthday cards have white children on them

another poem about white privilege written by a white, middle-class poet

for Lucy McQ

as a baby, you played babies in your colour
at the doctor's, the toy box cradled mini-clones of you
your first birthday cards were covered
with cartoons painted pink
under bedtime lamps, stories whispered beauty into mirrors;
fairy tales questioned *'who is the fairest of them all?'*
no one substitutes this phrase
her skin is white as snow / you giggle at the dwarves
the prince is tall and pale and handsome

you did not spend hours searching
for that nineteen-ninety-seven
version of cinderella where brandy begs whitney houston
to get her to the ball,
just so your children grow up believing
they can ride in pumpkins too; believing they are beautiful
you did not cry over *the princess and the frog*
you did not cry in tesco's over the new range of birthday cards
with doc mcstuffins on
you do not question the colour scheme of pixies

ditto mermaids
ditto fairies
ditto heroes
ditto elves

you watch the harry potter series for the seven-hundredth time
do not wonder if all wizards are white, they are
do not wonder if all witches are white, they are
when someone questions hogwart's inclusion policy
you point out that one scottish girl
(you do not call her scottish though)
and the black boy with no lines

as you grow up, you take ballet shoes for granted
slip custom pale pink slippers over custom pale pink feet
criss-cross ribbons around ankles;
open arms and legs in first position
you think selena robinson is making slightly too much fuss
painting over silk

as a teenager, you covered puberty's frustrations
with *skin coloured* foundation
teachers were much less likely to
underestimate your academic talents
overestimate your interest in sport and dance and song
you are less likely stopped and searched
on your way home from the youth club
you do not become too frightened to ask an officer for help
you do not watch your father mishandled every holiday
his sides tapped by uniforms begging him for badness
you have never been pulled over
because your car is a nice car
you are less likely to be sectioned for shouting in the street
if you suffer from ill mental health later on in life

if you stab another person with skin colour like yours
the crime will not be labelled white on white crime
if a person with skin colour like yours

stabs another person with skin colour like yours
the crime will not be labelled white on white crime

when twenty young people with skin colour like yours
stand on stage behind their favourite rapper
the tv standards agency is not inundated with complaints

you do not prefix 'white' searching netflix everyday
just to see an actor who vaguely looks like you

you did not rush to watch *black panther*
there are lots of other sci fi films
you thought star wars was diverse

on stage, you see your skin speak
in books, you see your skin speak
on the news, you see your skin speak
in ads, you see your skin speak
in films, you see your skin speak

you can claim not to see colour
because your colour is the norm

still, you worked hard for your place in life
you are not rich, you are not racist,
you did not take part in the slave trade
you are not one of the privileged
you have problems of your own

you open birthday cards again
white people on the cover
you laugh easy at the jokes

shopping with my daughter on glastonbury high street

for Bryony Dick's beautiful illustrations, thank you for these

for Shelly-Ann, thank you for all the books

there are no mermaids
darling, sorry

there are no fairies
darling, sorry

there are no pixies
darling, sorry

not even witches
darling, sorry
here, who look like you

these creatures may be mythical
but even myths in the hands
of this most spiritual of artist towns
have forgotten all the browns
brushes dipping in and out
of pink paint only pink paint only pink

your list unticked, let's stop
your eyes are sunk too much already
fuck their mermaid dolls
pixie pictures, key-ring fairy
crystals to hang inside excited
dreaming children's bedrooms

windows twisting sunshine into
rainbow's flecks

let's head back home
play make-believe
pick up your wings
and wands and truths

and wait until the world
of fantasy and fable
no longer paints like
hitler youth

getting out of the cereal aisle

'. . . 'cos mr kellogg was a racist.
a bigot. a eugenics fan.
thought interracial couples
were a curse upon the land'.

she looks at me. rolls her eyes.
holds my hand. we walk away.

she has not asked for
coco pops again.

TOASTED CORNFLAKES:
COCO POPS AND COCK CAGES

What I didn't say to my daughter when she begged and begged and begged for Coco Pops and then moaned all the way home when I said no, was that as well as being very racist, the American inventor of cornflakes, John Harvey Kellogg, was also puritanical about pleasure. He even invented a machine to strap onto boys' penises which hurt when they got an erection.

The invention of cornflakes – the first Kellogg's cereal – was apparently based on this puritanical belief. The story goes that John Kellogg thought that spicy and sugared foods caused too much sexual arousal in people and were therefore sinful, so he invented cornflakes as a food so bland that nobody could get off on it. I learned these things from a friend and writer called Luke Wright after I wrote this poem and posted it online. All I knew before that was that Mr Kellogg was racist.

Luke also informed me that the lesson I gave my daughter in the supermarket was actually wrong because Mr Kellogg would've in fact hated all the sugary new flavours draped over his original anti-masturbation cornflakes. Therefore, if I really wanted to protest against this pleasure-damning, racist bigot, I should let my kid gorge herself silly on the pleasure that stuffing her face full of commercially branded Coco Pops can bring.

Thing is. The small boxes of Coco Pops are what I steal from hotel breakfasts when I'm on tour and if I brought them home to her more often then it wouldn't be a treat and I'd have to think of a new guilt-for-being-away-working gift.

I should make it clear here that there were two Kellogg brothers: one called Will, one called John. It is John who I'm talking about in the poem. Whether John or Will is the rightful founder of what became the Kellogg's we know today remains contentious.

From what I can gather, the two brothers invented the first cereal – cornflakes – together. Will was more of a business person. He wanted to make money out of cornflakes. John had more moral reasons for wanting folk to eat this toasted goodness – celibacy. I can't stop delving into the history of John Kellogg; it is both fascinating and disgusting. John Kellogg was a medical doctor and nutritionist and an outspoken supporter of another medical practitioner, Isaac Baker Brown.

Baker Brown was a respected English gynaecologist from the mid-nineteenth century. He performed habitual FGM (female genital mutilation) operations, which he saw as a cure for masturbation, 'hysteria', mental illness and 'unfeminine behaviour', the last being a vague category which included 'distaste for marital intercourse'. I'd like to repeat that last one; this man advised cutting out the clitoris, the main source of pleasure for the majority of people with a vulva, as a *remedy* for those same people not enjoying their husband's penises inside them enough.

Whilst the majority of gynaecologists of their time did not agree with the extremes of female genital mutilation that Baker Brown advocated, John Kellogg was one of his most famed supporters. Cornflakes and FGM; two fierce weapons in the fight against immorality.

The best summary of John Kellogg's relationship with sexual pleasure I found in Lynn Enright's *Vagina: A Re-Education*, which reads:

He [John Kellogg] was married but apparently never consummated his marriage; he was vehemently opposed to masturbation and even sex. He believed that female masturbation was responsible for a range of problems, including mental illness, birth defects and cancer ... He advocated for the use of bandages and ties to restrict children from masturbating; when that didn't work, he suggested the use of a cage. In some circumstances, when other methods had failed, he advised a clitoridectomy or the burning of the clitoris with carbolic acid ... While other doctors performed clitoridectomies with a degree of discretion, Kellogg, like Baker Brown, was vocal about his support for them.

There is a whole section in this book about John Kellogg, and the use of FGM more generally in the UK. Whilst the use of bland breakfast cereals to put children off masturbating may seem fairly amusing, the rest of this 'history' is little less than horrific.

In the UK, we often deem FGM, or FGC (female genital cutting), largely as a thing of the past (if we admit it has a past in Britain, which we seem very happy not to do), or as a cultural phenomenon used solely in certain communities in certain countries by certain religions. This is not the case. FGM has a long and bloody history, and the 'justifications' given for this ongoing form of woman and child abuse crosses cultures and continents and class. In the United States, according to *The Vagina Monologues*, the last recorded clitoridectomy for curing masturbation was performed in 1948 – on a five-year-old girl.

Though clitoral burning may not now be prescribed legally for screaming females by highly honoured medical professionals in any country worldwide, and though the fight against forced genital mutilation has gained huge legal tract, FGM is still rife, with activist Leyla Hussein stating that a girl 'still continues to be cut every eleven seconds'.

In addition to this, there is another form of female genital cutting – labiaplasty – the practice of which is currently rising.

This is not the same as forced FGM. Labiaplasty is a choice, in no way comparable to past medical or present forced clitoral mutilation. In addition, the surgery is not internal or life-threatening and is, in most cases, done by medical professionals.

However, I think that the surge in this largely cosmetic surgery does needs to be scrutinised much more as part of a wider look at FGC. That this 'trend' has been labelled 'designer vaginas' across much of our media is an immediate red signal for me in this respect.

What an amusing tone this bestows on the process. Designer vaginas. A light-hearted label, a rhyming jingle to describe a supposed fashion choice involving the surgical shaping, reshaping, enhancing, beautifying, or whatever verb is deemed appropriate for the cutting of the inner and outer labia of a person's vulva.

There are many women having their labia surgically altered for comfort-centred reasons, in particular to reduce the rubbing of longer, protruding inner labia. If we look beyond these examples, at pure aesthetics, though, this surgery could be seen as being just like any other cosmetic surgery.

I am not getting into a bashing of cosmetic surgery here because I am not opposed to it and I'm sick of people who have undergone it being treated as if they are morons. I'm done hearing jokes about satsuma fake tan faces or boob job airheads or botox bunnies or self-righteous celebrities being praised for refusing to have any treatments. In a world where we are constantly judged on how we look, it is unsurprising and in many ways the sensible option to inject away each wrinkle, bash each bullied feature into the accepted shape. It would be great if no one judged anyone, if no one felt the need to look constantly younger or skinnier or bigger breasted or rounder arsed or straighter-haired but jesus, we are so obsessed with looks in culture right now that we even often buy food based on how it looks rather than tastes.

Still, there is one stark difference to me between most of those cosmetic procedures and aesthetic labiaplasty, because unless you are a regular user of a Finnish sauna, this part of the body is not on show daily or judged constantly by strangers and friends and colleagues. This is a part of the body that for the majority of people for the majority of their lives will only be seen by lovers, people who you are intimate enough with to be pantless and who should be grateful to be in that pantless moment with you, labia symmetry aside.

So why the rise in surgery? Two things are often pointed to; porn and spin class.

The effect of mainstream porn is perhaps obvious. The vulvas tend to be as monotone as the screams and hair flicks, many of them altered for better camera views. In terms of spin class, this relates to the rising trend in women's fitness gear. Because of the increased visibility of the vulva shape through these Lycra outfits, women are increasingly self-conscious about their camel toe (as it was called in my day). Hence, the rise in cutting.

It would be interesting to know whether those going for this labia surgery are primarily heterosexual women. I say this simply because these are the women who are least likely to have seen any other vulvas close up. Most heterosexual women do not see other vulvas; unlike penises, they are not easily viewed on the outside of our bodies to grab a glimpse of at urinals or changing rooms.

I have a book at home with one hundred photographs of people's vulvas and a story about how each person feels about their vulva next to the photo. It's part of a series by Laura Dodsworth. There's another one on penises and one on breasts. I leave them out with all the other books but do still worry when my daughter's mates (always) flick through them that their parents might ban them from ever coming to my house again. The vulva one has made a massive difference to me, knowing there are so many shapes and sizes to this body part. When my gran visited, she said, 'Do you have to have so many books about vaginas on the shelf?' before she started to talk about men's bottoms again. I imagine that heterosexual women who haven't seen this book and who don't work in gynaecological professions might be very prone to believing they have an abnormal vulva, especially if porn is used as the only point of comparison.

Designer vagina might sound amusing, but we're not talking fucking handbags here, we're talking vaginas. Only, we're not talking vaginas, which is the second red signal for me.

Even when directly discussing the surgical process of slicing our labia, we are still unable to correctly name this body part. We are not cutting vaginas, thank god, we are cutting vulvas. Labiaplasty is related to the labia. The vagina has no labia. The vulva does. Vulva / Vagina. These body parts are as different as throat and mouth.

As a society, surely we should be able to at least name this body part correctly before we begin creating snazzy headlines to describe a re-emerging trend to cut it, especially if this desire for surgery might spring from both a lack of understanding of what a normal, healthy appearance is and a deeply rooted socially constructed shame about this very lovely (too lovely in fact, that's been the main problem for centuries) part of our bodies.

Worldwide, we are still cutting up this body part in vast and various ways, some undoubtedly much more dangerous than others. It is not a thing of the past. It is an interlinked and continuous history of censorship and embarrassment and shaming and scarring.

My dad once introduced me to a friend as his daughter *who is desperate to say the word 'vagina' in every sentence.* I'm not. I'm really, really not. I don't want to write poems about vulvas or vaginas. I find it hard enough to say those words. I don't want to think about them, except when I need or want to. It makes me cringe talking about them. I said this to my dad. Then I said I needed to go for a wee. *There you go,* he joked, *talking about vaginas again.*

No, Dad, I laughed, *I'm actually not.*

Parenting is a huge part of changing culture. Despite often being treated with about as much respect as any other unappreciated voluntary workforce, I think parents and carers can change a hell of a lot simply through normalising things for the next generation.

I once heard Nimco Ali – anti-FGM campaigner and author of an excellent book *What We're Told Not to Talk About* – speak. When she was asked whether she thought FGM could be eliminated in her lifetime, she said yes. Yes, just like that. I'd never heard such a confident response to such a seemingly overwhelming issue.

Her reasoning was this: with FGM, if, as a parent or carer, in a community where FGM prevails, you are able *not* to cut your daughter, then that daughter is then extremely unlikely, if she has one, to cut *her* daughter. If you stop the process with your generation, it is highly unlikely to continue. I feel the same about the vulva; the word, the shaming of it, the knowledge of what it is and what is normal and healthy.

I was not brought up with this word in my vocabulary. It was the only major part of my body I did not have a word for. When I started hearing it, initially it was absolutely horrendous to say. In fact, I simply wouldn't or couldn't say it.

My mum was a nurse and when I was younger, she brought back a lot of metal objects to the house, which she had to sterilise. I asked what they were for and she said, 'I have to put them up people's bums to look up their bums.' I of course naturally ran out of the room screaming. When I was twenty-one and went for my first smear test, I saw one of these objects again and for a moment panicked that the nurse was about to hoof it up my anus. She did not. She put it into my vagina and I realised my mum had just been too embarassed to say one of those two dreaded 'v' words.

According to the charity Eve Appeal, only 1 per cent of parents will use the word 'vulva'; 44 per cent use euphemisms like 'fairy', 'flower' or 'tuppence'; 22 per cent never refer to female body parts in front of their daughters; 19 per cent use 'vagina' either because they don't know the difference or at least find it easier to say than vulva.

It amazes me that this word – five tiny letters – is so difficult to get out of our mouths. Mine included.

If someone's son pointed to their penis and said it was his balls I'm pretty fucking sure we'd correct him and say, 'No, those are your balls (or testicles), that's your penis,' before he spent the rest of his childhood and adult life continuing to confuse his penis and testicles. It would seem absurd not to say anything. But with the vulva, no. Just let the girls either not know what it's called, or call it a vagina, even though those are two completely different body parts.

I have to say here, I did think it might be quite funny the first time I babysat a neighbour's kid to teach them heads, shoulders, knees and toes in completely the wrong order.

Watching the next generation of kids whose carers and parents *have* swallowed their inherited trepidation and begun using the correct words, and *do* try to name the vulva and vagina with as much normality as they might say 'shoulder' or 'eyebrow', the shame all but vanishes. The kids still giggle of course, we are talking about private parts here, but they name them, know what they are, know where they wee from (the urethra, part of the vulva) and no one self-combusts because of it. It's very unlikely they will then un-name it if they have kids. *Well, I called it a vulva, but with my child, I think I'll go back to 'front floofy bottom' again.*

if flowers had disposable income

daffodils would be warned their trumpets are too crimped
tulips advised to have their petals snipped to standard shapes

lopsided curving carved away in cut out tulip templates
convinced this is the only shape a tulip cup must grow

roses would be warned they smell too strong of rose

the golden pool of buttercup that glows a promise
on each waiting chin, convinced of faulty colouring

the heavy headed alliums belittled for their skinny stem
the barrel-bellied cacti belittled for their chubby trunk

and the honeysuckle buds, oh poor honeysuckle buds
how bees would swarm to sip upon your sticky perfumed wares

with just a little nip tuck here and there.

vulva in the playground

for the first of my friends to teach her daughter the correct word
– i'm sorry we flinched

she says
my knickers are stuck in my vulva, mum

and everybody turns
and all eyes fix on you
and the children playing, freeze
and the swings in mid-flight, stick
and the autumn breeze breathes in
and the earth, mid-orbit, halts
and the rusting leaves, half-fallen,
hover, anxious in the air

and you try to answer her
as if that word is as normal
as a boy's hand down his pants

stealing their innocence

> *If I have a daughter I will tell her*
> *that there are some things*
> *which people will tell you as truth.*
> *Don't believe them*

NADINE AISHA JASSAT,
'Things I Will Tell My Daughter'

*for the parent i spoke to at a book signing worried about
'stealing her kids' innocence' by telling them about periods and
body parts and sex*

for Juliet, who inspired me to be more open about these things

i told my child
that i bleed every month
that this started at twelve
maybe fourteen
showed her cups
and tampons and pads
she stood by the sink
watched as i washed
blood from my hands
wrung out the towel
pink circles marbled
the drain, she asked
if it hurt me, i told her
some days it feels
like i've eaten my
own weight in muscle

some days i feel faint
most days it's ok
we spoke of wombs
building walls every month
she yukked at the blood
and she still did not stop

i told her i have a vulva
i have a vulva
i repeated the word
as much for myself
as for her, she giggled,
repeated a *yuk!* i said
that's what great-grandma
means by *front bum*!
she giggled again
and she still did not stop

i showed her a drawing
of labia and clitoris,
hood and urethra
i told her in puberty
the clit will get bigger
the hood might ease off
she giggled, said *mum!*
too much information!
and she still did not stop

i told her
her body was hers
and she still did not stop

i told her sometimes
when i touch my own body
in ways that i like
i feel tingly inside
like a bubbling bath
or a really good poo
she laughed at that too
asked at what age
that started to work
i said it depends
and she still did not stop

i told her
no one should touch her
that inside her pants
was as private as minds
      (she sighed, *yes I know*
i was told that at school)
your own hands excepted
i said, she said *yes*
and she still did not stop

i told her that
adults do not just have sex
to make babies, despite
what so many will tell you
and she still did not stop

i told her that grown-ups
play each other's bodies
like harpsichord strings
that sex can be rainbows of songs
that under sixteen is illegal

non-consensual is illegal
and wrong; that feelings
she might have are
perfectly normal and
she still did not stop
she still did not stop

she still did not stop
playing dollies and train sets
kissing teddies each night
picking conkers from forests
for more conker fights
she still did not stop
watching cartoons on tv
giggling at farts
begging for ice cream
holding my hands
and looking both ways
before crossing the road
dancing round chairs
till the party tunes stop

because that's not
how a child's innocence
is lost

eating whole carrots

I am no bird; and no net ensnares me: I am a
free human being with an independent will.

CHARLOTTE BRONTË, Jane Eyre

When a man is denied the right to live the life
he believes in, he has no choice but to become
an outlaw.

NELSON MANDELA

as i sit on the train, eating a whole carrot just munching a
     whole carrot,
i get funny looks

if i buy a packet of carrots, chopped into small finger-
     sized oblongs of carrots for five times the price, just
     munching these carrots, these pre-chopped carrots
i don't

my daughter asked if i *can please not put a carrot, like a whole*
     carrot like a whole carrot in her lunchbox, mum

i said *what if i chop up the carrot, like the carrots you get in*
     those packets of pre-chopped carrots that cost five times the
     price

she said *yeah*
that would be fine

slingshot

after a shopping trip into town and another argument about
not buying sweets at the till and then seeing the headline
'scientists blame working mums for UK's child obesity
epidemic' screaming from the Sun *as we stopped for petrol on*
the way home

for the people in charge of marketing crap to kids – fuck you all

take her just take her
i can't do this any more
you are too rich   you are too strong
i am too weak   i am too small

raise your billboards   sell those dreams
too high for her to ever reach
make fiction of her flesh
until each breath heaves insecurities

go on   tell her she's too fat
then tell her she's too thin
till she is petrified of any life
which creeps across her skin

go on and take her   i can't fight you
i'm so fucking tired with trying
david did not beat goliath
i don't believe this any more

so pour your sweeties
at each checkout where we're waiting
coat your cereals in cartoons

your 'happy' meals in shit 'free' toys
your fizzy drinks endorsed by all
her favourite youtube stars

til she's begging me and begging me
my calm ground down to dust

i'm told mothers are to blame
for obesity and body shame

she's begging at the checkout
i prepare to tell her no again

feet scream. i am *the worst mum*
heads turn. my cheeks ablaze

slingshot in my pocket
just in case

mother me

Mother is a verb. It's something you do. Not just who you are.

CHERYL LACY DONOVAN,
The Ministry of Motherhood

sometimes, i want to be the one
someone else brings the tea to
tucks under covers – a story, another
the light left on dim; kiss on the forehead
forced into rest

sometimes, i want
the towel wrapped round me
body rubbed lightly
pats drying skin as i step from the shower
my head to be towelled, my hair to be brushed

sometimes i want
my fears hugged away too
life called and told
i've to stay home from school

sometimes i want someone
to mother me
just like
i mother you

late night channel 4 documentary about men who like to pretend to be babies for kicks, which made my gran say *jesus, what has happened to this world*

i know you find it sickening
those grown men donning nappies
building giant play pens
their partners playing 'nanny'
to feed and feel their 'willies'

lolling in a crocheted quilt
fed adult food from baby spoons
hugged into the afternoon
woken wanking from a nap

heads patted for hours
chores put off until tomorrow
nipples licked at their request
silence stuffed between their
moustached dummy lips

i'm not saying i would want this
there are other role plays i prefer
i'm just asking
if it's really *that* absurd

FUN RUN

I live in a place where kids as young as three cycle better than I can; where people go camping for holidays, even when they can afford to stay in hotels; and where most of my daughter's friends have run a 5k, often each week on a Sunday. This is called a fun run.

I got so worried that my kid was the only one who didn't want to do this Sunday fun run that I started to panic that I had raised a really lazy child and that I was so lazy myself and that that was why she was now not wanting to go run round the park in her free time. I said to her one Saturday night when I felt like I was a particularly shit mum, *Right, tomorrow I think you should do this fun run thing.*

She didn't want to. She said so and screwed her face into the back end of a skunk.

I said that she was the only kid not doing it and it was meant to be really fun – *It's called a fun run,* I said. *A fun park run,* I repeated. *It sounds really good and loads of your friends will be doing it. Fun.* I tried as hard as I could to convince myself too.

Her face did not change.

I said she should maybe just see if she likes it and then I'd not ask again.

She asked me if I was going to do it because all the kids who do it do it with their parents.

I said no. I said I couldn't think of anything I'd rather do less with our weekend lie-in than get up and go run around the park in the rain.

We decided we'd stick to the three hours of TV (her watching, me sleeping) followed by breakfast at 4 p.m. I'm exaggerating, of course. I do things with my kid at the weekend, I just don't like running unless there's a ball between my legs, that's all. (I rewrote this sentence three times to make it sound less like I was speaking about testicles but I couldn't make it any better than this. I mean a football here.)

I also love the people around me and don't dislike anyone just because they run on Sundays. Admittedly, I used to mutter 'Fucking joggers' underneath my breath, but I've stopped now. If anything, I realised I was a little jealous of their motivation, or just annoyed at them because they made me feel like a lazy cunt when I didn't want to join them.

Driving with my parents as a child consisted mainly of a times-table tape that all my friends for some reason loved and were jealous of, the game where you try to spell your name out of other passing car registration plates (it was only as a parent that I realised this game was purely intended to shut me up and, I'll be honest, it broke my heart a little bit) and a constant abhorrence of cyclists from my dad: 'Look at those tossers in Lycra,' finger-pointing at people zooming skinny wheels up and down Scottish hills, all fit and ball-tight and happy.

I'm not sure if it was the cycling or the fact that these *wankers* felt it apparently necessary to wear that posy Lycra that infuriated him the most.

Like most of us, I notice all the sides of other people's lifestyles which I don't or can't mimic, and all the shit sides of my own, and I am trying not to translate that jealousy or self-reflection into scorn.

I don't jog but I am an adult roller skater. I feel the need to say that here. Not a serious one, but I really love to move with wheels strapped to my feet. I can feel the hate as I skate or scoot past other adults. Maybe I'll buy some professional Lycra to make it worse, though I'm pretty sure sweating in tight leggings would reignite the hell fires of thrush.

I am very glad to have friends who do things I don't. Friends who parent differently. Friends who do fun runs with their kids. Friends who take me camping. Friends who make me question things. Friends who make bird feeders out of lard and seeds stuffed inside a half-empty coconut shell to put in children's party bags, instead of shit plastic toys, for example.

This happened when my daughter was five. When we got home from the party, my daughter pulled this thing out of the party bag and asked what it was. I had no fucking idea. I assumed it must be a sort of sweet, nougat or marshmallow maybe, because that's what I knew filled party bags – sweets. I therefore tried to scoop the 'filling' out of the coconut shell before gagging and realising it was likely not for human consumption. I texted my friend Vicki to ask what the coconut sweet thing in the party bag was. She told me it was a bird feeder made with hardened lard. I told her I'd tried to eat it.

On days when I worry about parenting more than anyone should when the kid is safe and loved and not starving – I think back to my own childhood and the best pieces of it that I remember; the brazil nut caramel Quality Street in the selection pack of memories. (Or whatever your personal favourite is. Mine is the purple one.)

I was, and am, bloody lucky; there are thousands of good bits I remember from my childhood and teenage years. None of them, however, are the bits I imagine my parents intended as the best bits. In fact, loads of them are the bits that my mum recalls busting her guts with guilt over.

I do not remember the days my mum or dad picked me up from school and we just went home. I stress a lot when I think I've been away too much or not been at the school gates enough but when I think back to my own childhood, the best times I remember are the exact opposite of this: the days my mum and dad didn't just pick me up and take me home.

I remember loving being picked up by mates' parents and going to other people's houses to play. Of course. For a year or so in primary school I was dropped off at my friend Caroline's house down the road every morning. We ate breakfast and watched the film *Ghost* together nearly every morning. I loved it. I have kids who I pick up each week for friends, and friends who do the same for me when my daughter's dad or grandparents are unable to, and it seems to be something that we all worry about all the time. But it's bullshit guilt. The kids are fine with it.

After a day at secondary school, I'd often have to walk to and wait at my mum's work a lot, sitting on my own in the nurses' staff room for hours till my mum had finished her shift. I don't remember this in a bad way, either. It's a joyous memory. I got to see backstage at a surgery. I got to drink staff room squash and eat biscuits without anyone watching how many I took from the biscuit tins. Before going to the staff room I would sit in the waiting room with all the patients and when my mum came out looking like a nurse, I felt like a superstar as she gave me a hug and all the patients realised that I was not in fact your average patient but the nurse's very own child.

At my local surgery now, there is a water machine with small paper cone cups to fill up and drink from. Since she was a toddler it has been my kid's favourite activity to fill this water cup for me and her to drink from. Of all the places I've taken her, I think that this may well be one of the things she remembers as the pinnacle of our outings together.

I do not remember museum trips, for example, except the one in year eight when Jordan said he had a bomb in his bag to a security guard and it took us about an hour longer to get in and the teachers were fuming and we all thought Jordan was amazing.

I do not remember how clean or tidy or well-organised any of my friends' houses were. I remember Jodie's Sylvanian Families, and the fact she had pink wafer biscuits and Tracker bars and a soda stream. I remember the fact that Caroline got boobs before I did and introduced me to Counting Crows and playing kerby for entire summers. I remember the climbing tree by the graveyard and the swingpark that was special because it had a roundabout. Of all the summer childhood memories I have, the one that returns to me the most is being allowed to jump in the bin to push down all the garden rubbish.

picking memories

perhaps you will remember
all the best bits of our bedtimes
clinging to each other
as impatient pages turn

your yawns slurring insistence
that you're still not even sleepy
till – halfway through our story
– you pass out on the pillow

but perhaps you won't remember
it's more likely that you won't

perhaps you will remember
all the sandcastles we forged together
buckets sloshing seawater
as moats dissolve in sands

perhaps i'll pace your memories
as the mum who always held your hands
kissed and cuddled colds away

or perhaps you'll just remember
the days i was quite tired
the days i wasn't there
the things we didn't do

i can't pick memories for you
(god knows i'd like to)

as a child i don't remember much
snapshots through the years

but
jumping in the garden bin
as mum or dad held both my hands
trampolining me on top of
piles of rubbish, cuttings,
branches, stamping
freshly mowed-down grass
is one that made it past

i often wonder what yours will be
from all these years we've played

if even one is half as good
as jumping in a bin
on smiling, summer days

i'll be ok
i'll be ok
i'll be ok

playing kerby with caroline

for caroline

those were the summers
bouncing the ball against the brick wall
then bouncing the ball against the brick wall again
then calling on caroline to come out to play
to bounce the ball against the brick wall with me
until caroline went, called in by her mum
and i'd bounce the ball against the wall on my own
until caroline came back, chores done or fed
and we'd bounce the ball against the brick wall again
until, bored of bouncing the ball on the wall
she'd run to the opposite side of the close
and we'd throw the ball back and forth at the kerb
just throwing the ball back and forth at the kerb
five points for a rebound, ten for a catch
just throwing the ball back and forth as we chat
just throwing the ball over cars as they pass
just throwing the ball over years as they pass
just throwing the ball till the sun overhead
threatens ever so slowly to fade

and the lights in the houses that domino streets
extinguish the day with a flick of each switch
yellow to black yellow to black
and one of us has to go in

the kids are alright

or

poem to make me feel better about my kid playing computer games for four hours a day while i attempt to work from home during lockdown

for my daughter, who told me that 'neon grown giraffes' is not correct but who i'll annoy by not changing it

offer your hands but stop pointing your fingers
the kids are alright, the kids are not stupid
the kids are not feckless, the kids are not slobs
the kids are still climbing trees, the kids are still cartwheeling
the kids are still discussing who they'd kiss or slap or snog;

on their ipads and their screens, the kids are building castles
out of pixelated cubes; the kids are raising mythic pets
the kids are trading unicorns for neon grown giraffes;

on youtube they have learned to make slime from your
            shaving gel;
on tiktok, mimic dance moves a million times more skilful
than your macarena days;

the kids, they're ok, i think; it's us i'm worried for
scowling from our sofas one generation up
parroting the guilt our elders felt with us

rainbow

*for my daughter again, a thank you for all the rainbows
you've given me*

on the paper, you draw yet another rainbow
it's rainbows you've been drawing
and rainbows you still draw

red into orange, orange into yellow
green into blue, a dash of quick illegal pink

blu tacked to each wall; a rainbow
beneath each magnet on the fridge; a rainbow
hidden in my suitcase to find when i'm away; a rainbow
raised up in your arms when i come back home again

when i was pregnant; and all we knew of you
were patterns on my skin, i imagined *i* would be the one
pointing out the sky to you; wrapping you in bows
striped with the sunbeams of each storm

i was wrong

SHORT STORY: THE LADYBIRD HERO

I bought the National Geographic *once when getting the train up to a gig in Glasgow because I forgot the book I was planning to read and didn't want to buy a shit magazine which made me feel ugly, which a lot of magazines make me feel. Two facts I read in the* National Geographic *sparked this story:*

1. *There are many ways that heterosexual male creatures compete with other heterosexual males for female attention and to ward off other males. Lions do it mainly by fighting. Peacocks, by prancing around with sexy feathers up in the air, and fighting. But some ladybirds, I learned, ward off male competition in other ways. They don't fight because, well, they're not really great at that physically. So what they do is once they start having sex with the female ladybird they ward off other males simply by keeping on shagging so that no one else can. Some ladybird species apparently have sex for up to eight hours for this reason. Simply to stop others getting their mate.*
2. *Ladybirds are one of the only species where males can ejaculate more than once during the same sexual act (except Sting, I imagine).*

I wrote this story after my daughter found two ladybirds 'fighting' in the garden.

Antoni had been a premature near-tragedy; waters burst unexpectedly in the local shopping centre just beside the cereal aisle. For months in hospital, Kamila was unable to carry out all but the most supervised of hugs, holds, kisses; the main contact with her newborn son being a thirty-minute syringing of banked breast milk, donated by a local mother called Tracy, between his doll-sized lips every three hours.

Kamila promised little Antoni certain things as she stared at him through that plastic box. One of them was a garden. A garden he could pick strawberries in. When Antoni was three and a half, Kamila was able to fulfil that promise. Unlike the rest of Kamila's life, their little garden was perfect. Antoni would only toddle inside the house to eat and sleep, the rest of his daylight hours were spent rummaging within this long-awaited pygmy plot of wilderness.

In winter, he relished melting frost from frozen leaves with his fingertips and tongue or prodding the ice on top of puddles with thick sticks. In spring, he would rub the lavender between his palms the way Kamila had shown him when the first purple buds had flowered. He watched the bees and wasps nibbling the sweet-scented honeysuckle, then rolling, pollen-drenched, in the hollyhocks' petals. As summer approached, Antoni adored searching for the white flowers sprouting ruby red fruits between thick leaves in the strawberry patches.

But best of all were the ladybirds. Antoni *loved* the ladybirds.

For hours each day from mid-May onwards, he would sit cross-legged as close to the geraniums as he could master, coaxing these beloved little pets onto his palms, forcing one after the next to climb across his knuckles' peaks, left hand followed by right hand followed by left hand, in an ongoing dance of mountain ranges. Antoni loved this game; loved watching the tiny ladybirds scuttling across his knuckles, the tickling of their little legs on his skin.

Antoni counted the ladybirds' spots meticulously. He noted the colours of the spots and the colours of the wings and the number of spots on each side and he made a chart of dots and smiley ladybird faces in his special ladybird diary to keep track of it all. If Antoni uncovered a ladybird with more than two spots, he would run inside and mark the occasion with a yellow star sticker and a small picture scribbled in a square. He would tick next to the picture to mark a sighting.

Antoni chatted to the ladybirds constantly. He gave them names and back stories, categorised them into human social units. His ladybirds fell in love; some got married; some had family fall-outs and dramatic reunions; some went to ladybird restaurants and ladybird pubs and ladybird schools and ladybird football matches and got interviewed for ladybird jobs. And some had ladybird fights. Antoni did not like the fights.

The day Antoni named himself The Ladybird Hero he was four years and one week old. It was the second week in June. As Kamila watched her son from the kitchen that day, she noticed him sitting for longer than usual, head and shoulders hunched like an elderly man, shouting and then gently, or as gently as young children are able, prodding at a pair of double-deckered ladybirds.

After a while, Antoni turned his head frustratedly towards the kitchen.

'Fighting, Mum!' he wailed. 'Kasia and Barry fighting, Mum. I can't stop them and Kasia is getting squashed and I am The Ladybird Hero to save them! I don't like fighting, Mum!'

Antoni ran inside to his mum and wrapped his arms around her thighs as if her thighs were the toughest bouncers in the life club, his face sheltered between her knees.

Kamila stroked Antoni's hair. She praised him for his kindness. She told him not to worry. She offered him some of his favourite orange squash which he nodded in agreement to, and then sipped it from the cup like spooned medicine. He waited a while in the kitchen's haven, as Kamila soaped and rinsed the dishes, then, presumably healed by the sweet nectar, ran back to the garden, kneeling next to his ladybird friends, prodding them once again.

After a few seconds, he looked up. 'Mum! They're still fighting. Barry and Kasia are still fighting.'

'Help them then, honey. You're The Ladybird Hero.'

Yes he was.

Yes he was.

He was, he was, he was.

He was The Ladybird Hero.

He lay right down on the grass, his cheek squashed against the earth, his eyes fixed to the creatures with professional precision. He prodded Kasia and Barry once more, whispering in his most ladybird accent that they must stop fighting right now.

Kasia and Barry were not fighting.

Kasia and Barry were fucking, and had been fucking happily for the last four and a half hours, before this arsehole of a child had interrupted them.

Keep going, Barry! Kasia yelled from below. *Just try to cum one more time, quickly.*

I'm fucking trying! Barry yelled back down, unable to turn his ladybird head. *But it's hard to keep fucking you with these giant fingertips poking at my goddamn wings.*

Barry held on as long as he could. He just managed to come again before he was plucked off and hauled onto Antoni's proud, flattened and now lightly ladybird-semen-speckled palm. Barry dashed to the edge of this new terrain, searching desperately for a way back down to Kasia before any of those other fuckers hanging around them tried to mount her.

Too late. She and Eduardo were already going for it. Gutted.

Antoni ran into the kitchen, twisting his hand over and back again to keep Barry upright. 'Look, Mum, I saved little Ladybird Barry.' He smiled. 'Look, Mum, Barry is dancing!'

Kamila smiled at the dancing bug.

Barry was not dancing. Barry fucking hated dancing almost as much as he hated being 'rescued' mid-shag.

After several forced mountain-range hikes across his excited little fingers, Antoni released Barry into the strawberry patch on the opposite side of the garden. Barry sat, nibbling on a nasturtium petal, still horny as hell, wondering if he'd ever be able to fly again.

Antoni went back into the kitchen and made a 'Ladybird Hero' badge out of a badge kit he'd received for his birthday. Kamila pinned the badge to his T-shirt and kissed him on the forehead and said what a good, caring boy he was.

Antoni spent the following few weeks searching for and saving his ladybird friends from the fights they seemed increasingly to be having as summer broke through spring.

As mid-summer approached, Antoni noticed a population problem. 'I can't find any new ladybirds, Mum!' he shouted.

And it was true.

He couldn't.

MIRRORS

An Unfinished Face

and if you're still breathing, you're the lucky ones
cos most of us are heaving through corrupted lungs
setting fire to our insides for fun

DAUGHTER, 'Youth'

we are the only species who puts make-up on corpses

we are born
without one worry
how we look
on the outside

and when we die
we'll look shite
but we'll be dead
so we won't mind

the only time
we waste with worry
about our body's
shape and size

is this tiny in-between-time
known as life

fairy tale

despite what adverts make-believe
sofas are no comfier to slump on if you're 'beautiful'

sand sieved between your toes
falls no more finely through thinner feet

the scent of perfume lingers
as fragrantly on shorter necks

sunsets burn as brutally
on any gazing irises

the birds would still have landed
on snow white's hands, and sung for her
no matter how she looked

monster

To lose confidence in one's body is to lose confidence in oneself.

SIMONE DE BEAUVOIR

at school, i longed for:　　julie's legs

maddy's skin

rowena's backbone

kathryn's lips

laura's glow

hanna's waist

joanna's
arm s

a n d　　　　　　　　　　　a r　s e;

255

friends mangled body parts
cut and pasted over mine;

a patchwork dream of frankenstein
to improve my faulty flesh

as if 'other' were the answer
as if my body were the test

as if no one's watching

for @wellness_by_norah, who said:
Dance like no one's watching. Everyone's on their phone.
Nobody is watching.

written after a weekend dancing with my daughter at home
and then dancing with friends at a nightclub and wondering at
what age self-consciousness fucks up so much of the fun

when we danced
just to dance
enjoy the dance
sweat and dance
before we worried
how we look
when we dance

when we swam
just to swim
jumping in
sweat and swim
before we worried
how we look
when we swim

when we sexed
just to sex
naked flesh
sweat and sex
before we worried
how we look
when we sex

when we ran
just to run
just to run
sweat and run
before we worried
how we look
when we run

i miss those days
i want those days
i want to get back
to the age
before appearance
steals the feel
steals the fun

ON HAVING AN UNFINISHED FACE

don't wear your body
as if this sacred patch of skin
nerves and blood-rush restlessness
were an accident

VANESSA KISUULE, 'take up space'

We are all Edward Hoppers here
Painting pictures of ourselves

LAURIE BOLGER, 'Tables'

As much as is possible, without ruining my own career, I avoid doing things that include having my photo taken by other people. I'm not hugely insecure about how I look, perhaps because of a confident and loving upbringing, perhaps more likely because I fit in to the standard white, soft-haired, young and thin category of the still largely racist and ageist and size-ist podium the beauty industry is slowly having to question. Still, I have no idea how people working in modelling or fashion, or anything that involves your looks being scrutinised, do it. There seems to be this idea that modelling must be the easiest job in the world. Fuck that.

The main filmed work I do do is live poetry readings or pre-recorded poems for YouTube and other social media platforms. These are really important to me. I want to do them. I like watching other people read online and I think these social media platforms make for a very democratic and much less means- and/or class-based access to art. But even this took me a long time to be comfortable with because, as always, there are arseholes out there on the internet.

Arseholes who immediately hopped online to tell me, amongst other more intimate insults and threats, how ugly I was. I was in my mid-twenties when I started posting videos online and I am almost sure that if I'd been younger, or more insecure, that would have been the end of me sharing poems that way. Maybe at all. Luckily, I didn't give too much of a shit by then whether or not a person cry-wanking in front of his pet turtle in Texas thought I was too much of a ginger cunt for my poetry to be deemed worthy of his time. I'm not prejudiced against Texas. I checked analytics for the location of some of the comments and Texas came up. I made up the bit about the cry-wank and the turtle in my head.

Of course, comments can be switched off on most of these platforms, but I like the comments. They've been really helpful in many respects. I've learnt a lot from people's opinions online. I just skim over the ones telling me I'm ugly, or, as often, that I need more cock.

On the occasions when I have agreed to be photographed or filmed, I have often found it incredibly shit. After one three-hour fashion shoot with a trendy London-based magazine, at which a team of albeit very lovely people stood around a screen and with every picture taken *hmmmd*, *ooohed*, said, 'No, it's no good, take another one,' I was done.

I like getting dressed up to go out sometimes and I don't mind posing for photos, but when a crowd of people are standing around watching you and somehow waiting for you to magically look 'better' so they can get the shot they need . . . Nah, I'm not into it.

An interview for the BBC News slot *Meet the Author* was

similarly dismal. It was presented by James Naughtie. In all honesty, I thought it was a radio show, and only realised it was a television thing when I got there. I hadn't put make-up on before I left the house – sometimes I do, sometimes I don't – and when I got to the backstage bit (the green room), there was another author – male, about ten years older than me, waiting to go on too.

After five minutes, a woman came in. She was the make-up artist for the show. She asked me what make-up I wanted. I thought about it. Although part of my brain was saying, *Lather me in it*, a louder voice was saying, *No. This is an interview about my bloody book, I don't need to panic and put a load of make-up on just 'cos I thought it was a radio interview.* So I said, 'Just put on whatever you have to for the cameras.'

The make-up artist started powdering me up.

She then asked if I wanted my eyebrows filled in because I had quite light eyebrows.

I said, 'If it's needed for the camera, cool, but don't worry if not.' I knew nothing about screen make-up.

After a few more questions like this, I said, 'Just treat me like the other guy, just make-up that's needed for the camera but I'm not wearing any today so that's cool.'

She said, 'Do you want just a bit of mascara?'

I said, 'No thanks,' smiling.

Then she offered me some lipstick. Then she asked if I had a hair-brush with me.

This is no insult to this person. Her job is to do people's make-up and I'm sure women do ask to be made up more because, in this fickle as shit society, we are judged on this even when doing interviews unrelated to how we look.

I went and did the interview and left feeling neither excited nor proud that I'd just done my first proper interview about a book that had been published, but instead feeling like a piece of ugly shit on a stick, wondering who else watching would notice my undressed face and crappy hair.

With no insult intended either, the presenter of the programme is hardly a fucking oil painting himself, as the saying goes (though it maybe shouldn't because oil portraiture tended to discriminate less on looks and more on who had the money or lineage or fame to have their portrait painted).

The other two people on screen were both men, faces full of wrinkles relevant to their age and hair which had definitely not been brushed or styled for their TV appearance. They were not asked if they had brought a hairbrush with them. Or given powder, which I'd assumed was for the cameras.

I've heard our current 'Age' called 'The Age of Aesthetics' because we are so obsessed with and judgemental about appearances. This relates not only to our bodies and faces but to many other aspects of our culture: houses; gardens; food. That Nigella Lawson does not put photographs in most of her cookbooks angers many people I know.

It's a sort of culture that has created that surprise moment of open-mouthed amazement when someone who walks onto *Britain's Got Talent* looking at odds with what we deem beautiful can actually sing and the whole audience is like, 'Oh my fucking god, what a fucking shock that that old ugly bitch can sing,' and faints, as if we've forgotten that vocal cords and musical ability are not biologically associated with appearance and fashion sense.

The Voice is perhaps a relief in this respect, until you see the shadows of delight on some of the judges' faces when they press the buzzer and their chair spins and, *thank fuck*, the good singer is also attractive enough to put in a music video.

It is for this reason that I'm appreciating the drift of poetry on social media from YouTube to Instagram, where words are being shared now rather than just spoken in video performances. I like watching people read their poems, and I love hearing poems read by the poets in their accents (especially if that accent is Scottish or Irish or Welsh or from Newcastle or Birmingham) but I've had a few too many young people in schools say to me that they love writing poetry, but aren't 'cool enough' for spoken word. Though it might be unpopular to say, I've also had a fair few young people absolutely believe they're 'cool enough' to do spoken word videos, but who seem to give not a shit about the poetry side of things. The worried, quiet pupils, for me, are always the better poets, so I'm glad there are platforms other than YouTube sprouting up. Video stole the radio and all that.

If I'm feeling miserable, I sometimes binge watch the 'best auditions' YouTube compilations and feel my faith in people rise as someone who has spent his whole life hating his job in Carphone Warehouse shows himself to be a self-trained opera singer on a par with Pavarotti. I've watched Stacey Solomon's first audition a few times. For her, it was classism that had everyone shocked, like, *Oh wow, someone that talks with an accent like that can sing Louis Armstrong so beautifully. What?* One day, I hope these things will not shock us quite so much. I love Stacey Solomon.

Another filming experience that stands out was a series of short recordings I made for a condom company about the orgasm gap between people in heterosexual relationships. (In case you're one of the very low number of women who do orgasm from straight p in v sex, the gap is 'men orgasm, women don't'.) The company had asked me to write some fairly serious poems on this inequality and the historical stigma surrounding female pleasure, following research sent to me by the team.

When I arrived on set, the director sent me down to get my make-up done with the instruction, 'We just want you totally natural.' Of course, natural never means *actually* natural for filming, it's more like those beauty instruction pages in magazines titled things like '500 Simple Steps to Achieving the Natural Look'.

I went down the stairs and met the make-up artist, so often one of a handful of women on these shoots. She was lovely. I said they wanted it natural. She said cool, and started putting on creams and then powder and foundation and stuff. I should note, I really like the feel of having my face made up, whether it's by a make-up artist or my daughter. I'm rarely that comfortable with the end result but the feel of it is lush.

She asked me how I wanted my eyes. I said I normally caked on the mascara but didn't really do anything else, so could she put loads of mascara on and leave the rest? She put mascara on me. Then, like the other make-up artist, she said, 'Your eyebrows are really light,' and started filling them in with pencil. My eyebrows seem to annoy make-up artists.

I asked, 'Could you maybe leave them? I don't normally use pencil on them.' And she said, 'I'll do a little bit.' I thought maybe it was for the camera. Then she got out blusher.

I hate making a fuss. I'm not particularly shy, but speaking up can be hard, especially when you might offend someone. After a few of these sorts of shoots though, I'm getting a bit better at asking for what I actually want. So I said, 'Can you leave the blusher, please, or just put on what's needed for the camera.'

The make-up artist replied with a sentence I will never forget: 'It's just that I don't want to put my name to something that's unfinished.'

I won't lie. In my head, my first reaction was, *Bitch, my face is not unfinished.*

She wasn't being a bitch though. It's her job, and her name will be on the credits of these films and if someone watches it and sees me looking like what – in that world apparently – looks like a shit-ridden rat's arsehole, then it reflects on her. I think this is the worst thing about it all. That my face is not good enough for a make-up artist to feel comfortable leaving 'unfinished', even for a low-budget shoot where I'm supposed to look 'natural' to read a poem. She put on the blusher.

The filming was of four poems about orgasm inequality in heterosexual relations, based on a study of what 'bad sex' meant for women compared to men in these relations. Initially, the study was intended to create a light-hearted ad relating to 'bad sex'. But the results were shocking. The general finding from what I recall (of course there are always exceptions) was that 'bad sex' for the men asked had been largely interpreted as boring sex, or sex where silly, embarassing things happened, as expected by the company. For the women, however, the phrase 'bad sex' had been interpreted almost exclusively as painful (but nonetheless carried out), non-consensual or consensual but highly unpleasurable.

So instead, orgasm inequality became the focus and I was given and researched the following rough notes from a number of sources:

- Women in relations with women have higher rates of orgasm during sex than women in relations with men.
- Men in relations with women have roughly the same rate of orgasm as men in relations with men.
- Women in relations with men have the lowest rate of orgasm during partnered sex.
- Women in relations with men are most likely to carry on having sex despite pain and without seeking help.
- There are many reasons for this, none biological.

One of the more positive results of this study was that over 90 per cent of all respondents were desperate to know what actually made their partner feel pleasure. They *wanted* to please each other. I think this is the bit to concentrate on. It was society and culture that seemed to be fucking things up, not the individual people. No one wanted to be a shit lover. Well, most people. There was still the 10 per cent who, according to that study, didn't give a shit.

I didn't twig when I took this job that it was actually attached to a new product: a gel you put on your clitoris which apparently makes orgasms more likely. It says on the label it has 'Up to 20 earth-shattering experiences in just 1 bottle'. I didn't get sent any as part of the work, but I ordered a bottle. I'd already agreed to do the ad.

I started to imagine these terrible relationships where instead of asking how to please the partner, some tired guy just rubs the gel into her clitoris and expects that to do the job, saying things like, 'Go on, I'm rubbing it in, have you cum yet?'

I think I could be sued if I say anything negative about this gel, and I do appreciate the focus it gives to this body part, but let's just say one truth, because you can't be sued for truth: I put some on my clit and it stung like fuck and I did not have an orgasm. I did this twice, once when I was not at all aroused and therefore very unlikely to have one anyway and once when I was highly aroused. Neither time did it do anything other than sting.

Once my make-up was done, I was taken to a room to film these poems.

The bedroom was supposed to have been chosen to look 'like a woman's bedroom'. Woman, not girl. Woman. A woman's bedroom in which an adult woman – me – would be sat on the bed discussing the orgasms society had been stealing from her.

First thing that struck me. It was a single bed, rare in the world of grown adult sex lives. Secondly, there was a giant teddy on the bed and some smaller teddies and a duck and another cuddly toy I can't remember exactly. There were a lot of cuddly toys. And some fluffy slippers at the side of the bed.

Strange, perhaps, that so many non-sexual parts of women's lives are overtly and often ridiculously sexualised by brands – eating yoghurt, washing cars, shampooing our hair, eating a penis-shaped chocolate bar in a bath which is overflowing across the tiled floor because you are so concentrated on giving the chocolate a blowjob that you forget to turn the tap off – but when it comes to an advert which is intended to actually open up conversations about pleasurable adult sex, almost the opposite is apparent. The sexual scene is filled with teddies and fluff. Not fluffers. Just fluff. Anyway, women in porn don't get fluffers, just Vaseline.

I hate complaining on sets, because photoshoots and filming take ages and most of the crew have little interest in the politics of it and just want to finish on time and go home. But the idea of reading poems about the prejudices against our adult vulva-loving bodies while sitting cross-legged on a single bed surrounded by a child's cuddly toys was a bit much. I asked politely, 'Can we take the kid's toys off the bed, please?'

One of the young women on the team grinned. I thought the guy would say 'Yeah sure' straight away, but he didn't. I assumed at first that the teddies were just leftover. It was a real house we were filming in. Instead, he argued the case that the teddies were there to give it a more feminine touch. Teddies. Feminine.

Sure, some adults have cuddly toys, I'm not judging that. But most thirty-year-old people I know of don't sleep with or have sex next to giant teddy bears. Fine, if I was reading poems about my teddy bear or soft fur fetish. But I wasn't. I was just a young woman reading poems about general sexual inequalities while being made to look like she either sleeps in her kid's bedroom or dreams of still being five years old. I imagined they might ask me to suck a lollipop, I mean dick, I mean lollipop, next.

I asked the guy how old he was. He was my age. I asked if he had teddy bears on his bed. He said no. He even laughed at the idea. I asked if his girlfriend had teddy bears on her bed. He said no, and I thought that would have ended it, but it still took a while of talking before I could get the big teddy bear off the bed.

It takes a hell of a lot for me to assert myself like this and by the end of the conversation I was sweaty and my hands were shaking and I could hardly remember the poem I was reciting off by heart next, so I can only imagine what it must be like for any less experienced, less confident person in this sort of situation where a whole crew of staff is getting increasingly annoyed that there are delays being caused to their working day and *would you just sit on the fucking bed, cuddle the teddy bear and read your bloody poem about painful sex, Hollie, so we can get this take finished and all go home.*

After all the discussion around this giant teddy and the final OK to move it, I went to remove the last of the smaller teddies. The argument started again. I was too shaky to bother any more and hold up everyone's day. So, sitting to my right-hand side in the frame of a film shared with the hashtag winwinorgasm, on top of the radiator, quacking at me in delight, is one fluffly duck. Check it out on YouTube if you fancy!

I have developed rules for these sorts of situations now because it is too confusing and pressurised when you're on your own (I don't normally have any colleagues on set with me) and don't know if you're 'making a fuss over nothing' or 'overreacting' (I've been told these two things so often in life, particularly when talking about 'women's issues', that I'm paranoid about it). So now I ask myself in situations I'm unsure of and feel uncomfortable with: *If I looked like Mr Big from* Sex and the City, *would they ask me to do this, and if not, why not?*

Would Mr Big be asked to sit on a bed to read poems about sex? Yeah, maybe.
Would Mr Big be asked, in this situation, to sit next to a giant teddy bear? Unlikely.
Would Mr Big be listened to if he asked for the teddy to be removed? Very likely.
Would Mr Big be told his face was unfinished?

screen sex

*one of four poems i recorded for a condom company about social
sexual prejudices whilst sitting on a single bed that most of the
teddies had been removed from*

in the sex scenes
on our screens
he will cum
she will cum

ten kisses. twenty thrusts
it's enough. it's enough.

in the sex scenes
on our screens
she is thin
he is muscle

she won't queef
he won't fumble
she will scream
she will not sweat

her mouth is
open wide
and confident

hair tossed back
yet glossed
and neat

in the sex scenes
on our screens
they have no marks
they have no scars

she's always wet
he's always hard
satisfaction guaranteed

bed sheets crisp
and white and clean

and we
we are watching

with our sweaty skins
uneven bodies
watching sexy packaged up
as if sexy is a look

now we're worried
we're not good enough
our turn-ons are not right

in the sex scenes in real life
we keep quiet, carry on
many feel the need to fake

in the sex scenes on our screens
automatic bodies shake

make-up retouched
between each take

this is fake
this is fake

ten kisses
twenty thrusts
directed moves
airbrushed lust

it's not enough
it's not enough

when i see the man's wrinkles they do not look like wrinkles to me

I was waiting in Berlin's Schonefeld Airport for hours the morning after a show. Berlin Airport is a brilliant airport to wait in because there's a pub outside it which looks like the sort of pub I imagine you'd find in mountain villages, with outdoor tables. After a couple of hours people-watching I realised that I was automatically thinking, she looks wrinkly, she looks old, whenever I saw wrinkles on women. I didn't even think about the men. I don't know if this is because I'm not a man or because I live in a place that has told me that wrinkly women have failed in some way, whereas old wrinkly men have lived. Either way, I wrote this to try to stop my mind from being a subconsciously sexist bitch.

when i see the man's wrinkles
they do not look like wrinkles to me

they look like wizard skin; like wisdom;
like dumbledore; like merlin;
like gandalf; like saracen; like morgan freeman playing god;
like silver hair on mountain top; like riding in on horseback;
like davos seaworth; like stannis baratheon;
like jorah mormont;
like president; like riches, like thirty years in business;
like james bond; like pretty woman;
like a twenty-year-old age gap
between co-stars in hollywood;
like quiz show hosts, like attenborough;
like gq feature interviews shoulder shot front covers;
like black and white photographs
of george clooneys zoomed in ripened face;

like caves of expensive wines to dust off and uncork
and savour for their maturity

when i see the woman's wrinkles
they look like wrinkles to me

dendrochronology

excitedly, we count each line on storm split trees across the park, in awe, at the widest trunks, the eldest stumps, the wisest barks, scornfully, we count each line, beside our lips, beneath our eyes, as if we did something wrong, to also mark the passing time

acting your age

when i have fun
people say
'you're acting
like a teenager again'

i'm not.

i'm acting like
a thirty year old
woman

being teenage
was never
as comfortable
as this

DO YOU MIND IF I TAKE A SELFIE?

*I paint myself because I am so often alone and
because I am the subject I know best*

FRIDA KAHLO

Sometimes when I go online and see one after another photograph of someone's face from different angles, I get really bored. Maybe there's jealousy of those faces I deem better than mine. Maybe there's annoyance when it's someone who seems to think they're the most gorgeous person on the planet seemingly wanting to rub that into all the other fucks' faces. Mostly, though, I think it's boredom. There's a whole world around us, and all we do is keep taking photos of our own faces. After a while it seems to feel a bit self-centred. I get especially bored if I've followed someone online for a love of their music or poems or comedy and all I end up seeing is their face each day.

On the other hand, I feel the same criticising selfies as I do about criticising my family. I can diss them all I like but if someone else tries, I'm all *Fuck you, don't you dare talk about my cousin like that.*

I overheard two rather 'well-spoken' (another phrase that might be rethought) middle-aged women on a train journey once discussing the vacuousness of 'young girls these days, caked in make-up, doing nothing but take selfies all day'. I felt rage at how openly these women were scoffing at this modern phenomenon.

Hearing them criticising selfie-takers as some sort of conglomerate glob of vacuous airheads made me certain that I didn't agree with what they were saying. I imagined these women on the train as wealthy keen gardeners, which of course they may not have been and which was as judgemental of me as they were being about these young girls.

I mention gardening mainly because I find it very two-faced the way obsessing over your own face is viewed compared to obsessing, for example, over your own private garden or house interior. Also, this 'caked in make-up' sort of criticism of women, I have only ever heard from the middle and upper classes, aimed more often than not at those from less wealthy family backgrounds, as if wearing more make-up somehow makes a woman less intelligent, or, gulp, less of a feminist. It does not.

Every time *Gardeners' Question Time* comes on the radio when I'm driving, trying to listen to Radio 4 as long as I can until the repetition of voices with no regional accent becomes too much to bear, there seems to be yet another lovely person desperate to fill their garden with flowers that don't want to be there, purely because they like the look of them. My gran was meticulous about the centimetre space between pansies in her garden, yet constantly criticised vanity in people.

Not everyone has a garden though, do they? Or a house they can furnish and decorate. For many people, especially poorer or younger people, their own body is all they have through which to represent themselves. Their one blank canvas. Caking yourself in make-up and taking a selfie is surely not so different from obsessing over the pansies in the front garden or posting yet another photo of your kitchen renovation.

There was an article in the magazine *Art Quarterly* entitled 'The Self-Portrait'. I don't know why this magazine keeps getting delivered to my house. I haven't subscribed to it and it's definitely not free but I'm not the one paying for it and I've learnt a lot reading it, so.

I found the article really interesting until it reached a line about selfies. While the author rejoiced in artistic self-portraits in general, writing, 'The Self-Portrait claims its unique place in the history of human culture because of its ability to map, or seem to map, the fluid transformations of human identity. Making yourself visible is an attempt to clear some space', he then went on to say, while discussing the self-portraits of Paul Gauguin, that his complex presentations of self 'read as especially pertinent in today's accelerated climate of personal aggrandisement through self-representation'. (Yes: selfies.)

Now, it is very possible that I misunderstood this article as I don't often read a lot (by which I really mean anything at all) about the art world, but his aside about selfies being 'personal aggrandisement' pissed me off. I don't believe that people take and share selfies merely for 'personal aggrandisement'. It seemed a very smug tosser of a comment to me. In fact, I think using big long words like 'aggrandisement' in an article is more of a cry for 'personal aggrandisement' than taking a selfie is.

In such an in-depth article about self-representation through art, this sort of throwaway comment about millions of people currently taking and sharing photos of their own faces and sometimes bodies too, for myriad different reasons in myriad different ways, seems weak and patronising, especially after praising people who spend months painting their own faces.

Most of the selfies I see online are of young women. According to selfiecity, a project looking at selfie culture worldwide, young women are the most likely selfie takers, most likely 'head-tilt' selfie takers, and age-wise, most likely to post selfies while under the age of thirty, at which point this hobby seems to fade.

Some studies found that older men actually post more selfies than older women. Maybe because as women age they have been scientifically proven to stop giving a fuck. (This has not actually been scientifically proven, it has just been my experience of getting older.)

Maybe, less optimistically, it's because as women age they disappear from the majority of mainstream TV and media representation (*The Crown* is a breakthrough in this respect), shut away in darkened rooms with Rapunzel's captor and Melisandre and the rest of the old hags whose magic youth potions have finally stopped working, forced to watch reel after reel of Hollywood romances with average age gaps of ten years between male and female co-stars. Hard to know; maybe they feel their faces are no longer the faces anyone wants to see, themselves included; maybe they've got better things to do.

Whenever people criticise a trend which is not only predominantly female, but also predominantly of the young, especially when it is criticised as being evidence of vacuousness or stupidity or mere vanity, the hairs on my nipples perk up like hedgehogs stuck under piles of branches on November the 5th.

For years and years and years and years, girls and women and younger men in particular have been used as 'muses', aka models or sex workers paid a pittance to be painted by mainly male artists.

In many cases, this model/artist dynamic is very intrusive. It has undoubtedly been abused historically. The majority of famous paintings I saw of women when I was younger were in a gallery or photos on a CD cover or a magazine front cover and they were nearly always images made by a man, often with the model wearing few clothes, or, especially in 'classier' art galleries, no clothes at all.

Now, despite some of the YouTube comments I get calling me a prudish whore who needs more cock in my life (quite a confused image there I'd say) I am all for nakedness but when there is not such a cultural imbalance of who and who is not naked and why they are naked and who is choosing what sort of pose and lighting they are going to be naked in. Naked saunas. Yes. Consensual naked orgies. Fine. Nakedness as the most likely way a non-royal aristocratic female can still feature in an art gallery exhibition. Not keen.

There's a group called Guerrilla Girls which formed in response to an exhibition at New York's Museum of Modern Art with the aim of attempting to address the gender (and later, racial) imbalance in art galleries. I found out about them after seeing one of their posters in Tate Modern, which read, 'Less than 5 per cent of the artists in the Modern Art Sections [of the Met Museum] are women, but 85 per cent of the nudes are female'.

Are. Not were. Are. I had never thought about it before. It was one of those moments when you've just taken something for granted all your life and then you're like, *Oh yeah, it's not because women are just shit at painting and really good at being naked*. Though, personally, I am very good at being naked and not very good at painting.

One of my favourite painters in this respect, or any respect, is a Manchester-born painter called Annie Swynnerton. I stumbled upon her by accident in Manchester whilst trying to tour during the 2019 blizzards. I was working in Salford fortnightly at the time, co-presenting Radio 3's *The Verb*, and was meant to be heading to Chesterfield after work for a gig, but all trains to either Chesterfield or back home were cancelled due to snowstorms. I booked a room in Manchester's Velvet Hotel, one of my favourite hotels to stay in on tour, and gave in to the thrill of the snow stop (and an enforced night of no parenting). Weirdly, I used to feel sick touching velvet. So did my uncle. I'm OK with it now. Still relapse at times.

I got off the tram from Salford to Manchester City Centre at the wrong stop, just a stop or two earlier than I should have, overkeen not to miss the target and striking too soon. Once I realised, the tram had gone. I was right outside Manchester Art Gallery. It was open for another hour and I had nothing to do but walk on my own in the snow and then sit in a hotel on my own, so I went in. The exhibition was by this artist.

I hadn't heard of her, which doesn't really say a lot, because I haven't heard of many artists other than Van Gogh and Frida Kahlo. I never go for the brown cheese in Trivial Pursuit. Or the yellow. Or the green. Or, in fact the blue or orange. Just the pink really.

I loved the pictures. Annie was apparently one of only a few painters to paint real depictions of working-class women looking genuinely pissed off and bored with their work and childcare chores, at a time when the majority of the art world preferred rosy-cheeked romanticisations of back-broken labourers. Annie also beautifully emphasised women's wrinkles in almost all of the paintings, which wasn't very fashionable in the late nineteenth and early twentieth centuries in which she worked, especially in portraits of women.

Most of her portraits in this exhibition weren't nudes, though she is also known for these and has been described as 'one of the most daring painters of the nude, often shocking audiences with her robustly painted figures', which I think implies that she simply painted average-figured women. My favourite painting in the collection was a nude called 'Oceanid' which made me even more desperate to go skinny dipping than I normally am anyway.

I got to the hotel, all excited that I had learned something new and that I was now 'stuck' in a hotel for the night to eat and read and rest and touch, my frozen face and hair littered with melting snowflakes. There's a word 'sapiosexual'. It means, 'someone who finds intelligence sexually attractive or arousing'. I realised I was turned on by art sometimes. Saying this, the Velvet Hotel is a very sexy hotel anyway.

Back to the selfies.

After years of being represented, or not, by other people, finally a hell of a lot of people who couldn't before are able to take their own photos, to show themselves in the light they want with the filter they want at the time they want doing what they want to show the world who they are according to themselves.

We can take sexy photos the way we feel sexy and God knows this has been defined for too fucking long by other, majority cis straight male gazes. Of course, what we even feel is 'sexy', let alone what we might put into the world in the form of photographs of ourselves looking 'sexy', especially when we are sexually inexperienced, is likely to be defined largely by what we have thrown at us by a media still largely dominated by the same male gaze.

Still, now we can take our own self-portraits more and more, new gazes are emerging into the mainstream because of this; a queer

281

gaze, a trans gaze, a youth gaze, a female gaze and people are unsurprisingly doing it in drones, and because of this, the world shouts back BIGHEADS BIGHEADS ARROGANT SELF-OBSESSED TRAGIC INANE. Vacuous.

And these insults are largely being yelled at the younger and more outcast members of society.

Motherhood selfies are another case in point. I have heard the mothers who take them criticised a lot for 'using their babies' simply to pose in photos which are really about the mother looking good while also mothering well and not really about the baby at all.

I'm not one for putting photos of my kid online. I have been told by PR companies that I would get more followers if I did. I've even been told, by a solely white team, that mixed-race children are 'very fashionable at the moment' and that this would be an even better reason to put photographs of my daughter and myself online. It's more fucked up than I can put words to, other than swear words.

I don't put many photos of myself up and none of my daughter, but I have lots of folk I don't know following me online, one of whom has jumped on stage and tried to grab me in the interval at a gig; some of whom tell me they hate me and my face and my hair and my mind, so I think it's a bit different for me in terms of sharing personal pictures. But, bloody hell, I can understand why carers, full-time carers especially, mothers mainly, do this. Especially during those early parenthood days when you are often alone busting your guts with a baby, trudging around parks or corridors or at home with no one to talk to and no one documenting all this work and love you are pouring over this small bundle of life, this small bundle of life who is also not able to tell anyone about how much you've tried or likely to remember any of it themselves and who you are not being paid to look after so you do not have financial proof of this work either.

Yes yes, the babies will remember it all through the connections you are building and the love and all that, cool, but they won't remember that time when you sat and made daisy chains for four hours, will they? I write about parenting probably for some of the same reasons someone else might take a thousand selfies of themselves making daisy chains with their baby.

So selfies, in a way, are a bloody revelation for charting those early lone-parenting days. *Look, please see what I am doing here because no one is noticing and I'm so fucking tired and all I keep getting told is that the pram is taking up too much space and that I need to get my pre-baby body back and whenever anyone takes our photo, which is rare, I look like shit because I haven't slept but here! Look at this photo I took of myself looking gorgeous because the sun is covering my sore eyes and look at the smiling baby in the park feeding the ducks. Look at me and my baby looking fucking gorgeous together. Please. Please? Anyone! Fucking look at us feeding the fucking ducks!*

Motherhood in particular has so often been seen as a private thing, a domestic thing, as women's lives have been generally. I hear so many mothers lamenting a lack of photographs of themselves and their child because they were so often alone with their children. Selfies seem a little like a new era of representation between the outside world and your domestic life. Finally.

Until public representation in the media and the art world is not so touted by racial and gendered and sexual and general aesthetic discrimination, the love of taking our own photos of our own faces (and bodies) is unlikely to fade any time soon.

Money and class also push me towards a passionate love affair with selfie-defending.

For centuries, it has been mainly, or possibly solely, the rich, the aristocratic or the famous, who have been having their portraits painted in a certain light, with flesh added or taken off, skin lightened or darkened, depending on their desires or racist or classist beliefs. Classical paintings have been filtered and photoshopped for centuries by artists and moaning inbred royals.

The aristocracy have been getting pictures painted to attract a partner (think fifteenth-century Tinder but with oil colours) and many a poorer artist has been left quaking in their feathered boots in case the king or queen or prince or princess or cousin of both or lord or lady did not like the likeness of the painting that the artist made of them. Then photography was invented, and though cheaper and a little more accessible, representation wasn't all-encompassing.

Now, for the first time really, many more people (who can afford camera phones) have control over their own portraits. We can take the photos ourselves and edit them ourselves and share them if we want to so that one lover or five potential lovers or a group of friends or the whole fucking world can see us how we want them to see us.

I, myself, may well have, on several occasions, put my camera phone on a minute timer and rushed back into bed and pretended to be sleeping with lipstick on and my hair slightly but beautifully dishevelled the way every Hollywood film star has ever slept in black-and-white movies. Even better, I do not actually have to have a stranger (aka photographer) in the room with me to do this. And you might say, but Hollie, no one *needs* to have a photo of themselves fakely dishevelled in bed wearing lipstick looking sleepy-hot as fuck, and to that I would concede that this might be true but that maybe, just maybe, I want one after having watched too many of these black-and-white movies and that it is still one of my favourite self-portraits.

So I am in two minds.

Although photography is a highly skilful art form and a self-portrait on a phone by an amateur can't replace this, I hate having my photo taken by other people. I feel awkward and, sometimes, very intimidated. I've left many photoshoots, which I've been told I needed to do in order to get a 'proper author photo', feeling like a pile of bog rot or just slightly intruded upon or stereotyped or used. There's almost always some form of bias lurking. Also, I am vain but I don't want to be vain but I am because it's fucking hard not to be in this world, so I end up being like, 'Yeah, that's fine,' when really I want to say, 'No, take another one, I look like a heap of arse in those.'

A bit like when you get a haircut you hate and say, 'Yeah, that's great,' and then cry when you get home.

I also get a lot of class bias in photoshoots by the posher variety of photographer. When I had my first 'portrait' done for a book, the photographer wanted to stand me outside a block of flats in one of the poorest areas of London or against a wall covered in graffiti, to make me look, you know, 'edgy'.

By 'edgy', these photographers seem to either mean 'poorer' or 'a shit graffiti artist', as if people with less money are anything other than just generally underpaid and more fucked over by our economic system. This sort of poverty safari backdrop makes me want to gag, unless it is actually related to the person in the photo. I have been asked to stand in front of high-rise social housing more times than I can remember, once by a very expensive clothing company. Darren McGarvey's book *Poverty Safari* is very good.

One of the very first portrait shoots I had was with a photographer who kept telling me to turn my shoulders like in a school portrait and gaze out of the window at the sky. I did as I was told and got a set of the standard 'girl looks into space like an empty-headed moron' shots.

So, though I am bored of photos of faces viewed from a top right angle while lips pout slightly, I'm trying not to think, *What a bunch of boring cunts we are* or, *God, we're becoming so fucking self-obsessed*, and am more likely to think, *Fuck, this is the first time loads of diverse members of society have been able to create and share their own self-representations within the world instead of seeing the myriad of portraits made of and for them throughout history or not made of them at all throughout history because they were not deemed rich or classy or white or thin or famous or handsome enough to have their history recorded in professionally created and edited pictures.*

In the Eurostar queue once, I watched a woman I'd say was in her forties absolutely unashamedly taking one selfie after another at every angle she possibly could, as a whole queue of fellow passengers stared at her, some shaking heads as if they were disgusted by the self-indulgence, others giggling to friends and secretly pointing, others I don't know because I don't actually know what people are thinking.

Personally, I was in awe.

Yes, this person *may* also be seen as wasting their life taking photos of their own face when they could be doing something deemed more useful like, you know, visiting National Trust properties or watching *The Chase* or reading *Ulysses*; and they *may* also be horrendously insecure and therefore this is a display of that and their own hatred of their face. But this person looked pretty fucking happy doing it and, as someone who often puts make-up on in the toilet cubicles of train stations rather than in front of the actual toilet mirrors for fear other people might think I'm as vain as I am, I was fairly impressed by how forthright she was being about it. I found it hard to plaster her with the low self-esteem that some selfie obsessives are thought to suffer from, and some undoubtedly do.

A month or so after this trip, I was in Dublin on tour thinking about these selfies and walking down the canal. There were loads of pigeons around but everyone was ignoring them. One of them came up close to me and for the first time I noticed its neck. I'd never noticed the colours on a pigeon's neck before. I sat on a bench and wrote a poem about these beautiful pigeons in Dublin. It's called 'dublin pigeon'. It's not just pigeons in Dublin who have great necks though, but they do have a better accent than other pigeons.

Quick fact about pigeons posted to me after I put this poem about pigeons online:

I went to a lecture on colour and light and apparently pigeons have twenty-four different receptors in their eyes (we only have three). So chances are, pigeons are absolutely spectacular, but we have no way of seeing them. It's the same way people with colour blindness see certain colours as grey as they only have two types of eye receptors.

(thanks to Chris Hellawell for this)

dublin pigeon

for Rhiannon, who has always loved pigeons

i see you pigeon!
see that neck!
all emerald!
all amethyst!

sick to death
of all the praise
those fucking
parrots get

if you were
on instagram
i imagine
your account

would be
everyday updated
with selfies
of that lovely neck

shouting:

look at me you bastards!
i'm beautiful as well.

if you take my photo while i'm dancing, i'll punch you

*for that friend who always takes photos of you on a night
out dancing and ruins your most gorgeous memories of
yourself for ever*

do not take my photograph right now, it will not work
your camera cannot capture this

one click of that finger tricks carriage back to pumpkin
driver back to mouse; glass slippers back to blistered heels
prince charming back to smarmy pervert lurking on the
     staircase

this sweat across my dancing face
like thawing snow on dickens' roofs
– will just come out as sweat

these legs will not be beyoncé's legs
this hair will not be mermaid glossed
these cheeks will not be blushed
goblets brim with wine

they will just come out as legs
it will just come out as sweaty hair
they will just come out as blotchy cheeks

midnight will strike soon enough
but this next song is mine
so put that phone back in your pocket
so i can fuck up these glass slippers
one more time

pre-cameraphone nostalgia

if you feel the same, I'd recommend Berlin

lord, i miss those days
you could fuck against a fence
finger behind morrissons
piss relaxed into a gutter
knickers swinging ankles
moony all your friends
from the back seat of the bus
without fear of some cunt
clicking fifty half-lit photos
filtering your freedom
tagging you in shame

ADVICE FROM MY COUSIN

a thank you, for some of the best advice I've had, which I hated at the time

I was sixteen, I walked into my big cousin's bedroom. He was lying on his bed in the dark, eyes closed, listening to Nirvana.

His bedroom was painted dark red, ceiling included, mainly because he wasn't allowed to paint it black. My bedroom at the time was light blue and sunflower yellow with friends' handprints plastered all over.

He once summed up the differences between us as: he drank black coffee and smoked, I drank tea and played netball. I disagreed with the analogy but agreed with the facts. I still don't like coffee. He also said that if I ever told him that I didn't need drugs to have fun because I was high on life, we would never speak again. By drugs, I'm not saying that he was trying to get me into Class As, he mainly mentioned coffee.

That night, I was getting ready to go into town, trying to decide between a pink Topshop dress and a pair of baggy grey trousers and a blue woollen boob tube that I thought made me look very sexy yet sophisticated and 'cool'.

I had been reading an article in a magazine for girls three years older than I was, about how to make your skin shine: swap Pop Tarts for porridge, for example; make cucumber slices into cooling eye soothers; rub semen on your face. That sort of thing. I have read several times now about the benefits of using semen as skin moisturiser. I sometimes wonder if any research has been done into the similar use of vaginal juices.

After ten minutes of putting on and taking off these two outfits, I knocked on my cousin's bedroom door and sat down next to him on his bed using that 'I want to talk' waiting-room tactic.

'All right, cuz?' he finally breathed out, not looking up.

'Yeah,' I said, attempting to be cool and calm like him for all of two seconds before I began spitting out all of my dressing-up woes, which mainly consisted of moaning about how I just wanted to be a bit taller, 'cos the trousers didn't fit right at the bottom because I was 'too short', and a bit less freckly, just a bit, because I was 'too freckly', and less pale because I wasn't sure if that pink was all right on me and because my gran said I shouldn't go out without tights on with legs that purple but fake tan didn't suit me because fake tan covers freckles and although I was 'too freckly' I looked weird without any freckles if I tried to use fake tan.

I sat on my cousin's bed for a while talking, almost forgetting we were meant to be having a dialogue.

After a few minutes, he sat bolt upright, begrudgingly took off his headphones, placed Nirvana on his bed, fixed his eyes directly on mine.

'Well you're not, Hollie. You're not tall and you are very freckly. You will never be anything else. You will always be short and you will always be very pale and very freckly. So you can either carry on moaning about it, and you will still always be short and freckly, or you can stop moaning about it, and you will still always be short and freckly.'

He then put his headphones back on and closed his eyes in his scarlet box of cool. I stood up, mouth open at the insulting shit of a cousin I had. I walked downstairs to ask the others which outfit they preferred.

attempt at a haiku of a conversation i've never had with any girlfriend in my life

you've got lovely legs, she said.
yes i do. you too.
she nodded. *yes. that is true*

beach body ready

jelly shoes buckled tight; stilettos of the sand
so we can strut across this shoreline
over burning, battered shells
as other soles around us curse the *fucking rocks*
not us! we are ready; sunhats over shades

hairbands for the seaside breeze
towels thrown like thrones onto a perfect patch of sand
not too far from the toilets
not too far from the ice cream van

malibu and coke cans; uv lip balm reapplied
bikinis double-knotted now, tits will not fall out
until it's scheduled tits out time
are we beach body ready?

are you arseholes fucking blind?
can you not see that hole i dug?
did you not see her frisbee dive?
did you not see us in the sea ride that giant pink flamingo?

we are nammu of these beaches
we are yam upon these waves
we are seals of the shorelines
and we will sunbathe till we sleep

so let us lie down with our books, please
sunshine on our backs
are we beach body ready?
bitch, you do not have to ask.

yes, but have you ever seen my tits?

i agree with you completely;
nature *is* a precious source
of constant inspiration;
the way swallows sleep in air;

those starling murmurations;
migrations of the humpback whale;
the balance of a mountain goat
on misted cloudy cliffs;

this planet is a wonder
of course i am in awe of it
i'm just saying: *have you ever seen my tits?*
because they are quite spectacular as well;

these marshmallow masterpieces
shape shift every single month
like elephants in an earthquake
to warn of coming blood

able, for almost
twelve months of their life
to shoot milk across a room
with the mere surrender of my arms;

cramping to a baby's charms
across a tesco superstore;
leaking at the mere mention
of another needy child;

at other times –
masturbation's catalyst
direct line to the clitoris
a wank between two clouds
for a very lucky penis

landing pad for happy endings
two pillows for a perfect nap;
faithful office stressballs;
comfort in a bun

i'm not saying that my breasts
are necessarily *better*
than some birds who sleep mid-air

i'm just saying
i understand why people stare

be the best

for Tracy, who actually is the best at making pancakes

you will never be the cleverest
the prettiest, the funniest

you will never be the wittiest
the fastest the sexiest

you will never be the best
at anything you try to do

so perhaps just be the best
at being you

timeline of my life within this body

no body no body no body no body no body no body
no body no body no body no body no body no body
no body no body no body no body no body no body
no body no body no body no body no body no body
no body no body no body no body no body no body
no body no body no body no body no body no body
no body no body no body no body no body no body
no body no body no body no body no body no body
no body no body no body no body no body no body
no body no body no body no body no body no body
no body no body no body no body no body no body
no body no body no body no body no body no body
no body no body no body no body no body no body
no body no body no body no body no body no body
no body no body no body no body no body no body
no body no body　　　body　　　no body no body
no body no body no body no body no body no body
no body no body no body no body no body no body
no body no body no body no body no body no body
no body no body no body no body no body no body
no body no body no body no body no body no body
no body no body no body no body no body no body
no body no body no body no body no body no body
no body no body no body no body no body no body
no body no body no body no body no body no body
no body no body no body no body no body no body
no body no body no body no body no body no body
no body no body no body no body no body no body
no body no body no body no body no body no body
no body no body no body no body no body no body
no body no body no body no body no body no body

mouth full

however much i peer into your mouth
i cannot see the words come out

just shifting shape between your lips
sung across the air;

invisible as god

SHORT STORY: CAT

for Michael

They hadn't always been so close, the woman and the cat. They hadn't always been best friends.

The first time she had stepped out of her back door, the morning after she moved in, she had seen it immediately. One small white patch beneath its left eye. Otherwise, black as sleep. Curious, it crawled slowly across the top of the fence which separated her small patch of grass from its small patch of grass.

She smiled. It smiled back, shy, then scarpered. No matter. *These sorts of friendships take time*, she thought.

She imagined how nice it was going to be to have the cat as her best friend; to sit in the sunshine all summer long, reading her books with its lovely fur coat curled up next to her, it purring at each page-turn.

Early afternoon each day she came out to the small back garden, book and laptop under her right arm, a cup of tea and two pink wafer biscuits balanced on a saucer in her left hand. The cat would watch as she sipped the tea. Watch as she dipped the first biscuit into the centre of the warm liquid. Watch her bite the softened biscuit, dip, then bite again; the second biscuit she saved for the moment when work was finished and an hour of late-afternoon reading could begin.

Over that first week as the cat watched atop the fence, its head leant gradually further and further into her garden until she was almost afraid it would tumble. A silly concern, of course, for such an agile gymnast. Still, she'd be the one to comfort it if it did.

So the cat watched her and she watched it and it purred and she purred. *No hurry*, she thought.

Each day, the cat appeared. It never approached while she was tapping on the laptop. Only once she'd finished all her typing for the day and had picked up her book, encouraged by the silence, save for the slow turning of each page.

It was the first day of June when the cat finally jumped down from the fence onto her grass. She was on page 68 of a new novel. It was a good book, though not as good as the last good book she'd read, or the book before that. From its usual position on the fence, the cat watched. Then, yes, yes, it began crawling along to the far corner of the two gardens. It stopped and looked at her again. Her heart jarred. It was going to jump down, she was sure of it.

It did. The cat jumped; first onto her green bin, then the blue, then black, until it landed. It didn't stop there. No. It crept closer still; across the grass towards her and finally onto the flat patch of tarmac just outside her back door, just beside the lounger she was sitting on. It turned to her. *Go ahead*, she smiled, and it laid its belly on the hot grey tarmac, purring in delight.

That purring!

She carried on reading, not wanting to make such a fuss that the cat might run, overwhelmed by what was happening, by the closeness developing, though she could hardly concentrate on the lettering with her soon to be best friend finally so near. *Keep reading*, she thought, *a smile or two fine but don't mess this up now*. After her hour of reading was done, she told the cat she had to go in, and they parted company.

The next day was a replay. Laptop down, book out, green bin, blue bin, black, and down till it lay beside her once again.

She could already imagine what her life would be like if it would just come another inch or two, sling its body across her legs, all snoozing cat snoozes, as she read. A perfect friendship. The perfect life together.

Spurred on by the thought, she placed the book lightly on her lap and put her right hand gently on the tarmac next to her leg, mapping a circle beside her. *Come closer,* she said, *it's OK.*

Yes! the cat shouted. *I thought you'd never ask!* and it stretched out its paw onto her hand and lay, belly still on the hot concrete, paw in her palm.

June bloomed into July like petals turned to fruit, each day growing sweeter in the summer sunshine. Each afternoon, sun high in early evening skies, she would read her book, her best friend by her side, paw in palm. She had never been happier.

It was mid-July when the sky darkened. A cloud! A bastard cloud covering the sun! Not a huge cloud, not the sort that says 'you're done outside for the day, you may as well go in now'. But not a small one either. Not one of those freckles. No, it was a medium cloud and, depending on the wind direction, it would shade her and her best friend from the sun for anywhere between one and maybe twenty minutes.

The cat stood up and started to walk down the path towards the back gate.

No! Not now, please don't leave, the sun will come back any second! She felt the cold space on her hand. She looked at the sky. *Please,* she begged, *please don't do this.*

The cat stopped at the gate and turned back towards her. It was waiting.

You, you want me to come?

Yes, it nodded, *yes, of course I want you to come, silly!*

She held up her hand slowly. *Just, just wait a minute, OK.*

She put the laptop quickly into her kitchen and locked the back door to her house.

The cat turned. *Come on, I'm cold!*

OK, OK! she said, running to the back gate. The cat walked out of the gate and onto the communal path which backed the row of terraces.

She looked up. The cloud was moving the thick of its belly fully across the sun now. The shade was going to last for longer. The whole pavement in front was doused in shadow. At the end of the path, the cat turned right onto the main street, turning towards her as it did.

Good, you're still here, it said. *Keep crawling.*

Crawling, yes, crawling, she thought, and she bent further and further towards the pavement, until her palms touched the concrete just as the cat's did. Her knees hurt a little at first, so she tried on her feet and hands, which was easier.

Nice, the cat smiled.

Her best friend was impressed. Great.

The pavement itched her palms a little but it was no matter. She was not going to let her friend down over a few scratches.

They crawled, the cat leading the way, she following behind.

Soon, she noticed a change. The pavement, just a little way off. A light grey shift. A paler shade.

Oh you! she smiled. *You've found the edge of the shadow.*

The cat turned, and nodded. *Of course*, the cat said. *Where did you think we were going?*

They both crawled a little faster now, her hands red and rubbed. Just a little further and they'd be there. Back in the sunshine together. Back holding hands.

At the edge of the shadow, the cat stopped. It put one paw tentatively into the patch of sunlight and felt the heat from the pavement. She did the same.

Oh, you're so clever, it's so lovely and warm, she said. She put her nose to its nose and they laughed.

The cat purred a long purr now and continued crawling until its whole body was hot and sunlit again. It stretched out onto the tarmac, resting on its belly, legs and arms splayed like a starfish floating on the surface of a warm wave.

You try, it said.

What?

Come into the sun, silly.

It does look very inviting.

She crawled into the sun patch as the cat lay, purring encouraging purrs. The sun was a hug once again.

Get down here, the cat laughed. *Feel the heat properly.*

She lay on her front and felt the concrete warm her clothes. It *was* lovely. Her palms pressed flat against the heat. Skin to sun. She looked at her friend, stretched and ready to nap again.

Good, huh? it giggled.

Gorgeous! she replied.

It turned onto its back and let its legs and arms fall open to the elements, the sun rubbing its belly now.

Oh, I suppose you're right, she laughed.

She sat up and unlaced her shoes. She put them aside. She took off her socks and put her soles to the pavement. Oh the hot concrete on her feet! She purred, delighted at this new discovery. All these years, all those summers! What she'd been missing out on!

Keep going, it said. *Doesn't it feel great?*

It really does!

She unbuttoned her dress and peeled it from her shoulders. She lay, face down, beside her best friend, stomach pushed to the pavement. It was like nothing else, the heat from the hard concrete rising through her ribcage, blending into her backbone. She turned her head to the side, her best friend smiling back, both purring in delight. She unbuttoned her bra from the back and pulled it from under her, pushing her breasts deep into the scalding hot. Her nipples tingled.

Watch this, her best friend said, turning onto its back again and rubbing its bum all over the sun patch.

Oh yes! she cried, pulling her pants down her thighs and calves and dashing them over her ankles and into the air, rolling onto her back, her buttocks now slapped with the heat of the summer sun.

They rolled giggling a while longer, until, all laughed out, they settled finally on their bellies for a much-needed nap, the sun-soaked concrete warming their bodies as they drifted, two best friends, holding hands, happy in the sunshine.

cat nap

stay like that, please
just like that, please

leave your hand
asleep
inside my hand

your skin
tucked in my skin

finest quilt
i've ever had

let's just stay, please
let's not speak, please

limbs on limb
all rag doll limp

let's just be, please

you breathe
        i breathe

just like this

like otters

maybe there's no fear
we'll float far apart
from each other, in these waters
as moon beckons tide

but, cosy in bed, still
i rest so much better
like otters, together
your hand warm in mine

MASTURBATION

Ringing the Devil's Doorbell

If it doesn't feel better after a wank and a biscuit,

reassess.

VANESSA KISUULE,
'Mantra'

the devil's doorbell

each time i ring it

someone comes

you call it sin

i call it love

la dolce arte di non fare nulla

'the sweet art of doing nothing'

even the clouds
are dawdling
today

                                        unswayed
                                            for
                                            hours

                    ice crystal
                        upon
                    ice crystal
                        upon
                    ice crystal

                they hover

                                    shape
                                    shift
                                    a little

                                        feather
                                            into
                                        backbone
                                            backbone
                                        back
                                            to
                                        feather;

i stay, watching; suspended on the world's crust
back against the grass, grateful for the gravity;
bare skin changing shade so very, very slowly;
sloth cross chameleon   soon,

                              the clouds
                                will shift
                              again

feather
 into
   backbone
perhaps
 backbone
     into
       dinosaur –

                  diplodocus's
                      tail
                          batting at the birds

as day darkens, i will start the short walk home
perhaps, later, in my room, search for stars out of the window
perhaps masturbate a while, perhaps just read a book;
perhaps just go to sleep, i really do not know

magician

girl

when
you are able

you will strike a fire
inside   your skin
your fingertip   magicians
if allowed   if not
condemned   as sin
will work out   every
slight of hand   ,   each
stroke of luck   each
nuanced   pause
till flames
inside your flesh, gasp,
like rapturous
applause

.

masturbation meditation

what if humankind had never worked out how pregnancy occurred
and reproductive sex had not become the moral norm?
what if certain shapes of bodies and certain shades
of sexiness were not plastered over billboards
on every path you walked? what if nobody
had sold hierarchies of your body parts?
what if nobody had made a dartboard
of your flesh? what if nobody
had told you which poses
and positions and cloth
cuts and camera
angles were
sexiest?
what if
you'd never
seen a sex scene
in a tv show or film
or read a sex scene in
a book or flicked through
adverts in a magazine? what
if nobody defined what sex was
meant to be and all you had to learn
from were your body and some time, a
paintbrush and a room entirely of one's own?
what pictures would you paint then? which strokes
would you perfect? which patterns and repetitions and
colours would you swirl across your ever-changing canvas of flesh?

ROCKING HORSES IN
VICTORIAN ENGLAND

I read somewhere that in Victorian Britain it was advised that, like women on real horses, little girls should side-saddle their rocking horses or be encouraged not to use these toys at all. European women had not always ridden side-saddle. The earliest depictions of women riding sluttily astride horses, legs apart like nymphos supposedly orgasming with every trot, have been found in carved images of Greek vases and Celtic stones.

The side-saddle technique developed in Europe because of the creeping attitude that it was unbecoming and immodest to be seated, legs astride, when you had a vulva between those legs. It was also said that sitting side-saddle would 'protect' the hymen of aristocratic girls, thus still enabling their virginity to be checked. Long skirts were a bastard for horse-riding too, I imagine.

A few famous figures – Diane de Poitiers (mistress to Henry II of France), Marie Antoinette and Catherine the Great of Russia apparently rode the slutty way. Catherine the Great even commissioned a portrait showing her astride a horse, wearing a male officer's uniform.

When British women started wanting to ride bicycles, side-saddle was recommended to keep their dignity intact. Unfortunately, even more so than with horses, it was pretty tricky to pedal a bicycle with an ankle-length skirt and two legs on the same fucking side of the bike frame. Slowly, as always, protests grew on both sides; women who attempted to cycle more easily were called sluts and publicly attacked, until finally they were allowed to cycle with one leg on either side of a bicycle. Little things.

I tried to side-saddle my bicycle the other day for the crack. It was very difficult. Also I do sometimes get a nice feeling on my vulva when cycling, especially if I lean forward a bit. So they were right about that. Cycling can be hot. (Long-distance cycling is another matter, so make sure you get the padded shorts especially made for the vulva, because, in pro-cyclist Hannah Dines's words, 'while the valuable parts of the male genitalia can be moved out of the way, female cyclists sit right on the money'.)

When people question why those of us with vulvas are in general more embarrassed to talk about, to try, or, if we do, then to admit to masturbating than many of our penis-clad counterparts, I find it quite ridiculous, when we've spent literally hundreds of years being banned from or slut-shamed for even straddling a bike, trussed-up in corsets and metal knickers to go and buy the daily bread.

According to the Oxford English Dictionary the definition of the word 'masturbate' is now gender neutral. Finally, we all officially do it. At least, those of us who want to and know how to or are allowed.

Masturbation:
1. *intransitive.* To stimulate one's genitals manually, or by other means, for sexual pleasure.
2. *transitive.* To stimulate the genitals of (a person), esp. manually, for sexual pleasure. Also *reflexive* and *figurative*.

This all-inclusive holiday, however, changes when we start speaking colloquially.

The most common colloquial phrase used about intransitive, i.e., doing it to yourself masturbation (I think I'm in love with the phrase 'intransitive masturbation' since writing this) is 'to wank'. However, according to the Oxford English Dictionary, harbourer of the English language as used by people since the eighteenth century, the definition of the word 'wank' *is* gendered.

Slang:
1. *intransitive.* Of a male: to masturbate. Frequently with *off.*

Since I saw this in the dictionary, I've been asking what words people with a vulva use for masturbating (intransitively – if transitive, we tend to call it fingering). There are a lot – 'flicking the bean', 'fiddling', 'having a fiddle', 'thrumming', 'having a touch', 'sorting myself out', 'jillin' off', 'pleasuring myself', 'flipping the switch', 'having a girl's night in', 'buttering the muffin', 'polishing the pearl', 'tinkering', 'diddling Miss Daisy'. I learnt 'ringing the devil's doorbell' from my friend Juliet. I learnt a lot from my friend Juliet.

The penis version of this last one is 'a devil's handshake' which I learnt from Michael Pedersen via the Blindboy podcast. The episode of this podcast was focused on the amount of people unearthed in Pompeii after the ash was cleared who were wanking or shagging, which was kept out of any mainstream viewings of this petrified city. There is an image online of one poor boy volcanically halted mid-wank which I stared at for much longer than was appropriate.

Despite this increasingly poetic assortment of choices for masturbatory euphemisms, most women I asked just used 'to wank', despite it being perhaps physically unfitting. 'Women Wank Too' is a slogan I've seen more and more online, as well as on T-shirts, recently, so it would be nice for our official language registry to catch up with common usage. I can't really believe there is a need for women to wear a T-shirt about wanking. I think that kinda says everything. I don't want one of these T-shirts. I don't like sloganed T-shirts much. I wonder if there was ever a time when men felt the need to wear slogans like 'men masturbate, you know?' or 'it's ok to touch your penis'. Maybe.

Whilst waiting for the Oxford English Dictionary to please remove the outdated 'of a male' wanking bias, I decided to make up some extra dictionary definitions that they might consider adding; things which I think are very cool about masturbating intransitively (I am going to keep using this) with my anatomy and which I think should be more linguistically celebrated.

1. A Water Wank
Masturbation using only water droplets; most commonly water from a shower head, tap flow or a super-soaker water gun, e.g.,

- *Kamila was prone to a quick water wank between application and rinsing of the conditioning treatment.*
- *'Good god,' screamed Dania, 'why do hotels always have these dreaded ceiling showers nowadays, I was really hoping to get a water wank in before the conference this morning.' Desperate, she lay on the shower floor, her legs wide as the Nile, but it was no use, the accuracy and pressure was simply dismal from that distance.*
- *The new chateau was lovely and spacious, with a rose garden to perfume the sweetest of dreams. But the bath taps, much to Lady Madeleine's horror, were not of the mixer type and lord knows, one cannot water wank between separate hot and cold streams.*
- *'Actually, Hollie,' Ian stated over the delicious Lebanese dinner Marjorie had made that night for the poetry group meeting, 'it is indeed possible for those of us with penises to water wank, if the shower spray is on its strongest, straightest setting. Whether or not we reach full orgasm is, however, doubtful.' (based on a true story)*

2. A Hands-free
Masturbation by using only imagination and clenches of the pelvic floor muscles.

- *After almost an hour sitting on the train practising her Kegels and fantasising about the trolley maid gently kissing her now erect nipples, Countess Vimela felt a hands-free stirring beneath her gusset.*
- *Bored by the lecture on Sigmund Freud's theories about the immature clitoris, Tammy crossed her legs beneath her desk, clenched her thighs together as tightly as she could and attempted to get as close to a hands-free as possible before the end of the class.*
- *While the personal trainer could be a bit of a bossy bitch sometimes, the final round of sit-ups seemed to be stirring an unexpected hands-free for a few of the women in the class. Julie, Joanna and Laura were the first to give in.*

3. To Buzz

Slang, verb, intransitive/transitive: to masturbate oneself/another person by using vibrations, for example of a washing machine, back massager, vibrator or bumpy train ride between Liverpool and Hull.

- *'Juliet!' Sally called, staring at the stains on the base of her wash bag. 'Have you been using my electric toothbrush to buzz again?'*
- *'Would you like me to buzz you a little this evening, darling?' her young lover asked over the fruitbowl that morning, as she sat watching the barking deer from the dining-room window. She replied that she would indeed, and forked a second slice of banana into her mouth.*
- *How Laura-Jane loved washing the Van Saxonburgs' clothes! All day long sitting on top of that glorious new electronic washing machine, clenching and unclenching, hands-free buzz after hands-free buzz until her own knickers needed to be washed out as well.*

4. Invisible Arousal
The state of being extremely aroused, with no outer appearance
of crotch-area horniness.

- *Thank goodness for invisible arousal, thought Vanessa, as she
  reread the chicken hut scene on the number 9 bus to work again,
  her pussy puffed as a gentleman's unsqueezed bath sponge. If I
  had a penis, she thought to herself, I'd have a whopping great
  gentleman's boner right now!*
- *Sitting in the pantry watching her husband's poker partner
  spooning the grapefruit juices slowly between his lips, Lady Carlie
  thanked the lord for invisible arousal as she got up to pour a
  second round of cognacs for the guests.*
- *'Oh clitoris, you clever beast,' Becky tittered, as she sat, legs splayed
  to each side of her hallway mirror, massaging herself, testing
  her invisible arousal face for signs of flush, before heading to the
  Arsenal stadium to watch the cup final.*

see also *poker fanny*
see also *derection (discreet erection)*
see also *clit wink*

fifty ways to wank

silent as study
as a library as death

loud as a lock-in
as a birth pool
as protest

paced as a snail
naked as a slug
expectant as a prayer
heartening as a hug

frantic as a hummingbird
pivoting its shoulders
wings chasing the time
trees blurred from train windows

a moth battles a light bulb
a fire spreads through thirsty crops
fleeting as a lifetime
from a deathbed
as a snowdrop

panda on bamboo slow
koala eucalyptus
lazy as a sloth
undecided as forgiveness

with one finger
or two fingers

or three fingers
and turn around

with a finger in
with a dildo in
with a penis in
and touch the ground

with your knickers on
with your knickers off
with your knickers
half and half

with legs parted for
the bubbled
spouts of a
jacuzzi bath

with a shower head
beneath a flowing tap
with your friend's
electric toothbrush

with an aubergine
a wash machine
the wheel seat
of a bus

with a pillow
with a cushion
dry humping
or wet

on a chair edge
on a cliff edge
on a table edge
(by accident)

with legs crossed
like bladder bursts
thighs clenching
extra friction

with legs wide
as smear tests
toes pointing
to oblivion

in circles
in stripes
in zigzags
in all of them

with a vibe
on a low speed
or high speed
or a medium

with lube
or without lube
on your front
on your back

with your breasts
squashed to the radiator

with your nipples
dipped in molten wax

with a rubbing
stroking, patting
pinching, pushing
prodding, press

fifty ways to wank
each one of them correct

the best thing about imaginative masturbating . . .

You are your safest sexual partner.

SELF & MORE, London

. . . is that the sand; the sand on the shore where you've scattered your clothes as the uncancerous sun does not burn your skin, never drifts through the cracks in your knickers forcing you to visit the pharmacy the next day to explain to the man, arms crossed at the counter, that your vulva is sandpaper sore, as he prescribes you some internal cream and frowns as if your mother could never have loved you as the tiny bell tolls your departure,

and that garden; that garden where your lover has conjured a picnic of endless chocolate eclairs that do not make you sick, your mouth smushing pastries like chain-smoking cream amongst blackberry bushes shaped into hearts never sets your hayfever off so you have to apologise and rush home to take your piriton again

and that stranger; that stranger who winks on the train, whose name you don't know, whose stop you get off at, who you grab in the snow that does not make your naked skins cold and who fucks you so long his tongue makes a pact with your womb

is *definitely* not going to murder you

if i could reply to the spam emails telling me they have hacked into my laptop camera and have footage of me masturbating to porn and will share this shameful footage of me masturbating to porn with the world unless i transfer loads of money into their bank account right now

WARNING!

your device was recently
infected with a software
i developed!

WARNING!

the software has recorded
you masturbating wildly!

WARNING!

we have all of your contacts!
we'll send it to your mother!
we'll send it to your family!
we'll send it to your friends!
unless you send us all your money!

*

WARNING!

there is nothing 'wild'
about me wanking

when i masturbate
i hardly even move

my face looks like a statue
of a concentrating fish

it would possibly be
the most tedious film to watch

my friends don't give a fuck
and my mother is much more interested

in birdwatching
and nature documentaries

than her daughter
jacking off

love hollie

showface

for Kat

the difference between
the face you make
when you masturbate
alone

(common examples
    1. deadpan
    2. gritted teeth
    3. tongue slightly lolling out of open mouth
    4. dribbling in your sleep
    5. licking lips like a perverted villain in a comic book
    6. pushing out a pleasant poo
    7. birth [without the fear]
    8. on the brink of minor vomiting
    9. double speed meditation breathing
    10. pretend snogging your arm)

and the face
you try to make
when it's turning
someone on

recurring fantasy caused by watching the video for 'don't speak' by u.s. rock band no doubt too many times during my teenage years

in the park in a blue cotton polka dot dress
i am the mirror image of gwen stefani
in the video for don't speak

a stranger approaches; asks if i actually am gwen stefani
in the video for don't speak. i smile, say, *no,*
but it's a common mistake

he likes the red lipstick either way, and the bindi
on my forehead which he doesn't
see as cultural appropriation yet

he unbuttons the first button of the polka dot dress
and says *it's like you're actually her twin*
i laugh, *yes, yes it is*

he laments how *we used to be together*
every day together even though we didn't
and unbuttons another button till my nipples show

he says, *i miss you you know*
i say *i know what you're saying*
even though i don't

so i tell him not to speak, just unclip this pointless bra
and fuck me from behind
like the best friends you appear to think we are

clitoris / ceasefire

And I'm thinking
If I happen to die tonight in my sleep
I'll have cum and not blood on my hand

WITHERED HAND, 'Religious Songs'

thank you to the two people on twitter who sent me the ideas of
'iceberg' and 'wishbone' as possible metaphors for the clitoris,
now we know how much bigger it is than we previously thought

clitoris –
what disservice we have done
comparing you to satan;
witch nipples; lift buttons

oh wishbone of this body –
are you baffled by it all?
all those battle declarations?
all those blades held to your neck?

all the hatred we have harboured
for such a tiny pound of flesh –

oh hooded hidden genius!
war button of the underdesk!
oh iceberg of our pelvic seas!
oh bouncer of the basement club!
poker face of public lust!
gateway drug to gasping love!
pinprick of a cosmos!

do you roll your beaten eye at us
beneath that hooded top
head poking from the trenches
praying no more friends will fall;

questioning relentlessly
the folly of it all?

BOYS CUM, GIRLS BLEED

Boys cum, girls bleed. I was taught this in school as if they were parallel spiritual experiences. It has taken a long time to rid my mind of the influence of these teachings.

For those with penises, sex and puberty education seemed to imply that you got horny, your penis was about to or had started to go even harder than before and, more importantly, may have begun to release semen in a potential orgasm of pleasure, onto your hands or another person's body if willing or, embarrassingly, onto your sheets as you slept. A few of my friends learnt to use the washing machine quickly at this stage and lost valuable sleep rushing to wash in the middle of the night.

The jokes amongst my boy friends at this time in our lives were mainly about how to deal with unwanted sudden erections, and how to slow down this riptide of pleasure as you held a sock over the head of your cock. Some of the boys soaked up these conversations joyfully; no doubt many of them felt pressure to join in or ham it up a bit, even if they didn't want to. Nonetheless, the conversations both in and out of the classroom were centred entirely around something which could result in pleasure. Orgasms and ejaculation were deemed a huge part of hitting male puberty. According to Adrian Mitchell's poem 'A Puppy called Puberty': 'It was like keeping a puppy in your underpants.'

In music class, years before, in year six of primary school, we sang songs from *Oliver Twist*. From the back row, myself and my friend Sandy changed the last line of the verse from 'Food Glorious Food':

Pease pudding and saveloys!
What next is the question?
Rich gentlemen have it, boys
In-di-gestion!

to:

Rich gentlemen have it, boys
An eee-rection!

We thought we'd made it up ourselves, but it may well have been one of those songs every kid thinks belongs to them and their school alone. Either way, it is proof that, by that age, I had already heard of erections of the male variety. Whispering the lyrics made music class a lot more fun.

Back to secondary school.

For the girls in class, there was no mention of desire or the physical repercussions of horniness as part of our move into puberty, though the poems I wrote at this age confirm unflinchingly that desire was there, none more so perhaps than the aptly titled 'fuck him like a pornstar'. I wrote this about my apparent aim to have hot sex in the back of my car with the boy I fancied after my birthday outing. The outing was at the local bowling alley. In the poem, there is no mention of who would be driving the car as we fucked. None of us were seventeen at the time and it was my mum who picked us up so I guess it was good that I never carried out this poetic fantasy.

The fact that the boys, perhaps humiliatingly so to some, were being increasingly talked about as if they were now some sort of uncontrollable ball of ejaculating sex bomb who could no longer concentrate on anything in life other than putting their throbbing penises into any sort of soft massaging substance (how any of them passed exams seems incredible in this light) made the absence of any such discussions relating to me and my girl friends even more stark.

Our horniness was not so visually obvious, or biologically important, and thus invisible in most of these discussions.

The supposedly 'uncontrollable' aspect of the male sex drive was perhaps the most dangerous part of these teachings. I know too many friends who have had lines like 'you've made me hard now, what you gonna do about it' or 'my balls are blue' or 'you need to sort this out' repeated by some pressurising arsehole as if it is that girl's moral responsibility to now empty the rabid bull's ballsack because he happened to get an erection.

The worst thing was that, in many cases, I believed it. But boys are not bulls, and their desires are not uncontrollable. Even if they were, those boys all have hands. I've had people cause my knickers to dampen in a variety of unsuitable locations, but not once have I insisted that this clit-tease must now hand over the cash for me to go to Marks and Spencers and get a fresh pair. At its extreme, this teaching almost sided with the myth that rape and sexual assault are some sort of farthest reaching consequence of male sexual needs, and not the violent crimes they are. Most men and boys do not rape people, even when blood is rushing full throttle towards their genitals.

On a similar string of thought, I was taught at school that 'boys have a penis, girls have a vagina'. This binary lesson of course ignored any experiences of intersexuality, sex and gender minorities. It is quite a standard thing children are still told in school and at home. My daughter has been told this at primary school already. For years, I believed the vagina to be the female sexual equivalent of the penis.

This is not the case.

Anatomically, the clitoris is the closest equivalent of the penis. Or, to add the urethra into the mix, the equivalent is the vulva. Biologically, the penis is very similar to the clitoris, both formed from the same erectile tissue in the womb, both responding in much the same way when aroused, though we still seem loath to admit this in our desperation to stick to the Men are from Mars, Women are from Venus binary train of thought.

I've heard grown men homophobically baulk in almost vomit-like form at the idea that their girlfriends might also get 'erections', just as I've heard women adamant that their clitoris is in no way a forerunner of their husband's penis. I have to add here that all of these examples come from cis-gendered heterosexual friends.

The wider effect of all of this education on us girls' comfort in discussing and owning our own pleasure was and still is evident. Many women I know had p in v sex before they'd ever had an orgasm. Many had sex for years before having orgasms. Many women had babies before they'd had an orgasm. Some women I know have never had an orgasm. This sexual timeline is very rare for men. Not the having babies bit, the orgasm bit and the masturbation bit. The vast majority of boys fastened their own seatbelts way before helping others.

I have many friends who tell their children 'Mummy and Daddy have sex because they love each other' but who flinch at the idea that I tell my child that I masturbate because 'I love myself'. Don't get me wrong, I also flinch at this, but am trying very hard not to.

When one of my friends told us all in the final school lesson of the day that he couldn't walk home with us because he had to run to get to the shower before his brothers and mum got back so that he had time for a wank, we all went into hysterics, the boys nodding profusely. None of the girls said a word about their own habits: maybe because we were less likely to have any; maybe because, if we did, we were more worried about admitting to them. Even touching your own body was enough for the slag label to emerge. Any girl who *did* admit to masturbating was immediately deemed either 'dirty' or 'weird' or 'up for it'.

When we moved on to learning about sex, by which I mean reproductive sex, we learnt that the penis had to be hard; aroused. We did not learn that the vulva and the vagina should be aroused too, wet, lubed. It just didn't matter. As for allowing these ideas within the biology curriculum in schools, the different wetnesses and textures of all the fluids in the vulva and vagina *are* biologically there for different reasons, one of which is in order to help sperm travel faster into the vagina.

When at the ovulation spin of my cycle (because the menstruation cycle is not just about blood I have only recently learnt – again, thank you, Juliet) I am wetter, juicier, more moist – all those words most of the women I know absolutely hate. So this Wet Ass Pussy (thank you, Cardi B, for mentioning Kegels in a pop song) *could* have been added purely from a reproductive point of view, or in a biology lesson on the menstruation cycle. But it wasn't. Of course it wasn't. It got worse.

Whilst female pleasure wasn't discussed, what I *was* told about was female pain. Pain figured very highly in my lessons on female puberty. Not just the pain of period cramps but the pain of sex. I was told on more than a few occasions that penetrative sex would actually probably be painful the first (few) time(s) for those of us with a vagina and this is something we should put up with until the pain eases. That many women think that painful sex is generally OK and normal to continue with is a legacy of this sort of teaching; a legacy that many organisations are still working globally to counteract, in the UK charities such as The Eve Appeal. Girls and women are told constantly to expect and put up with pain, especially when linked to menstruation and sex and menopause. And they do put up with it, often to the detriment of their health and sexual well-being.

The boys in class were not told to expect pain. Fine, they generally don't have periods. But they were never once told that heterosexual sex will or should be painful. Because it shouldn't. Sex shouldn't ever be painful, unless it's part of a consensual sexual interest in pain play.

The 'sex will be painful the first time' lesson is something I hope we will stop giving young girls as soon as possible. It is a philosophy taken from historic and present-day cultures in which sexual timelines have been socially constructed to suit those in power; in which girls were or are married very young, expected to have had no

337

previous sexual experience and to then have immediate p in v sex, often with much older men, in order to consummate the vows on their wedding night, bridal sheets checked for that infamous red sign of painful female purity.

If you have masturbated, if you are stimulated and comfortable and excited and wet or lubed and mutually compassionate, if you have done other types of sex before penetration, sex shouldn't be painful. I wish we would make this more clear. Vaginal pain in sex is not something to put up with. It is something to see your GP about. My first time having p in v sex did not hurt but I was constantly told that it would. I even thought that there was something wrong with me because it *didn't* hurt. My sexual education made me think that I was weird because p in v sex felt really nice the first time. I cannot quite get to grips with how fucked up that is.

That the UK school biology and PSHE syllabuses are finally taking on a new puberty mantra, other than the 'some of you will get hard and horny and some of you will bleed and cry', makes me exceedingly hopeful that the culture will slowly shift with it. Obviously, I'm not a teenager any more and maybe things have changed already, but I'm not sure that's the case.

My most memorable interaction in this respect was after a poetry reading I did in Strode in 2018 to a group of around two hundred fifteen- to eighteen-year-old school pupils. It was the first time I'd ever mentioned masturbation in a school talk and I was petrified about the reaction of the teachers. It wasn't *in* a poem, but as part of the Q and A after the reading.

I was asked by one of the pupils why I don't work from home, after saying during the talk that if I can, I often go to libraries and cafés to work. My standard response tends to be a mix of: it can be lonely working from home; I like the inspiration of people around me; the library is full of poetry books I can pick 'n' mix from; I get less distracted by all the things at home I need to do, like cleaning.

All of these are true, least of all the cleaning one.

That day, however, I bit the bullet and added another truthful reason: *If I'm home all day reading and writing I often get distracted by the possibility of masturbating.* I said it as one reason within the list, didn't linger on it. There were some giggles, of course. Then the next question came: *Who's the most famous person you've ever met?* and we all moved on.

At the book signing afterwards, I had never had so many female students wanting to talk to me. Almost every one of them to nervously comment on or thank me for mentioning, just *mentioning*, the fact that I masturbate. As if it were just OK. As if it were normal.

One girl burst into tears as she was speaking. That week, she recalled, whilst the boys were laughing about wanking, she joined in and agreed it felt great. In her words, the girls in the group immediately isolated her and she was called a slag by one of the boys; one of the boys who had just been jovially joking about their own techniques. I thought back to the similar day I'd had at school twenty whole years earlier. No wonder we all kept schtum.

I don't tell this to brag but rather to suggest that young people are often desperately *wanting* these conversations and I think it's about time we gave them them in whatever form we're able. It was nothing to do with my poems that had them thanking me, just one three-second reference to the fact that I masturbate. I realise I may never get booked to do a school reading again after this.

That solo masturbation for anyone of any gender has been so culturally frowned upon throughout many stages of human history is so curious to me, because, as hobbies go, it is one of, if not *the,* safest, most sustainable, cheapest, most equitable, most environmentally friendly activities on the planet. Perhaps this is exactly the reason we do demonise it so much.

blueballs

for anyone who's had this pressure

he said his *balls were blue*
fit to fucking burst
hot air balloon fire full
stifled throbbing hurts

a need for men, he clarifies
this outpouring of love
he needs inside me now,
they'll kill if he can't cum

i look at him,
sad, to lose your mind like that
mistook my pussy for a dustbin
forgotten he has hands

tissue box

perhaps
a box of tissues by her bed, too

she might not spill like he spills
it might not save a sock

but good to offer something
to wipe her daydreams on

when faking seemed the simplest solution

for the first boy who asked me to explain how I liked to be
touched 'there', which was a lovely thing to ask me, but it just
seemed too difficult and embarrassing and intimidating to
explain at the time, firstly because I had learnt that admitting
to knowing my own body could make me look like a bit of
a slag and secondly, because I also didn't know if the way I
touched myself was the same as the way other girls touched
themselves because we never spoke about it with each other
and there wasn't much in the media about it and it wasn't
such an obvious thing physically as it is with a penis, so what
if, I thought, I told him how I liked to be touched and he'd be
like 'what?' or 'that's weird' or 'that's not how other girls like
it' and I'd feel like a freak, and thirdly because, if I did get
over those first two hurdles and started to explain and show
him, then I wasn't sure if I could actually explain it to him
very well because it didn't always work in the same way, and
I didn't want to explain it and keep correcting him and then
not orgasm when he asks for the millionth time if I've cum,
which will make him either feel bad or make him want to get
back together with Tanya, who he said he did please a lot even
though we know he didn't because she told us all that she faked
it too, so i just nodded shyly and said he was doing it right
already as he shoved his finger in and out a few times and I
started a long teenage romance with faking pleasure because it
was easier than all the tiring social and cultural hurdles you
needed to overcome in order to just tell a guy how you liked
being touched

i used to think mathematics
was the epitome of precision
until that question came

grappling for a formula
to explain my fledgling flesh
hot spots shifting daily

in constant metamorphosis
depending on the time of month
the time of day; the type of day

isosceles to scalene, scalene to
equilateral; sometimes the hypotenuse
sometimes the right angle

a millimetre difference
between a first class and a try again
trial and error, the sole method available

open brackets close brackets
flip the fraction square the root
$x = 25$ right now but in another

two days' time who knows what
x will do;

so instead, i stay silent

let the poor boy guess

as his fingers poke at y
between my legs

dirty talk

how simple
if lovers could say

i do not have your body
i've no idea the things you like

perhaps, tell me
what feels nice

undressing one another

for Michael

and you are baffling
and awkward
and your tongue
won't stop exploring
my skin
and the english language
have more
in common
than i thought

you are wizard
and apprentice
and your bottom
tastes like medicine
and your watermelon
socks are the best
socks i've ever
seen

you eat passion fruits
for breakfast
your cum comes
sweet as fruit juice
and you prepare
by buying pineapples
like the pineapples
on your pants

and you are santa claus
and christmas elf
and your breath smells
like i want to smell
and your foreskin is
a silken crotch
of the silky cloth
you rub

and i like it
when we touch
each other's
'special' parts
at the same time

and if you let me take
your shyness off
i'll let you take off mine

things i have been shown by media and advertising industries that will make me orgasm

shampooing my hair under a waterfall. eating low fat cream cheese in the middle of the night when i'm on a diet. eating a cadbury's flake chocolate in the bath as if i'm giving it a very loving blowjob. hoovering my house with a really good cordless hoover. buying overpriced lace underwear. buying more overpriced lace underwear. standing next to a male model in overpriced lace underwear. any US hollywood lead actor twice my age putting his penis in my vagina three times. any US hollywood lead actor twice my age lying on top of me under expensive, clean bedcovers grunting while i scream yes yes yes. buying a new sofa in a furniture shop sale. sitting on a car bonnet in a bikini. having really, really smoothly shaved legs like the goddess venus. buying lots of small pots of skin cream and carrying out a daily skincare routine. having really, really, really, really silky straight hair as i walk out of a hairdressers

things which actually make me orgasm

five to twenty minutes of targeted massage;
probably any of the above, if combined with five to twenty
minutes of targeted massage

MASTURBATING FOR A ROBOT

I once agreed to do an advert for a well-known audio company where I would read a poem while walking round a room directing voice-activated electrical appliances – lights, speakers, television – to dim or quieten or switch off in order to create a romantic setting for a night in by myself masturbating. The idea was as shite as it sounds.

It wasn't meant to be about masturbating at first.

The initial script they sent to me was about commanding these appliances in my house (dim the lights, put soft music on, switch the TV off) for a reason that would not be revealed until the end of the advert. Then, the doorbell rings and da da, you'd see my boyfriend standing with flowers or something equally 'normal' for a romantic night in and realise I'd been preparing the house for that. In the script the boyfriend had the same name as my brother, which added to my dislike of the script.

So I turned down the advert. I don't like doing adverts in general, unless they can be in some way positive, more positive than just selling the shit they're trying to sell. I thought that this script was really boring. I wrote and said that I wasn't interested but thank you very much for asking.

They came back with a new script, asking if I'd reconsider.

Everything was the same but then when the doorbell rang and I opened it there was now *da da daaaa*: a woman awaiting my romantic night in. Thing is, the name (a gender-neutral name) was still my brother's name. Also, I'm pretty straight and was not about to take the limited script and screen jobs that the LGBTQ+ community already doesn't have by pretending to be romantically interested in this woman. Perhaps if I was an actor it would have been different. I'm not saying people shouldn't be allowed to act parts of characters with different romantic preferences to themselves but I'm not an actor. It was a writing job, writing from my own perspective about my own preferences and feelings and then reading on screen. I said no.

They sent a few other scenarios in case I changed my mind again.

The oddest of these was the one in which a man was walking around (in this case I was just being asked to write the poem, not be in it) getting his house ready for someone by, again, commanding his home electronics. Directions for this inspired script went as follows: Man 'switches off the war film' and 'puts on slower, calmer music'. At the end of all the preparations, the doorbell rings and standing in the doorway is his smiling wife with … their newborn baby in her arms. The idea was that his wife had just had their baby and he was being a lovely partner by getting the home ready for them to come back to. I wrote back with a few issues.

Like, why isn't he at the fucking hospital to pick them up but instead sat at home watching 'war films'? Also, after giving birth, which I assumed or maybe hope now that none of this creative advertising team had experienced, a woman cannot drive – whether she's had a Caesarean or a vaginal delivery – and therefore I'd have to assume she'd got the bus home from the hospital while the father of her newborn baby had been watching war films and was now quickly and, at the very last minute, setting some soft music on the stereo as if that was all he needed to do.

All in all, I thought his wife would definitely not be smiling sweetly at the door when he answered it and was worried he might instead be bludgeoned to death by her with the hospital bag she would also have just heaved home.

They agreed to scrap this script.

*

After a gig in Bristol that week I stayed with Vanessa Kisuule, fellow poet on that night and close friend. I love Vanessa but also blame her for everything that happened next. We were talking about this job and we started joking about what if the romantic script, instead of being about a partner, ended up just being about having a night in masturbating. Like getting the house ready but then the doorbell rings and it's someone delivering a vibrator or something.

Me and Vanessa drank some more wine and within a couple of hours were convinced that this new idea was great because masturbation was such a taboo, especially for those with a vulva, and this would be an advert on mainstream TV so I had to do it, even if my whole family disowned me afterwards. The next afternoon, I realised I'd sent an email to the company suggesting this idea while I was pissed. They had replied with a yes.

Ah.

So I did it.

I wrote a poem, if you can call it that, about setting up electronic devices in order to have a romantic night in by myself to watch films and masturbate.

At the end of this script, when the doorbell rang, I would answer it to a postman with a delivery. I was to take the box he handed me and go and sit on the couch and look down at the box and open it. The camera would then cut away (because seeing an actual sex toy – even a non-penis shaped one – on TV might cause some sudden deaths) and then you'd just hear a buzz and I'd grin like a fucking arsehole at the camera.

When I arrived at the video shoot, all possible humiliation became worth it, if just to see the set design. The set designers were all men and they had set up this room to look like 'woman having a night in masturbating'. I walked into this very posh, trendy, open-plan London flat and saw more candles than I'd ever seen in my life outside of church. Records playing soft jazz music. Very dim lighting. Red wine bottle on the side, a large glass waiting to be filled, which

I was to hold in my hand as I walked around the room speaking in a soft 'I'm about to masturbate' voice to the record player, light switches and television set.

We had a few toings and froings about certain things on set, like, 'Do the lights have to be quite so dim, I mainly close my eyes anyway?' and, 'I'm not sure women would light *quite* so many candles just to have a touch?' Compared to the condom advert though, this idea of sexy was a lot better suited to me. Wine and candles rather than single bed and teddies.

I asked for a few changes to the set but mainly just did it; thought of the message, thought of female masturbation being hinted at on mainstream TV, thought of the money. I didn't even complain when, of course, I was told once again to get my eyebrows darkened for the shoot, even when they put my hair up into a two-poodle bunch ponytail and curled each so that I looked like a bridesmaid in a Jane Austen novel. I walked around the set reciting lines about dimming my light switches and topping up my wine, then did the most awkward 'yay, my vibrator has arrived' grin at the end of the script. I can't act for shit.

Don't get me wrong, the actual set probably would have been lovely for a night in touching myself, but I couldn't help wondering as I left and took one last look what the reaction would have been if the set designer had been told: prepare this room to look like a man is staying home to have a wank. It was like a dimly lit Catholic shrine but for the worship of my fanny.

Maybe I *should* make more of an effort for myself, though trying to actually masturbate surrounded by all those candles would likely have me so distracted by fire hazards that I'd never be able to concentrate for long enough to cum. Comfort is such an underrated sexy beast.

For a while online there was a news story that went around about women wearing socks in order to orgasm. Lots of friends sent it to me. The reports were all based on one 2013 study by the University of Groningen in the Netherlands. The results of this study showed that 80 per cent of the women taking part orgasmed when wearing socks, compared to only 50 per cent who were not wearing socks. The conclusion of the study was that 'women need to feel safe and comfortable in order to orgasm more easily'.

This seems like a fairly obvious point but the way that this study was portrayed by the multitude of women's health and lifestyle magazines and online blogs made me want to retch. A lot of write-ups simply stated that 'women should wear socks to orgasm', as if there were little else to it than sticking on a pair of foot mittens. A lot of men's magazine's unsurprisingly used it as an excuse to post photos of appropriately shaped women wearing just their socks.

However, the article that most made me feel like vomiting into my own arsehole was not in a men's magazine, but in *Cosmopolitan*. It was entitled, 'Ten Sexy Socks That Will Help You Orgasm'. After quoting the conclusion of the study the writer then continued, 'The problem here is that no one feels super sexy in nothing but yellowed running socks or mid-calf black dress socks. So I enlisted Cosmopolitan.com style editor to find some cute, sexy socks that you can wear to bed to help get you there.'

The entire point of the research study was that when women feel comfortable in their own skin, which includes having warm, cosy feet, they orgasm more easily than when their feet are cold and uncomfortable. When they are comfortable they orgasm more easily. When they feel safe they orgasm more easily. Now the magazine takes this finding and flips it head over arse, full circle, into an article telling women once again what is and is not sexy; what they should and should not feel comfortable in; which socks will or will not make them orgasm.

Honestly, what is this line: 'The problem here is that no one feels super sexy in nothing but yellowed running socks or mid-calf black dress socks.'

desires and wants and abilities of bodies like mine, just in order to appear normal or to please a guy or to orgasm faster or to fit my way of orgasming into the sort of heterosexual sex I thought I should be having with a guy is staggering.

If I'd spent all that time learning about my own mind and body and working out how to communicate my desires, rather than reading shit articles about why or how or with what sort of fucking footwear I should be feeling sexy, I'd be my own tantric pussy expert by now.

Last thing on the masturbation advert. The week after filming the terrible poem, the company emailed me to say that they were so, so, so, soooo sorry to disappoint me and to thank me for all my hard work and that I'd still get paid, but the advert could now not be used because of timing issues.

I think it was probably because the poem was absolute shite or the theme too controversial to use, or my acting ability just too dismal, but maybe it really was timing issues. Either way, my debut 'how to prepare your lighting for wanking' poem would not be slathered across mainstream TV. I lit five hundred candles in my bedroom, put on some soft jazz music and lay back to celebrate in a pair of £40 lace ankle socks.

women orgasm more easily when they feel safe and comfortable

on those rare days
when home is a
honeycomb abandoned

and quiet makes
a concert of your waking
birdsong breaths

cheeks creased
in pillow maps
a single sock lost in the bed

on those rare days
of solitude;
everything is sex

the lie-in. the silence
the heat between your sighs and skin
the non-ticking of alarm clock
the non-opening of curtain
the stumble to the kitchen
the countdown of the kettle click
the clicking after bubbling
the dipping of the tea bag in
the whispering of rain on roof
the grab of book, the back to bed
the dressing gown, the buttered toast
the unplanned doze, the waking haze
the rain, more rain, the takeaway
the movie on, the blanket up
feet snuggled into woollen warmth

no wonder
when in storms like these
thighs slowly open up

the sky sparks
in an instant
lightning hotter than the sun

little death

inspired by the T-1000 terminator and the french phrase 'la petite mort' *(little death), a euphemism used to describe the feeling post female orgasm*

my body, liquid metal now, melts into its flesh;
lips, the first to soften, dribble mirrors down my neck
and chest; fingertips, once knife-edged,
seep silver from my palms;

    a final gasp for life until, puddle soft
    i'm gone;

resurrected, seconds later, twice as strong

fruit salad

*inspired by Stephanie Sarley's artwork and a comment about
me eating a banana (I learned that strawberries aren't actually
fruit a week after writing this but I can't accept this as truth, so
I am leaving strawberries in this poem because I love them)*

yes,
i get it.
this banana
i am biting
looks a little
like a dick. but
have you ever
sliced in half
to gorge inside

a strawberry?

or a grapefruit?
or a passion-fruit?
an apple?   or a pear?
a pineapple?   a melon?
or a gooseberry?   or a fig?
or a mango?   or an orange?
a raspberry?   or a nectarine?
a peach?   or an apricot?
a cherry?   or a quince?
or a plum?   a papaya?
a pawpaw?
or a kiwi?

because they *all* look like me.

a winter tale

for anyone who loves snowfall

like fingertips
and fannies
no two snowflakes are the same

COMING IN(TO) NEWCASTLE

'. . . your open
thighs' honeyed wetland,
summer rain, puddling'

MICHAEL PEDERSEN, 'Deep, deep down'

Vulvas are great. I believe this now.

Not the way they look. I don't mean that, though I am happy there are an increasing number being graffitied next to the twenty billion cock and ball scribbles in public toilets and on pub tables around the world. I'm not saying they don't look nice, just that no matter how happy I now am to have one, I am never going to spend hours with my legs spread around an unhooked mirror trying to force comparisons of this body part to a dewy rose or a precious pearl in the same way I'm never going to put my face up to a mirror, open my mouth and stare at the inside of it till I find the underside of my lips, my tongue, my gums, throat and tonsils beautiful. I like them because of what they do, a functional love: kiss, snog, taste food I like; send signals to my hand to grab another slice of that really good pineapple and sweetcorn pizza and stick it all in my mouth.

I don't think many parts of the human body are essentially very beautiful on their own. I think we need to get over ourselves a little in that respect. Even the common pink-tipped daisy trumps us fairly easily I think. And what about hollyhocks? Or those colour-changing chameleons or those fancy furred leopards. Really, humans are not that special to look at no matter how much cash and time we spend trying to be.

Maybe you've been told you have nice tits by a charming gentleman in your local nightclub. I was told that once and held it up as a tit trophy for years. I have nice tits, I thought, excellent, thank you, man four times my age, for letting me know this fact about myself.

I'd wanted to be told I had nice tits since another man had told me on the bus on the way to that same nightclub a year previous to that that I didn't have nice tits. He said that my tits were in fact shit. Very loudly, so the whole bus could hear. *You've got shit tits.* So I understandably took the compliment when I got it that second time around. But really, what does nice tits even mean? I agree with the statement of course. My tits *are* nice. Really, very nice. The man was on point. But he hadn't actually seen them, or touched them, or been fed warm milk through them.

Tits are nice for so many reasons; mainly because they're soft, warm most of the time, lovely and squidgy to play with, often very nicely sensitive; when pushed together in certain bras they resemble arse cheeks, which is a turn-on for some folk; in some cases they produce sweet antibody-packed milk that can save a baby from imminent death in the midst of a hurricane. I'm not saying breasts are not aesthetically beautiful either. I like curves as much as the next person. I'm just saying that the looks aren't as relevant as we seem to want to make out.

Thinking back to the guy who told me on that nightclub bus that I didn't in fact have nice tits, it seems weird now. *What's not nice about them?* I should have said. *What the fuck are you on about?* Calling my breasts ugly now seems on a par with calling a pillow ugly, or a cup of hot chocolate ugly. Ditto with my vulva; its loveliness has nothing to do with how it looks and even if it did, I'm not planning on sending it into any beauty pageants. I'm not going to deny it a compliment if my boyfriend wants to give it one and I don't necessarily mean that it's *not* beautiful, whatever beauty is, just that, as much as I love it, it will never beat the view of the bridges over the River Tyne as you come into Newcastle by train.

I didn't always think the vulva was great. Like many people, I used to think it was gross. Even the word itself. Just a bit weird and a bit, you know, ugh. Definitely, it was much shittier than a penis, as if the two genitals were in some sort of global beauty competition. At university, I learnt about Penis Envy. This is a theory of Sigmund Freud's that, simplified drastically, does pretty much what it says on the tin; claims a jealousy of those without a penis towards all those with a penis because those without one must want one.

Alongside this train of thought is another of Freud's theories: the Immature Orgasm. Freud concocted a scale of worthiness relating to female orgasms concluding, perhaps unsurprisingly, that for women to orgasm via massage of the clitoris was 'immature' sexually. Real women, he declared, ought to orgasm via the vagina only, and using solely their husband's penis to do so. This is the pinnacle of womanhood. He did not know the full dimensions of the clitoris in those days.

For his remarkable work on the female anatomy, Freud became a household name, a master of the problem they call women; from our wombs to our clits to our hysterical outbursts and back to our wombs again. I studied Freud as part of my German Philosophy course at Cambridge. I didn't study any women. Despite disagreeing with many of his ideas, I still undoubtedly let a whole heap of them seep into my brain, in the way I often did with the writings of most so-called (male) experts or (male) geniuses or (male) intellectuals I had been recommended to study.

This idea that an orgasm achieved via any stimulation other than. pure p in v sex is not quite grown-up enough is perhaps the theory I found stuck more than the others, probably because it is a theory that is still widely touted in the world of hetero-love. After years of extensive research, however, I have come to the conclusion that this is a load of crap; and that vulvas and vaginas are (also) incredible, if given the confidence to speak up for themselves. I'm annoyed I wasn't simply told this from the beginning.

This is not to say that if given three selfish wishes one of them would not still be to have my own penis for a day. It would. I would drink water constantly throughout the morning so as to enable me to pee in as many different places and positions as possible – pot plants spring to mind first here, flowing rivers second. I would then spend the rest of the day playing with my penis, including doing the helicopter, slapping it against my thighs and stomach and learning to touch it really nicely. In all honesty I would probably want to flash people but I wouldn't.

The other two wishes would have to be the ability to fly and the ability to breathe outside of our atmosphere – infinite wishes aren't allowed, it just ruins the game.

arriving into newcastle by train

fuck me, newcastle, you are so hot
all bridge upon bridge upon bridge
muscle built beauties of sweat into steel
of hardening fires, solidified metals
all banging of bolts, all hammering hail
as the river gulps raindrops, panting below

foreplay

the fact that foreplay
is called foreplay
is all the evidence i need
to be certain
that our language
was not forged
by equal tongues

finger me

for Danni, Erin and Elaine
for drunken discussions about fingering in the Róisin
Dubh, Galway

if you want to make me shudder
with zero fear of pregnancy
or thrush
or cystitis
or stds

– finger me

fingering to ed sheeran's shape of you

if you are not a fan of ed sheeran's music, feel free to replace his name with a singer-songwriter of your choice

in the hope ed sheeran will now write a song about fingering

i do not want fingered *first* today
i do not want this fingering to be the warm-up band
you arrive late for but have to watch a little of
in order to get in a better position for the person
you actually bought the tickets for

no, i do not want fingered like
james bay to the ed sheeran tour
or zara larsson to the ed sheeran tour
or the darkness to the ed sheeran tour

no, i want this fingering to *be* ed sheeran
to be ed sheeran
strumming his guitar with hard working red-head hands
holding the microphone to the crowds
singing the final line of 'shape of you'
over and over again, at a continuous slow and steady pace

i want fingered like you have just pulled out
onto a roundabout on the way to the concert
and your sat nav has just stopped
so you keep driving round the roundabout
dizzied as to which is the correct exit now
and if you take the wrong exit you will be going
the wrong way down a motorway for miles and miles
you cannot risk it so you fiddle with your phone

you fiddle and you fiddle
at a continuous slow and steady pace
as you drive around the roundabout again and again

i want fingered like it's illegal to finger me
i want fingered like you are driving around a roundabout
fiddling with your phone
until you realise there is no exit any more
until you realise the driving around the roundabout itself
is the reason for the trip
and there is no ed sheeran concert
because ed sheeran is already sitting in the roundabout
eating sushi from a conveyor belt
from one of those restaurants
where different coloured plates of sushi
just keep going around and around
at a continuous slow and steady pace
around and around
at a continuous slow and steady pace
which does not speed up *ever*
because if it sped up the customers would not
reach the sushi bowls they need
and ed sheeran would be off beat
and we would all have to start again
from the beginning of the song
and the chorus line would never, ever come
and eventually the phone battery would die

no, i do not want this fingering
to be spring rolls before the pad thai
not wings before the burger
not like the recap before the first episode
the meet and greet before dinner

the introductory lecture
the tapas *is* the meal today the fingering *is* the tapas
i want my pussy to be that happy hamster running
round and round the little wheel
stuffing sushi in my mouth
until the hamster is exhausted
until the car engine explodes
i want to keep on passing go
i want two hundred pounds each time
i want ed sheeran singing 'shape of you'
in the middle of the roundabout
until the hamster breaks free
and i am covered in wasabi
until we are in love with the shape
of our gorgeous, gorgeous bodies
as much as ed sheeran claims to be.

reducing our carbon footprint

for anyone else who cares about the environment

getting fingered nicely
in the toilet of a pub
is better for the planet
than a takeaway coffee cup

i have two lovers

you, and my left hand
i won't lie –
there are certain things
it's better at

i do not feel the need with it
to comb my hair or nip
a metal blade across my ankle
bones, do not feel the need
to moan, the way my lungs were
told to moan, the way my back
was told to arch, the way my breasts
were told to perk to help it
search the darkness
encouraging its progress
like a patronising boss
midwife to a birthing mother
an oversmiling gift unwrap, like

yes, i really like it
yes that's really nice like that

making of my pleasure
an overzealous sat nav

take that tiny turning on the left
yes that tiny, tiny turning there
keep going, do not stop

– a theatre absurd
it does not panic

if i do not say a word
it cannot read me stories
it cannot force early bedtimes
it cannot interrupt my day
with answer message songs
it does not surge and pop
bubblegum inside my swelling skin
it does not smell like berlin nightclubs
it cannot dance topless
it cannot get me tea in bed
it cannot get me pregnant
it cannot juice me lemons
to ease a common cold
it does not dance in stripy pants
or pound me into walls
it does not ask if i'm ok
if i cry after i cum
it does not ask me if i've cum
no need –
the pope is always catholic here
i do not fear the clock with it
tick tock stress of orgasm
it does not get excited
by mealtimes or a film
it does not know the platform
before the train is in
it is quicker;
it *is* quicker;
and sometimes, despite a love
of kissing over tablecloths
beside the spanish seas,

a fast food drive through bag of chips
is all the time i've got

i have never dreamt
it hurt me; i have never dreamt
it turned me into god

rush

i cannot predict you
you pass through my body
like weather; i try to prepare
a thick coat; a sun hat
a back bent umbrella
i cannot control you
i've tried to stop guessing
what shapes i might see
in the clouds overhead;
you drench me like storm
dry me like sun beam
rub me like mist
fuck me like hail
kiss me like snow

SHORT STORY: THE DAY KELLY SAVED THE HUMAN RACE FROM A VAMPIRE APOCALYPSE

As the vampire's fangs skimmed the nape of her neck, Kelly leapt back. *Wait!* she yelled. *Give me one minute, OK?*

One minute, but that's it, said the vampire.

Kelly ran into the bathroom and closed the door. She squatted over the toilet and rummaged in between her thighs and bum for the thin string stuck to her skin. *There!* She tugged gently until she felt it escape. She held it up in front of her. She pulled up her pants and leggings and rushed back into the living room.

Here, she shouted.

The vampire stepped closer. *What the hell is that?*

A lollipop, Kelly declared. *Try it.*

The vampire took it. Sucked. Smiled.

You got any more of these? it asked.

As many as you need, Kelly replied.

BLOOD

Rambo in Finland

When she bleeds, the smells I know change colour. There is iron in her soul on those days. She smells like a gun.

JEANETTE WINTERSON,
Written on the Body

contraband

it's not the blood that bothers me most:
i've never been too bothered by blood

never one to hold up my hand in dissection class;
ask to sit out when the lamb's hearts were placed
in bags next to tabletop scalpels
and chris stuck his finger right up the aorta
and we all laughed
and joanna threw up

it's not the blood that bothers me most:

it's not holding the tampon string up
while i wee that bothers me either;*
not blood dripping into the shower;
bath mats freckling red
as i step from the water; not pants
more pants dashed in the dustbin
when wings do not stick;
not worrying at work about leaking
in meetings running over and over;
not my professor insisting
i sit on his sofa in each supervision
pausing to check if i'm listening
when all i am thinking is

---

* For anyone reading this poem who doesn't have first-hand knowledge of tampon
use, this line is because i'd just changed my tampon minutes before and didn't
realise i needed to go for a wee at that time and it's a waste to then take out the
tampon again afterwards but you don't want to get wee on the tampon string so you
have to hold it while you wee (or poo). Good fun.

this sofa is expensive and white
this sofa is expensive and white;
it's not the cramping of thighs
as if my muscles are punching
a path through my skin
the way my mother's did too;
it's not continuing to smile
as my insides implode
as if my body does not own a womb
– which bothers me most

no.

it's sneaking the products;
contraband carefully cradled up sleeve
the way my grandmother taught me
to smuggle past grandad, dad,
my brother, every boyfriend i've had,
every colleague at work,
every train passenger
i brush past on the train,
every person i pass
on my way to the loo

as if carrying a bomb
sure to go off
if anyone sees

blood, grandad

for my grandad, who left the room whenever the sanitary towel adverts came on tv

don't worry, grandad, it's not *that* blood

it's just scuffed knees blood, weak nose from a cold blood, finger cut on paper blood, tiny line of red blood and you sort of wish blood there was more blood, 'cos paper cuts never look quite as painful as they are blood

so don't worry, grandad, don't get up
it's not *that* blood

it's just kid's blood, just tom and jerry blood, cartoons before school blood, cat brains bashed with saucepan blood, just fairy blood, just story blood, snow white's lips as red as blood, aurora pricked her finger blood, rapunzel's lover fallen blood, thorns blinding both his eye balls blood

so don't worry, grandad, don't get up

it's just pg blood, just fortnite blood, harry potter's horcrux blood, just fake crime blood, just true crime blood, just crime book blood, just rocky's blood, just rambo blood, just arnie blood, just bruce lee blood, just war films blood, more war films blood, more war films blood, just young boys barbed wire close-up blood, a pan of all the bodies blood, corpses piled on poppies blood, just saviours nailed to crosses blood, just thorn of crowns, just game of thrones, just house of cards, just house of lords, just fighting blood, just violent blood, just dying blood, just dead blood

so don't worry, grandad
don't get up

it's not *that* blood
it's not *birth* blood
it's not *urgh* blood

HAS THE DEVIL VISITED YET?

This is the question one of my mum's patients asked her nineteen-year-old daughter after she had dragged her to see the nurse (my mum) because she (the daughter) hadn't started her periods yet (according to her mum).

The conversation continued:

Girl: No, the devil hasn't visited me yet.
Girl's mother (to my mum): You see? She's nineteen years old and the devil still hasn't visited her. I think there's a problem.
My mum (to the girl): Have you started your periods yet?
Girl: Yes, when I was sixteen.

My mum told me this story when I was sixteen, which is the same age I was when I watched *Carrie*. Because of this, in my head, I have always imagined this girl and her mother to look like the characters Carrie and her mother, but this is unlikely to have been the case.

The girl had no idea what her mum meant by the 'devil's visit', which by that point she had been referring to for years, and had spent that time half-petrified at what this meeting with the devil entailed. Upon hearing the above, the mother was fuming for the years of worry incurred by her daughter not telling her that the devil *had* in fact visited her, and the girl, just relieved that there was in fact no visit with the devil to ensue, sat in silence staring at her own mother and my mother.

Obviously, this is not a common occurrence but of all my mother's nursing tales it stuck with me (alongside the patient with the boil the size of a tennis ball on his head which popped out and rolled along the floor as soon as she touched it and who then thought she was a genius boil extractor, and the lovely woman with diabetes I mentioned earlier, who lent us DVDs).

I read a book called *Period Power* when I was on tour in Ireland in 2019. It taught me more about my bloody body than thirty years of being inside it (if I am inside my body or if I am my whole body but that's a much bigger question). I also realised, the first day I took the book out with me, as I sat in a café in Cork having a bowl of vegetable soup (which in Ireland is so creamy and delicious and served with soda bread and Irish butter, which is about as sexy a soup as I've ever had the pleasure to put to my lips), that I was still too embarrassed to read that book in public unless the title was placed flatly out of sight. How stupid, but still, centuries of shaming are hard to shake. If you too want to eat delicious Irish soup, I recommend the Farmgate Café above the (unfortunately named?) English Market in Cork.

Another place that does amazing vegetable soup is a sort of posh travelling stop-off in the North of Scotland called House of Bruar. The socks and soaps in this place are like £500 each but the soup is not, and you fill the bowl yourself so you can fill it up to the brim *and* you choose your own hunk of bread, most of which are about the size of a small cat. I eat a lot of bread and soup on tour. Even more than I do normally.

Back to blood.

When I started my periods, I genuinely thought I had shit myself. The colour was not what I'd expected. All the blood I'd seen gushed the same colour whenever cracks in the skin were opened. But that blood I'd previously seen came from everywhere else on the body except the vagina. The only blood I'd ever seen which supposedly came from a vagina was the translucent blue liquid poured in sanitary towel adverts. I often wonder what action films would look like if they had been forced to use that same blue liquid. Perhaps it would've worked for Braveheart.

If television taught me that period blood was blue, it taught me that birth blood was either non-existent or invisible. The few scenes of screaming labours I saw on film when I was younger showed no blood whatsoever. The baby came out shiny and clean as my gran's wedding crockery. Must have been Jesus. Now that I have given birth, I find most birth scenes laughable on television. *Call the Midwife* and *One Born Every Minute* excluded, I watch most birth scenes on screen like an ardent football fan watching a match in which they constantly disagree with the referee's decisions. I find myself sitting forward in my chair, staring at the screen, my hands playing havoc in front of me, shouting things like:

Why the fuck is she lying on her back to give birth?!
Where's the fucking mess, man! How is that bed that clean!
That's not a newborn baby, that kid is like two fucking years old and already dressed!
How the fuck is she in a full face of make-up right now?
What do you mean you can leave? She's not pushed out the placenta. She needs to push out the fucking placenta!

Watching these sorts of blue or bloodless phenomena, it's no wonder I grew up fairly ignorant about these bloody matters. I find the limits of what we can show of menstrual blood ridiculous. A constant 'almost'.

We show a sanitary towel on TV but only – until one advert finally broke the mould in 2020 – if the blood is depicted as blue liquid. We can show a woman giving birth and screaming and sweating, but the baby is then born as if it has just been scrubbed through a car wash. We can show bottle feeding but hardly ever breastfeeding unless a comedic parody of a teenager still on the tit. We can show the pushing of birth, but not the pushing of placentas. We can almost show the truth, almost, but not quite – a camera zoomed in but still left just that little bit out of focus. The phrase 'a bit much' springs to mind here.

When I was in biology class in my GCSE year, the teacher said we were going to learn about the menstrual cycle. One of my good mates, a boy, who was sat next to me, groaned, 'Miiiiisss, do we *haaave* to learn about this, we know about periods!' and everyone giggled.

When the teacher started the lesson with, 'So, when a girl bleeds . . . ' the same mate jolted his head up, turned to me and Julie and spat out the words, 'What! You actually bleed!' and the whole class pissed their pants laughing again.

I remember swimming lessons at school and the confidence of a few girls to say 'I'm on my period' to the sports teacher to get out of swimming (or rather to get out of wearing a swimming costume in front of the whole year – that's really what we all wanted out of).

I remember the teacher once saying, 'You've been on your period every sodding week, Gemma,' and Gemma just nodding her head and shrugging her shoulders with a 'Yes, miss, they're irregular'. I was totally in awe. Gemma (not her real name) also owned a vibrator shaped like a dolphin, which added to my awestruckness (not a real word I know but this is what I mean here) and also slight confusion about why sex toys were animal-themed until I realised that fantasies came in all shapes and species.

Before I got my period, one of my friends tried to huckle me into lying to the PE teacher that I 'was on', so we could both sit out of swimming together. I couldn't do it. Perhaps this is because I didn't want to lie, but even when I *did* have my period on a swimming day I still found it excruciating to tell the teacher, even on the days I was desperate not to have my flat-chested teenage body seen by the boys at swimming. Which was every day after the age of thirteen.

I hadn't always been bothered about having a 'flat chest'. I was informed of it during a game of what we then called Chinese whispers (but which in most other countries they less racistly call telephone) in history class, in which one of my friends changed the teacher's 'Everybody loves elephants' into 'Hollie still has no tits' about halfway around the curve.

I watched as snigger after shocked face after sympathetic glance my way ensued, until my friend Kathryn, three people before me in the whispering gallery, said, 'I'm not repeating that,' and eventually told me what they'd said. I wasn't upset as such. The boy who'd done it was a good friend and we paid him back enough by deciding I should run out of the classroom pretending to sob. He chased me out, apologising continuously until he saw me laughing. I called him a dickhead and he said sorry again.

Years later in sixth form, a similar event occurred. This same friend was acting like an arsehole again, teasing one of the other girls about her appearance, this time about her face not being as attractive to him as he deemed it should be. Instead of a fake dramatic sob, we decided – the girls in the class – to put a tampon covered in ketchup on a tissue inside the boy's school bag. We planned meticulously: grabbed the ketchup sachet from the canteen at lunch; hovered round the leaking Terrapin classroom till he was out on the far fields; smothered just enough of the condiment over a tampon as we thought believable (as if he was likely to know the amount of bloodstain the average tampon would incur); and placed it carefully on the tissue inside his bag. We weren't total bitches. We didn't want to get ketchup on all his stuff.

His reaction surpassed our expectations. He opened that bag during afternoon registration and screamed as if we'd put a live tarantula inside it. Although I was still fairly embarrassed about my periods at that time, this boy's reaction gave me my first sensation of I don't know what; a pride maybe. Pride, I guess, in our ability to handle something bloody better than the boys could. Boys, who in our same stereotyping minds, were much more often associated with blood and bravery and, well, not screaming loudly like that. Not even pleasurably in porn. You have to watch gay porn to hear men make any noise. In heterosexual porn, it's only the women who tend to have vocal cords. Thanks to Vanessa for this.

Seeing someone leap back so vehemently from a mock-up of something we regularly pulled from inside our bodies, a blood which some of my friends had dealt with from the age of nine or ten, was a shock. There were slight equivalents of this trick through my teenage years: a dissected lamb's heart put in one of our classmates' school bag in year ten; a used condom thrown into a crowd of us at a field party; the boy's genital guards removed from their sweating crotches after sports matches and thrown at our faces as we ran away screaming, half of me disgusted, half of me feeling like I'd just caught the bouquet at a wedding. But this was different. It was pure disgust.

He was so disgusted by this fake blood that he wouldn't speak to us for days afterwards. We did apologise, but in his words, we'd gone 'too fucking far' this time.

It is still the most petrified of a harmless object I've ever seen anyone in my life and despite also feeling fairly sorry for him, I can't deny it left a slight tingle in me. For once, the utter disgust at our menstrual blood, which for years had caused us regular pain and shame and worry about even the tiniest leak being visible to the outside world, had finally worked in our favour. It was like we'd just this once claimed a little bit of it for ourselves.

Anyway, back to the small tits.

From that day in history class, until I was eighteen, I worried about my small tits. I stopped worrying about them on 27 August 2001. This is the date that 'Whenever, Wherever' was released as the lead single from the album 'Laundry Service', the fifth studio album and first English-language album of Colombian singer-songwriter Shakira.

When Shakira's song came out with the lines 'Lucky that my breasts are small and humble / So you don't confuse them with mountains' I sang this line in my head on repeat for years. I still

392

do sometimes. For all I'd love to admit that I was the sort of young poetry lover who sat reading Leonard Cohen lyrics in my darkened room or scribbling 'Howl' onto my skin with purple ink, I wasn't. I did read them later. But I think these lines from Shakira are possibly the lines of poetry that had the biggest impact on my young life.

I went to Finland on tour recently and after looking up things to see on my free morning between gig and the next afternoon's flight, I realised I was staying right next to one of the country's oldest swimming baths. I love swimming. I searched for the opening times and found it was open the morning I had free. Great. Then I read that you don't need to wear a swimming costume in this swimming pool. You can, but most don't. And you aren't allowed to wear any clothes in the saunas.

I'd read this was the case in most saunas in Finland and I'd decided I had to go for it if there was a sauna nearby. I'm not too bothered by nakedness any more. When I was pregnant I read a report about mothers passing their body insecurities on to their daughters (just one more thing to blame ourselves for, excellent) and was determined not to do this. So since motherhood, I have acted like an arrogant arse in front of my kid, strutting naked, shunning any comment on my body as a compliment. We had an argument recently about me not being as gorgeous as I think I am, which went like this:

Her: Mum, you're not *that* beautiful.
Me: Yes I am. Look at this bum.
Her: It's not *that* great a bum.
Me: Yes it is.

When I got there, the day of the gig, the day before I planned to go naked into the Finnish waters like a fucking glorious confident mermaid, I got my period. I was gutted.

The gig was really lovely in a gorgeous venue called Korjaamo, organised by poet Harri Hertell. Afterwards, I was chatting to a bunch of women in their twenties and they asked me what my plans were. I told them about my sauna aim and how annoyed I was about my period starting. At first they just looked at me like there was more to the story, not understanding the issue. So I clarified, 'I really wanted to go but I just got my period and I assume you can't go if you've got your period?'

They laughed that sort of laugh that people who come from countries which are way more relaxed about these things do. They joked about my Englishness and when they finished giggling, one of them finally explained, 'It's OK, you clip the tampon string,' as nonchalantly as if she were telling me how to put the kettle on. They then gave one of those group nods, still grinning at my prudish English ways.

There should be a word for this sort of laughter. We have so many words for laughter in English but I think there should be a word for that sort of friendly 'you silly uptight fool' Finnish-at-the-English laugh. Maybe like a cross between 'to giggle' and 'to pity' and 'to smile'. Maybe 'to smiggle'. Oh no, that's a shop which sells stationery to kids and makes you feel like you're on an acid trip and you have to pull your kid away from the £30 pens which smell of Coca-Cola car fresheners. Maybe, to 'spiggle'. Like: 'The girls in Finland spiggled a little at my ingrained English fear of my own naked body.'

I went to the baths with all the awkwardness of an outsider; the nervousness of not knowing where the lockers are, where you're meant to hang your coat, where to pee, who to pay, what coins mean what. All that. But I went in.

I don't know why I'm so proud of this, but I am.

Some of the pools and saunas are mixed but this, one of the oldest baths in Finland, alternates the days for men and women. The lifeguard was a man though. Walking into the main area I looked around. There were all sorts of people. From teenagers to ninety-year-olds (if I guessed correctly). Teenagers in groups just hanging out naked with their friends. Just hanging out naked. Talking to each other while naked. I could not fucking believe it. I thought back to our changing rooms at school, our desperate attempts to learn the taking-your-bra-off-under-shirt magic trick; our British beaches full of four-month-old girls in bikini tops to cover their illegal baby girl nipples.

I got in the water. I kept my bikini bottoms on for this – I had been told people did this with their periods – and I swam, breasts bobbing, finally free.

I couldn't, and still can't, get over how good swimming nude feels, and as weird as this might sound, it felt like I was in some sort of mermaid cove. Finnish swimming pools will bring you as close to being an indoor mermaid as you can get. No tails, but breasts out swimming with a bunch of women. That's basically what mermaids do while there are no seamen in need of being saved. Of course, we censor mermaids in the same way we censor every other image of women's nipples, starting with the post-biblical placing of leaves on Eve's breasts. We also mainly show long-haired, young, thin mermaids and, of course, cover their mermaid nipples with shells or long hair worn in a centre parting and hung over the breasts like the Starbucks logo. But in the Finnish mermaid pool there were all sorts of shaped and sized and aged mermaids splashing about.

I sat in the water at the edge of the pool for a while, trying to emanate total coolness in this setting, while thinking, oh my fucking arse, everyone is fucking naked.

I swam, surreptitiously watching women going in and out of the saunas to check whether they took their towels in with them or left them outside, where they put their costumes if they'd been wearing them, all that stuff. Of course, also looking at their bodies because all my life I'd had such a photoshopped sense of our bodies that this was utterly spellbinding. Even the most stereotypically beautiful of women looked, well, normal naked.

Once I was certain what to do, I rocked up to the sauna door, whipped off my pants and hung them up with the towel, as if I was not even red-faced about it, awkwardly checking my tampon string in an unnecessarily subtle way which probably just made it more obvious. No one was looking at me. It's a funny self-centred thing that we're always so bloody worried everyone is interested in us over anything else going on in the world as if we're that fucking special to look at.

I lay in the sauna averting my eyes from the others, not wanting to seem to stare, the way I still do when mates breastfeed and I'm not used to it even though I did it for years. Stupid I know. But I still feel awkward. I don't agree that awkwardness should be seen as proof that something's not OK to do. I feel awkward when certain people chew loudly or snog too vehemently. I feel awkward about a lot of things in this life.

It felt so good to be all skin. I realised that, after my breasts, of all my body parts, it was my vulva that had hardly seen the light of day or felt the warmth of burning wood, air or steam, and felt the best uncovered.

When I went back to England and went swimming, the costume felt crap, clinging coldly to my flesh. In the open showers afterwards I washed myself over my costume as you do, and felt all the soapsuds still stuck over my nipples and vulva and arse crack as I went to dry myself.

My boyfriend took me (in England) to a hotel with a spa a few months after this. It was one of those spas where there's a glass screen between the pool reception and the pool itself and then small doors leading to a sauna or steam room off the pool. A group of women walked in, late-twenties, chatting to one another, their towels wrapped round themselves. I guessed, from their voices and appearance, that they were Swedish, but I could have been wrong. They scanned the room, then took off their towels. They were totally starkers. Not a strip of cloth to be seen. They continued chatting just as easily as they hung up the towels and walked slowly towards the pool.

The woman at reception saw them through the glass. I have never seen someone move so fast. She sprang up from the counter, mouth agape, pointing at them as if she had just witnessed a group entering the spa with AK-47s. She bolted in, frantic, flustered. I watched as she started blurting out to these women, who stood there, listening very politely, very nakedly, to her red-faced English babbling, with looks of slight incomprehension on their faces as they made sure they'd understood correctly that it was necessary to *wear costumes in the sauna?*

Yes, yes, you must wear costumes. Yes! Yes!

The receptionist left and the group of women very calmly shrugged their shoulders and walked slowly back to put on some small smatterings of material over their bottoms and vulvas and nipples. I imagined they did so discussing how strange the English were.

A little later, I went on tour in Ireland and when I turned up at the local pool, still nostalgic for the Finnish dream, I was told I couldn't go in unless I was wearing a swimsuit *and* a swimming cap. I don't think the Irish and Finnish would get on in swimming pools.

Just to say, swimming nude was not the only thing I loved about Finland – there were also amazing markets and, well, Lapland is in Finland which means Santa Claus officially lives there, and I bought some brilliant wolf-print socks and the people I met were gorgeous and the city centre of Helsinki was beautiful, including of course the old baths I went to. But the naked swimming stands out. It felt like taking an exam in my own self-confidence and passing it with fucking distinction. If England had slowly morphed me into believing I was a bleeding devil, Finland finally convinced me of the truth: that I am in fact a mermaid.

i have become that naked woman in the swimming pool showers

for Finland

i have become the naked woman in the swimming pool showers
lathering her tits, back firm against the tiling walls
as the woman to my right grapples soapsuds
from her shoulder straps
pulls her costume just a little open at the front
as if catching rain in a cleavage basket
pickpocketing her own breasts,
subtle shooshings of the shower gel
in places nobody can really reach
while still wearing a swimming suit

i have become the naked woman i would look at from below
as i stood naked in the showers as a child
holding my mother's hand
and thought of the chips i'd get later in the café
lathered with ketchup, and thought nothing of my nakedness

i have become the naked woman i would look on as a teenager
and wonder when that happened
as i washed and brushed my hair
tried to hold my towel up, pull my costume off, pat my crotch,
put pants on still damp skin
as if all the world were watching me,
hook my bra on top of towel and pull it out from underneath,
tits still covered, *thank fuck*, like that trick where china cups
stay upright on the tabletop
when the cloth is whipped beneath them

now i'm naked in the changing room full drying my crotch
like the woman i saw last year and assumed *she must be dutch*

so much easier to wash now
now i've stopped giving a fuck

(again) (almost)

bad manners

i find it hard to trust a culture
where a photo of my nipples
is more weighted than a photo
of a pointed, loaded gun

where traffic can be murder
but fucks and cunts are far too rude
is it really any wonder
the kids are so confused

sometimes i wish i had legal man nipples

for you, next to me, topless, on the beach today

my nipples would like to sit next to your nipples
and chat about this hot weather; in my garden
they would like not to have to cover every time
the neighbours come to hang their washing out
dry in sunny skies; they would like to sunbathe
in the park un-fearful of police or shouts
they would like let off the leash for a stroll
on the beach like your nipples not checking
for signs that dogs are allowed here or my nipples
are allowed here, i envy your nipples,
the way they are treated, your legal male nipples,
which look very similar to my illegal nipples
just a bit more deflated, all cherry no cupcake,
sauntering, unsweating in the sunshine
as i slip my bikini top just to the edge of my
nipple blind spot and you look at me like *what?*
i didn't make up the rules, Hollie!

sometimes i really wish i had legal man nipples

another poem about my nipples written during lockdown
because I was very hot, walking in the sun
and saw a topless man in his garden looking very happy
and got jealous again

so soft and so hot, you pant on my chest,
i'm so sorry, my loves, to cover you up
all stifled and sweating under this dress
i know you'd delight in the light of the day
i know that you're sick of hiding this way
embarrassed, always at odds with the shade
that the rest of my skin has soaked in the sun
yes, i know what you've done – all that milking
and loving and looking hot as hot air balloons
swelling in balconette bras, i know it's not fair
i can see him as well, digging his soil,
whistling his tunes, his nipples all free to the world
despite how useless and tiny they are
nothing compared to your factory flesh
but don't worry; i promise once this is all done
we'll find you a beach we can walk on together
cleavage sweat no longer trapped in the heat;
bitches both let off the leash

BECOMING A WOMAN

I started my periods when I was about fourteen, I think. I can't remember for sure. I do remember not knowing what it was for a while, because it was not the colour of Rocky's nosebleeds and I also remember being one of the ones who always hadn't started when we asked each other at every sleepover who had and who hadn't.

I also remember, when pissed at one of these sleepovers, after the standard quizzing of everyone on periods, someone asking who had pubic hair and everyone being like, *yeah, yeah course* and then one of the girls saying we needed to get into pairs to 'prove it'.

I found myself almost subconsciously rushing to the two friends I knew who also hadn't started their periods and whose chests were as flat at mine, falsely thinking that this would be directly correlated to pubic hair growth. In this case, my guess was correct. We stood in silent acknowledgement, flashed the top of our fairly hairless vulvas to each other and then all turned and nodded, *Yep, we all have pubes. Yep, definitely, loads of pubes there all right. No, no, not too many, we mean, like just the right amount of pubes, yeah yeah.* Fuck. How have we made pubic hair so fucking complicated. How have we made everything so fucking complicated.

Growing up, I felt embarrassed and ashamed about so many things: like spots; like sweat; like masturbating; like the hairs around my nipples. Like the hairs on my toes. Like the hair on any part of my body other than my head; like periods. Not a rare story. In fact, so unrare, that the period story which stood out most within our

403

group of friends was the one about the friend who, on starting her periods, was taken out to dinner by her folks. When she told us this, we all almost fainted.

This wasn't even in an overzealous period party sort of way. Although, I don't know why I'm judging that, as if it would be a terrible thing. Compared to the horror that many girls go through when starting menstruation, I should probably be less critical of people who throw their kid a party and more critical of those who are silent about it. I am just far too removed from that sort of culture for my first reaction not to be, *A party? How fucking weird.*

I didn't go out for dinner. I didn't tell anyone. For some reason, despite having a consistently great relationship with my mum, I was still too embarrassed to tell her and I wouldn't have dreamed of telling my dad or brother. Instead I spent the next year – in my head it was a year but maybe it was only months – nicking sanitary towels, which were actually panty liners but I didn't realise, from my mum's middle drawer when she was downstairs. Lucky I had a light flow.

I plucked up the confidence one night when I was in bed. I called Mum back into the bedroom and took about an hour explaining to her that I had something to tell her, but actually don't worry but yeah well, I've sort of . . . and so on until she dragged the information out of me. That feeling really stuck in my gut, the nervousness about telling my mum this new fact about myself; something I hadn't caused and which wasn't something I'd done wrong but felt horrendously awkward about.

It's so strange when your body changes, especially if it happens fairly swiftly. I don't think puberty is easy for anyone. I remember all sorts of trauma amongst the boys: those teased for early beard growth and those teased for the bum-fluff opposite; voices breaking in one moment between bird chirruping and lion roars; the pressure to become muscle-clad action figures; the obvious penis-size debates; the difficulty of hiding this area of your body due to the urinal set-up of the boys' toilets; erections. But a large part of so much awkwardness is massively influenced by silence and thus shame about these changes.

When our 'baby teeth' fall out, that is a sign of growing up too. Literally, from baby teeth to adult teeth. But most children don't hide their shed baby teeth in shame, even though teeth falling out is pretty weird and gross, especially at the hanging from a bloody thread stage. No, it is often seen as an exciting thing. Perhaps because there are treats associated with it in most cultures, for me a fairy bringing cash, perhaps because it's a non-gender-specific physical development which we haven't sexualised and awkwardised. (I know 'awkwardised' isn't a word, but I think it should be because our culture makes so many parts of life more awkward than they need be.)

One of my worst memories of starting my period actually wasn't the blood or the pain (though to be fair, I've always been fairly lucky with my cramps compared to lots of people). No. It was when a friend's mum, when I was at their house after school, told me, smiling, that I was 'now a woman'. It was meant kindly, but the label made me want to gag.

I was fourteen years old, studying at school and playing rounders and drinking WKD in the park with my friends. And now, just because I'd started menstruating, I was, from one moment of my life to the next, 'a woman'. *Fuck off*, I thought. *I don't want to be a fucking woman.* The idea made me feel sick. Whereas most other transitions in puberty comprised fairly slow and ongoing changes, this one was sudden. You don't bleed. Da da! Now you do. A split-second shift of your entire being.

Even the word itself – 'woman' – seemed like some sort of dirty insult. It was certainly never used as a compliment in day-to-day conversations. If anything, it was a word we seemed to avoid using. I only really heard 'woman' said in very formal talk, or in the context of a man talking about 'his woman'. Or I might come across it on a sign for a bra shop for people with larger breasts saying that these were for 'real women', by which measurement, I'm still definitely not, and in the pop music and poetry of those attempting to change this status quo.

In most contexts, in most *positive* contexts, grown women were referred to as either ladies or girls. Sports teams of adult women were 'ladies' teams' when I was little. Sports teams of adult men were not 'gentlemen's teams'. As I got older, these labels shifted to a more equal footing, increasingly becoming 'women's teams', and the anger that this change provoked in some of the men around me was fascinating. *Why can't you just be happy being ladies, why do you have to say women women women all the time?*

In the shops, if an assistant did something nice or served us well or whatever, I'd be told to say thank you to the 'nice lady' whereas if it was a man I had to thank the 'nice man'. The only time the 'gentleman' equivalent was used was on toilet doors and in theatre announcements to 'please take your seats' and golf tees, where the 'ladies' and 'children's' were aligned.

I have been pulled up so many times by family and audience members for using the word 'woman' that I became almost scared to use it for a while, for fear of people thinking I was being a deliberate pain in the arse. Before a gig, I'd remind myself not to do too many 'womany' poems in a row.

Perhaps it's just my experience, but the word 'woman' is so stigmatised in my head that I still trip over it if I try to use it in normal conversation; to just refer to someone as a woman. I'm not bothered if I get called a lady or a girl or 'duck' or 'hen' or 'lass' or whatever, I think there can be a sweetness to all of them, I'd just like to be able to use the word 'woman' without looking behind me to see if anyone's there ready to be like 'oh god here we fucking go again'.

I have friends who hate being referred to as 'girls'. I don't. Mainly because men are often referred to as 'boys' in jokey or light-hearted contexts. Ageist, maybe. Sexist? Personally, I don't think so.

When I started reading my poems at gigs in my late twenties, I was labelled a feminist poet in the first online article that mentioned me. I almost puked. I asked them to take this word out. After a few years of reading poems, and this label coming back again and again, I was still iffy about it. At one of my London gigs somebody asked if I had one of those 'this is what a feminist looks like' T-shirts. When I said no, they asked if I'd like them to send me one. *Are you fucking kidding?* I wanted to scream. *Feminist? Written across my chest? For everyone to see?* Christ, give me a minute, I've only just managed to say the word 'woman'. I politely declined the offer.

It took a few more years, and the friendship of in particular Sabrina Mahfouz and Deanna Rodger, for me to realise I needed to scrap this shame. Yes, it is OK for someone to call me a feminist. I still would not wear the T-shirt though.

I did not grow up in a place where my period signalled a womanhood of forced removal from education, or marriage or sex or isolation. I was not desperately trying to hide the blood from family and friends for fear that someone would find out and force these things onto me. My family was also sufficiently well off that I never had to struggle not to bleed through clothes in public, missing vital education and socialising. It's shocking that we have been bleeding this way since, I believe, the beginning of humankind, but still this menstruation = woman equation has so many dangerous connotations for young girls worldwide.

The most concise summary I've heard of this ridiculous and dangerous battle we still have with menstruation was in a talk by Adita Gupta, co-founder of Menstrupedia. She began: 'A natural biological process . . . a phenomenon that is so significant that the survival and propagation of our species depends on it. Yet we consider it a taboo.'

How great it would be if our society had got to a point that we could say to young people:

Yes, you will start menstruating, but you already have all the information about that and we'll help with how to deal with it all practically and you'll get your free protection if you can't afford it and don't worry if you leak a bit, no one bats an eyelid any more.

The distaste I've had for becoming a grown-ass adult woman is so much more annoying now that I'm in my thirties and am one hundred per cent certain that this age, compared to being fifteen, which I also liked, is so, so much better, even with blood released by my body each month. For my mother, she says it was her fifties that have been a highlight. My gran said her seventies were some of her best.

When I was in my early thirties, I was asked to help a well-known London football club who had funding to try to encourage girls back into sport. According to their research, girls' interest in sport appears to lag around the age of twelve.

I was invited into their offices with two other female poets, both of whom also liked playing football. At the meeting a man in his twenties talked about what they'd been doing trialling a programme in local schools and asked if we had any ideas as to why it wasn't working. He described all the incentives they had come up with, from assemblies about the benefits of sport for girls' bodies (I am still reeling this was one of the things they promoted) to dance classes.

I raised my hand and asked if they'd offered the girls any advice on periods or sports bras. The man immediately went red-faced and stumbled, *Errr, no*. I didn't intend that question to be controversial. I don't think the correlation between twelve-year-old girls doing less sport and menstruation and bra-wearing is rocket science.

After my questions had been awkwardly fumbled through, I was asked if I thought I might write some poems for this football club to help encourage girls to stay in sport; perhaps something inspirational about how great sport could be that I could read in an assembly; perhaps a theatre piece about the joys of sport for girls. I wrote one poem but it wasn't used.

inspirational poem written for well-known london football club to change the minds of teenage girls about sport by writing an inspirational poem about how fun it is to participate in sport as a girl

for maddy and stu

first stanza: instructions on how to increase government funding for individual shower cubicles in schools

second stanza: advice for those who've started menstruating on how to talk to family or staff members or friends about period protection

third stanza: teach everyone, not just those who may menstruate, about the ins and outs of the menstrual cycle so that it becomes destigmatised and the idea of having a leak of blood through the tiny gym pants my school for some fucking reason deemed it appropriate to force us girls to wear or the white skirt for tennis matches or the short netball skirt and on and on does not feel like the end of the fucking world if it happens which it does and will because sanitary protection is never infallible

fourth stanza: talk to coaches who coach teams where people may begin or have already begun menstruating, so that they are aware of this and can bring it up in team talks without fear: a quick 'some of you may have started your perods, so if you're feeling more tired or uncomfortable playing at certain times of the month, don't you worry'. Also, cycling shorts are very good kit to hold pads in place better.

fifth stanza: practical instructions on reusable period pads and pants and sanitary towels and information about different absorbencies of these at different times of the month and funding for those who can't afford them (well done scotland)

sixth stanza: detailed instructions and advice on how to insert tampons or mooncups when sanitary towels are not soaking up enough blood or when sanitary towels just keep moving and screwing up in your pants or the sticky glue if you use disposable ones gives you a rash round your vulva lips (get used to saying vulva in the talks) and therefore once a month sport might be an absolute fucker for you to feel comfortable doing even if you love it.

note: do not equate using these internal sanitary products with becoming a non-virginal slut

hint: i inserted a tampon for the first time with a friend in my bathroom. if you have a close friend to help, even from outside the bathroom door, shouting things like 'is it in?', 'you've got to bend forward and like push it towards your back', 'touch your clit and see if you can get it a bit less dry up there because wetness helps get it in without hurting the skin on each side', then this can be helpful. Family is also good if you have that sort of relationship, which i did, but my personal experience was with a friend.

seventh stanza: instructions on how to buy a good sports bra if needed. funding for this if needed.

eighth stanza: recommendations on how to reply to that person in class making jokes about your tits bouncing up and down when you run across the field. Personal preferences include: ignoring them and realising they have their own shit and are just projecting this onto you because they are also awkward as hell with their own bodies; telling them to fuck off outside the ears of a teacher; telling them to get a bra for their balls (if they have balls) because you can see those waggling about (this is less kind but it's also a pet hate of mine that there was no ball bra ever invented or that balloplasty isn't pushed by plastic surgeons onto people the way labiaplasty is, not that i want people to start worrying about their balls more than they do, i just want everyone to worry less)

ninth stanza: instructions on doubling up on a normal bra if you can't afford a sports bra. (A lot of my friends did that. i didn't need to because, as mentioned, my tits are the size of satsumas)

tenth stanza: list of possible replies to that person telling you how sweaty or red-faced or ugly you look when you go back to class after playing sport at lunchtime (I got this a lot after sport because my face goes genuinely beetroot with just a line of white above my mouth like a pale moustache): my experience includes crying (this was the first time it happened in year seven, my teacher made me stand at the front of the whole class because he couldn't believe how red my face had gone after netball); other responses i mastered after that were: *thank you, yeah i know, or fuck off* (a go-to throughout most of secondary school)

closing stanza: hire someone who doesn't blush at the words menstruation and sports bras to give your fucking talks

do you?

*written as part of an always ultra advert describing
period poverty*

you know those days?
when you're so worried stains will show
and three socks stuffed in pants
won't soak it up
and tissues scrumpled up
and newspaper paper cuts
but you're so petrified of leaking blood
that you skip school maybe
three, four, five days every month?

you know?
those days?

when you miss lessons
miss your right to equal education
miss grades miss break time
miss information miss the latest gossip
miss romance miss homework
miss getting into college
miss mates miss school miss fun
miss not feeling afraid
of your body as it grows up

you know?

dip-dye

for the childhood friends who i dip-dyed pebbles with

only halfway in we dipped them
never going all the way
the dramatic line of colour change
from natural to marbled paint
was where the beauty lay

crouching on the toilet
on those days when blood is rosehip red
tampon string eased out
swollen bloody cotton binned
i unwrap the yet expanded
new bottle cork contraption
back arched to ease the entrance
finger push into position

finger out again
i cannot help but stare
the top half cherry-dipped
the base still skin-plain

i think back to those afternoons
pebbles dipped in paint

DRIP TRAY

At the age of thirty-five, I ordered a pack of five reusable Modibodi period pants to try. By period pants, I don't mean the comfy pants that we sometimes refer to as period pants (or granny pants) as if old age or menstruation are the only time we should allow our arses this comfort; I mean actual pants designed to bleed into. These period pants aren't even big pants, unless you buy the larger styles. They just look like normal pants but with inbuilt period protection. Like a sanitary towel inside, but one which you don't have to remove from the pants.

Even writing about these pants makes me want to sob a little. I get very excited buying underwear in general, mainly because I've tried to stop buying new clothes, so underwear's the only thing I regularly buy that's not second-hand. Still, of all the fantastic pants I have seen and purchased the world over, none have got me teary.

Actually, that's not true. There was one pair when I was eighteen. I was at an Ann Summers party. If you haven't been to one of these, this is a party where a saleswoman from the Ann Summers store comes to your house – or in this case my friend Rowena's house – and tries to sell you underwear and sex toys in a fun way. There are activities like testing out all the vibrators on your nose (apparently the most legally sensitive area of your body to test them on at non-sex parties) and strapping a dildo round your waist and attempting to fit it in a hoop dangling between your mate's legs.

Once our noses had been buzzed to a numbness akin to sticking your face in a bucket of snow (actual snow I mean here, not cocaine,

414

though both would likely have a very numbing effect), the assistant got round to showing us all the products. Amongst an array of the standard naughty devil/nurse/farmgirl/bunny/dinosaur/astronaut costumes (the last two are not yet available but I'm hoping will exist one day) and nipple-peak peepshow bras (which I still think could be re-imagined for breastfeeding), she lifted up a pair of white, crotchless pants and said what I then considered to be one of the most disgusting phrases I'd ever heard: 'Great for a quickie in the office, girls, but no drip tray for the dregs.'

I'm not sure I cried out of laughter or shock or because of the horrified expressions contorting every one of my school friends' faces. I still cannot walk past a pair of crotchless pants without thinking of chip shop grease.

So I've cried twice over what you could say are the opposites of the pant world; the first, lauded for its non-gusset freedom, the second, lauded for the fabulous absorbency of its drip trays. I can't quite get over how much shame (and possibly ocean life) could have been spared if I'd used these sooner – the period pants, not the crotchless ones. Especially if they'd existed in my teens. You just rinse the magic pants in cold water when you take them off (yes, you have to see the blood, but fuck, we have to see it anyway) and then put them in the wash with everything else. Not even embarrassing on a washing line. Just some pants drying with all the other pants as if nothing had happened.

The first day I wore these pants I felt like my world had changed. This sounds like I'm getting a backhander from this company, but I'm not. I just cannot write about periods without talking about them because these pants have literally changed my bloody bloody life. (I also wanted to write that sentence because I think the word 'bloody' is a great example of how fickle language is. The same word, but one is a swear word and one is perfectly acceptable simply due to their position in the sentence.)

I hear the same life-changing claims made about menstruation cups, but I haven't used one of those yet. I also have a love–hate relationship with the internal period devices. Sometimes, it's a joy not to feel the blood coming out. But sometimes, I just get so sick of and sore shoving things regularly into my vagina, especially when it's less lubricated. I have friends who extol the joy of contraception that stops the bleeding altogether, but I've never been on any that does this so can't comment on that either.

What I can comment on are my new pants, which I have now worn leak-free whilst carrying out the following activities: watching television on light-coloured sofas, riding my bike, dancing in a night-club in a short skirt, doing Joe Wicks workouts during lockdown whilst my daughter shouts 'I hate you' every time he says the words 'Captain Serotonin' on screen.

Using these pants has been a pivotal moment when I've been simultaneously ecstatic my daughter will have this sort of option, whilst being sad that my mum and my younger self didn't; let's not even mention grandma's rags. I think for my grandma, the most comparable feeling of elation could have come in 1957, the year in which Mary Kenner of Charlotte, North Carolina, finally saved up enough money to patent her life-changing invention for women worldwide: the first sanitary belt; an adjustable belt with an inbuilt moisture-proof napkin pocket, precursor to the modern day sanitary pads. Unfortunately, the move from invention to production took another thirty years because, despite corporate interest in the invention, 'when they found out I was black, the interest dropped'. Despite this, Mary Kenner continued with her invention with one mantra: 'making people's lives easier'. So please think of her the next time you don't have to stuff rags in your knickers.

Fast forward to the present day and the inventions are improving still. If every person, on starting their periods, now got sent a voucher to purchase a set of these period pants, I swear on my bleeding soul, a grand part of menstrual shame would cease overnight. Also, ocean life, I imagine, would enjoy swimming without the possibility of our old sanitary towels choking them to death, which in my head is probably one of the more gruesome ways to go.

The drawback to these pants is that, like everything else that's good in this world (except hugs and public park fruit trees and dancing), they are currently very expensive. In my dreams, the government of every country will one day subsidise them, if not from a newfound love of us bleeders, then from a preventative environmental or waste-disposal budget.

Weirdly, the fact that these pants have made my period so much easier to deal with has made me sort of in awe of this bodily cycle, or at least not so disgusted by it. Having a period has been shit for so many reasons for so many years. However, now that I have got over the shame of this aspect of my body and have these new magic pants, it's not quite as shit and I have started to attempt to find positives.

Aside from the ability it gave me to have my child, I've been wondering things like: does this monthly cycle mean that my body is having to replenish itself of this blood loss each month and therefore I am maybe sort of like going through a deep-cleanse each time? Does seeing this blood mean I am more aware of my own body or mortality maybe than someone who doesn't see this monthly blood? Even the fact that I get more teary or 'emotional' just before my period starts, something which for years has been a running 'oh god, the PMS' joke amongst colleagues and friends, perhaps has something positive in it. I must say here, I do not have PMDD, which I'm told is a lot worse and much harder to be positive about.

I do definitely cry more just before my period starts – I have tried to deny this for years, seeing it as a sign of some sort of lack of control or weakness. I have also denied it because I hate how we so often blame hormones for everything to do with women's feelings, often in a sort of hysterical fucking women gag fest or a *you got your period or something?* style insult. I've been told many times 'must be your hormones' whilst I'm on my period and it's always felt like a dismissal. I've had to deep breathe in order not to scream something like,

417

'Maybe it's the fact there is blood dripping out my vagina as I leak into a sanitary pad, which has given me a fucking rash again, whilst my thighs and stomach feel like someone is slowly squashing them down like a car squished into a scrapyard.' Or, 'Maybe I'm annoyed because having my period in this fucking society is an absolute shit storm of shame, you tosser, maybe it's not my fucking hormones.' But of course, an angry outburst like that would just make the perpetrator feel like I've proved their point even more.

I felt the same in pregnancy. Any time I started to cry or became angry or anxious, I was comforted with a standard 'your hormones must be all over the place' response. On most occasions I thought, *That may be so, but I am crying because I have to tell my boss I'm pregnant and I'm petrified of her reaction and no one gave me their seat on the train and I thought I might piss myself.*

I still get extremely fucked off when 'it's your hormones' is used as some sort of catch-all belittling of actual practical and often political obstacles to menstrual and pre- and post-natal ease. Despite this, I also have to finally admit to myself that I do cry much more frequently just before my period starts.

Sometimes it really is like clockwork.

I finish crying about an overwhelming sadness in the world, go to the toilet and am like, *Oh, I've started my period*. After one particularly upset day, my boyfriend, very tentatively, said, 'I'm not saying anything but is there any chance your period's coming?' I said I didn't think so. Then went to the toilet and, well, there was the mud.

So I am no longer denying the hormones or tears. I am just wondering if the negativity of phrases like 'hysterical', 'over-emotional' or 'hypersensitive', which I've often heard attached to these outbursts, is fair. Maybe, I suddenly thought, sitting mid-sob in my bedroom in my new period pants, maybe it's not so bad to have a couple of days a month when my body is like, *Yes, tears, you may flow, flow to your heart's fucking content, have a good, good cry. Scream if you like, you'll feel better afterwards.*

I've heard that some people actually pay to scream and cry. As therapy. Like, go to a field and talk about their problems and then scream out all their anguish. Cry. Sob. Release. So from now on, I'm no longer referring to my menstrual 'mood swings' as 'fucking PMS' or 'that time of the month', I am going to refer to them as 'my monthly VIP access to a heightened state of awareness of the strength of emotion and insight my body and mind are capable of'. Like LSD, but with blood.

I don't believe that menstruation *makes me a woman* any more than sticking on a pair of high heels or giving birth or having 'real-woman'-sized breasts does, in the same way that not menstruating does not make someone *not* a woman. But maybe it does make me special in some way and maybe I need to think about it like this. Maybe the fact that every month my body creates a house and then lets it out or demolishes it, depending on the housing market, is kind of cool. A sort of internal, exceptionally talented architect. Maybe we should be in awe of it in the same way we should be in awe of so many of our different bodily processes. Maybe not.

I must add here that I wrote these last few paragraphs about embracing my periods in all their hormonal, bloody glory whilst I was not actually *on* my period. I was really enthusiastic about the writing. Then, about three days later, I started getting cramps all through my thighs and stomach as I do most months. I was driving to Scotland. I pulled over into a service station to stretch and rub my belly and to wince in pain a bit. I made a voice-recording note on my phone as I often do when I think of new ideas or poems or edits. I listened back to the voice recording the next week when I was editing this book again. It read: 'scrap the bit in the blood section about embracing your fucking periods, you have just started getting cramps again and you feel like absolute shit.'

So maybe I'm not quite the womanly guru I was hoping to be. Still, I do believe, that like so many other things, periods, with the right knowledge, response and, in more extreme cases, medication, needn't be anywhere near as horrific as they so often are. If we could stop comparing them to the visit of Satan, that would also help, I imagine.

If I think of the difference between my gran and me, I can see the progress more easily. My gran pretty much had to hide everything about every single bodily function she had. She even had a woollen dolly with a really long knitted skirt that sat on top of the spare loo rolls at the side of the toilet to make these less shameful.

I had my toilet rolls, mainly for lack of storage space, piled in a pyramid next to the toilet. She found that difficult and would comment on it in that sort of critical-but-pretending-not-to-be-critical way whenever she visited. Like, 'I see toilet rolls are in fashion these days,' or, 'Do you not have enough cupboard space, my love?'

What was one step too far for her was that I also always leave a box of tampons and a bag of sanitary towels next to the toilet too. I wanted it all out in the open from a very early age for my daughter; as normal to see as soap and loo roll. Also, because a few times, in the days before I was more confident about just asking, I came on unexpectedly at other people's houses and couldn't find any products whilst scavenging for some to steal from their bathrooms.

My friend lived with a guy at university who used to complain if the women in the house (two-fifths of the household) left the 'women's drawer' even a little open because just the sight of a box of tampons was enough to *make him sick*. The other boys told him to stop being an arsehole and the problem was solved. I cannot emphasise enough the impact of boys and men being 'on side' in moments like this.

I spent years hiding sanitary products from my dad because my gran had told me firmly *we musn't embarrass the men*. In my twenties, on a visit to my gran's house, I needed tampons. My dad was going to the shops. *Fuck this*, I finally thought to myself.

Dad, will you get me a box of tampons from the shops, please? I asked.

420

My gran almost choked. She gave me the stare of death across the room.

Yeah sure, he said, like it was nothing.

Our family business on my dad's side, from my great-great-grandfather's time until the shop closed in my dad's thirties, was a Spar grocery store, where my dad had helped out all his childhood, stacking the shelves with all sorts of products, including, he later told me, as we laughed about the telling-off my gran had given me when he was out at the shops, sanitary products. All those years I had been shoving those fucking tampons up my sleeve and it turned out my dad wasn't in the slightest bothered. I wondered which other men in my life weren't bothered either. I'd say it currently sits at about seventy-five per cent non-botheredness.

A similar moment of release and wonder came when I met my boyfriend, who was so nonchalant about the blood that he almost made it sound like a sexy lube. Which, well, yeah. Good point.

The first time I awkwardly apologised to him – as I had a tendency to do in any romantic situation from the age of about nineteen whenever I was on my period – he simply laughed and said something along the lines of 'I'm aware you have a body that bleeds but I'm not sure why you're apologising for it'. I honestly felt as if my entire body was collapsing in on itself and re-emerging. Like I'd just walked back through the wardrobe and realised that I was still the same person but now knew all about the magic of Narnia. Really, that's not a good metaphor at all but I really love that book so much and wanted to mention it. The excitement was similar, that's all really.

So every time my grandma visited me, she'd put the sanitary products back into my bathroom cupboard and every time she left, I'd take them out and put them back beside the toilet.

My gran died before I had a chance to show her my magic pants, but I'm almost sure she'd have scowled at me for talking openly about periods and/or my underwear and then asked me hundreds of questions about them. That tended to be how all of our conversations about taboo topics went.

Writing specifically about these pants has been very helpful for my family life because my daughter is currently so bored of me strutting around the house in them every month pointing to my own crotch exclaiming, 'I can't believe it, I can't believe how much easier this could all have been, look at them, just like normal pants, aren't they, how nice do they look, huh!' that she rolls her eyes and says, 'I get it, you like the pants, Mum.'

But she doesn't get it. She really doesn't. Hopefully, she never will.

showering on my period

for the days I can embrace my bloody body

i'm told not to admit it – not to write it
sick girl to speak of a beauty in blood
but i must. because at that peak of each month
when the brown soils have sulked away
mud phase at its end, when all that i'm left with
is red: cherryade soup; neon blood sunrise;
vertical life-line; lava spills straight
from the insides of earth, in the shower, look down
as red ribbon rivers map out my thighs until
thrown by the bone of my ankles
the bath's floor dotted with poppy field pools
expanding in watered down circles
like litmus test patterns
until rain comes to wash us to sea

no, i take it all back, periods are just shit

*for the days I can't embrace my bloody body no matter
how many empowering books I read about the strength
within my cycle*

my walls have begun crumbling
i can feel it in my thighs again

it happens every month
but each month i'm still surprised
as stomach cramps force forth
my lips in constant curse

like yes, it's normal, yes i'm fine
but fuck off, this shit still hurts

view of the world in the three days before my period is due

yes, i might get angry
and no doubt i will cry,
for the world in all its glory
is essentially shite

for every petal patterned butterfly
there is a caterpillar slayed
for every march of fluffy ducklings
there is a mother duck gang raped
for every transitory rainbow
there is flood and there is drought
the world would work much better
if the human race died out

hot-blooded

i used to hold it like a fisherman queasy at each catch
ease it from the waters – resistance in the tug until
with sudden lunge the fish erupts flailing wildly from the sea
sometimes spattering the tiles with its final bloody spit

i'd recoil then; hold the string in front of me
like mum held out my brother's socks
dramatically disgusted, as if the cotton bullet bit

the first time i touched it, wrapped it up in loo roll,
squeezed it in my palm, i didn't think it would be warm

i was jealous of them then; the men i'd let inside me
easing in and out my flesh – *how cosy it must feel in there*

hot chocolate for a frosty night;
sleeping bag tucked up neck high;
thick slippers on a marble floor;
a towel, radiator hot, wrapped around their skin;
bathtub after storm

in the holocaust camps

the women swapped knickers sometimes
handed blood-laden gussets
to girls too young to have started
or women whose blood
had been shocked back to childhood
by famine or fear;

so the women swapped knickers sometimes;
saved blood-laden gussets
for those who needed them most

protection from soldiers who
pacing past ditches of bodies
shot face down in mud

still deemed *this* blood
too dirty to rape

no. no, it isn't

for you, who did not flinch

you know when you tell a guy
i'm sorry. i'm on my period
apologising, as if you've scheduled it yourself

and he looks at you, bewildered
and says *what?*

then gets what you mean and jokes
oh, my sheets wash!

then sees you staring silent
gets nervous and stammers
i mean, only if you want?

before he questions
just to check
he hasn't got the layout
of your body wrong
and asks

your clitoris isn't covered by the tampon anyway
– is it?

and you look at him cooking dinner
and you say, no
no
no   it isn't.

modern art

after sex
you sit up

stark bollock

my tampon
on your rug

your penis
stained with
all my blood

sipping on
your coffee cup
you offer me
the frothy bits

i'm thinking;

we could win
the fucking
turner prize
for this

ON LITERARY SUBJECTS

Many years ago I was at a poetry night for a brilliant magazine called *The Dark Horse*. There was a young poetry editor there from another literary magazine I won't mention the name of. We all make stupid comments sometimes, and he seemed a very lovely man who made one flippant remark.

At the end of the night, I was standing in a group of a few people, all men, including this editor. He declined a final drink, saying he had to get back to read all the submissions for the magazine he worked for. Then added something along the lines of: *At least you can get rid of the periods and birth poems first, and then you can focus.*

Everyone went silent and stared at me, jostling me, as if I would have a response.

My daughter was about three by then. My friend was going through surgery for a prolapse. I had just interviewed a woman for a radio series who had jumped out of her top window onto a green-house below two days after her baby was born due to post-natal psychosis. I still had flashbacks to birth every time I tried to relax in a bathtub. I had recently released a book of poems on parenthood and we'd all *just* watched Clare Pollard on stage read the most brilliant poems on the pressures of new motherhood.

But I didn't say anything. He had just implied that the two physical processes he could not have had first-hand knowledge of were not fit subjects for literature. Not worth reading about.

I don't find it easy to argue with someone I don't know, especially when it's over something really important or a bit gut-wrenching, or when I really want to get my thoughts in order first, or when the topic makes me imagine holding that person's face and squeezing sweat out of it like a hardened lime because I've heard this sort of shit said so many fucking times during my thirty years on this planet.

It's one of the reasons I started writing poems. To not scream before I'm sure what it is I am screaming. So I said nothing. I maybe imagined biting through his armskin a bit and watching the blood drip onto the tip of his trainers, but I said nothing.

He left, dismissing two of the most momentous events of my life to choose some very suitable poems to publish in the literary magazine he worked for.

To be clear, this comment wasn't about the quality of the writing, which would be fine to comment on. He hadn't already read any of the poems in question. It was simply about the themes: no periods, no birth, get on with the real literary subjects.

I often think about the laughter and the gulps of air taken by those other men standing there. The amused shock, the immediate turn of their heads towards me as if it were for me to start debating, a fun challenge for me to rise to. But I just felt gutted.

When people speak about the perils of any form of positive discrimination in any line of work, I think back to this moment and I imagine what this sort of bias was like ten, twenty, two hundred years ago in the publishing world.

It has also made me sadder over the years, as more people I know have suffered due to childbirth or pregnancy or periods or menopause or miscarriage. Also because I have learnt more and more about those aspects of our bodies so carelessly disregarded in that moment, how fascinating they actually are. I've now read poets like Sylvia Plath, Clare Pollard, Maya Angelou, Kim Addonizio, whose poetry on motherhood is, in my opinion, exceptional and could not, even by the most literary of magazines, be deemed unworthy of being labelled literature. This is obviously not an issue related only

431

to motherhood or 'women's topics' but a small part of a much larger systemic prejudice in literature and life to any minority voice.

I finally wrote a poem about this poetry editor's comments during the end credits of the film *Mary Shelley*. The poem is not a well-written poem but I don't want to edit this one because I wrote it in a flurry of tears after this film and it did me a great service of just getting something down on paper so that I could stop having continuous fake arguments with this editor in my head, which is a massive waste of energy.

I don't know what this poem is called.

I called it 'smug tosser' at first, then decided on 'i have read so much fucking poetry by men about sex and blood but the minute a woman writes about sex and blood you think it's too moany or vulgar or domestic to be considered literary'.

In all honesty, I don't care what the title is. Sometimes I really care about titles and spend ages playing with them. Sometimes I don't. For now, I'll call it 'cunt'.

cunt *(working title)*

if you could fathom just one hint
of those themes you deem too illiterate
to place into pages of literature

if you could bleed as we bleed
pop pills, meticulously labelling
each hour of each day of each week;
open legs to the nurse
copper coils uncurled in your cervix
hormones injected in veins
just to be able to play

              the way burns
and byron and percy and baudelaire
rabelais, chaucer and dylan and dylan
deemed so very poetic:
                if you could
fall pregnant; sense life expand in your flesh;
feet and fists kick inside of skin;
a human head burn through bloody-soaked thighs
as you push and you push and you push
fearing your ribcage is fleeing your lungs
or scalpels slice open your womb
as a baby's first scream jolts you from death
legs huckled apart to patch up the path
ripped from your hopes to your arse
hold a baby still tubed to your flesh
watch lips suck life from your breasts

if you could give birth
after pushing and pushing and pushing

to an unbreathing child
feel fistulas spilling out faeces for life
as your body still floods with warm milk;

if you could feel a miscarriage slip;
then a miscarriage slip; then a miscarriage slip
appear from the toilets as if nothing had happened
for fear they will know you were trying to get pregnant

spend years after labour
leaking in pants

cursing your womb
as a prolapse protrudes

or stumble past picketed signs
denying abortion
comparing women to Satan

if you could imagine the gamble
that all the above could easily happen
every time you open your legs to lie naked
and fucking so liberally in love;

the way burns
and byron and percy and baudelaire
rabelais, chaucer and dylan and dylan
deemed so very poetic:

you might realise why sex or why lust
or why passion or why battles or why bodies
or why war or why blood

might be scripted
slightly differently
by some

SHORT STORY: CATCHING SLUGS

so disgusted
by the texture
of a slug
yet we kiss
with their cousins
in our mouths?

*

The sunset was the colour of Cherryade that evening. Greg didn't notice. He was busy preparing for the slugs. The little fuckers had already demolished half of his lettuces and he was almost certain that they were plotting to go for his strawberries next. Greg was not having it. No fucking chance. These slimy little bastards would not get the better of him again. He was, as he had said to Cathy earlier that evening, ready for battle.

Greg sniffed deep and loud, swallowed the phlegm into his stomach, pushed the last of five pint glasses of beer firmly into the soil. He twisted each glass a final time. Once he was certain that no toppling would occur, he turned to Cathy and she nodded and they smiled to one another. They smiled most often when catching slugs.

Cathy and Greg made love most Saturday nights. They would drink a few glasses of Sauvignon Blanc, watch a TV programme they agreed on. They would brush their teeth, Cathy would remove her make-up and they would have sex in bed before a kiss goodnight and sleep.

Blowjob Sunday used to be a thing, but that had fizzled out about two and a half years after their tenth wedding anniversary, alongside Cathy's enthusiasm for the reverse cowgirl. There had never been a cunnilingus night. Greg had tried to establish this a few times, but eventually given up.

When Greg and Cathy made love, Cathy imagined her vagina as the inside of a hot-dog roll being stuffed with one of those long, firm but gentle sausages, before mayonnaise is haphazardly squirted inside. The thought often made her giggle. For Greg, sex with Cathy was like dipping his penis into a cup of warmed Heinz tomato soup; always there in the back of the cupboard; a little bland perhaps but nonetheless comforting and sweet.

On that particular Saturday, as she lay with her husband, Cathy's mind drifted to the weekly hairdresser's trip: the warming shampoo suds rubbed into her scalp by caring hands; the chat she would get to have; the questions she'd be asked about herself; the space she'd be given to answer as her scalp was pressed heavily by forceful fingertips.

She thought of the soft sensation of the hairdresser's comb running from roots to the tips of her hair follicles; the sound of the scissors' light snipping; the feel of falling hairs tickling the nape of her neck; the soft brushing away of leftovers.

Sometimes, Greg imagined he was kissing one of the two presenters from *Strictly Come Dancing*. He didn't mind which, really. Both were lovely; *physically, of course, and* – he would often point out to Cathy as they watched the programme together – *personality-wise too*. Cathy would nod because she did agree that both the women were beautiful and seemed very friendly. Greg often pointed out women on the television who he thought were both beautiful and interesting.

Sometimes, the two presenters would morph into one person; blonde-haired but short-framed; brunette but with a stronger sense of humour than normal. Sometimes Greg would picture them dressed in the dancers' outfits rather than their own elegant evening-wear. Greg wasn't sure which attire he preferred. Cathy preferred the gowns, she would say, though secretly she had often imagined herself spinning across ballrooms in the fancy leotards.

Outside Cathy and Greg's bedroom window that night, two leopard slugs were having sex the way leopard slugs normally do: spinning intertwined and suspended from a long piece of glittering silver mucus. The silver mucus hung from the top branch of Cathy and Greg's cooking-apple tree, sparkling like the semi-final costume of Giovanni's partner in 2015. Possessing both male and female organs, and being, for their size, mightily well-endowed creatures, both leopard slugs wrapped their long sea-blue penises around each other and thrust simultaneously. Intoxicated by the scent of the ripened fruit, the mating slugs spun a tiny while longer until both ejaculated, both received, and they made their way slowly and surely across the branch of the tree, down the trunk, and onto safe ground, the night-dew grass tickling their muscles as they slid.

That night, after they made love, Greg kissed Cathy lightly on the lips and tucked himself deep into the warm covers. He loved that moment, when the covers hugged him to sleep after sex. He closed his eyes and drifted off. Cathy looked at him for a second, smiled and kissed his forehead, before she got out of bed and walked, pelvic muscles clenched, to the bathroom. She sat on the cold toilet seat and waited until the majority of Greg's sperm had oozed from her insides, dropping quietly into the toilet water below her.

She wiped herself, the quilted paper she had treated them to that month slipping across her skin. She washed her hands and walked back to their bedroom. She took a sip from the glass of water that she kept by her bedside in a bid to prevent her cystitis from returning and read a chapter from the latest of her Jilly Cooper novels. She glanced at her husband sleeping beside her, kissed him once more on his forehead, switched off the lamp and fell asleep too.

Below the window, the two slugs followed a sweet scent of post-coital beer and strawberry leaves. Discovering the glass edge, they slid thirstily up, peered over the ridge and fell, splash, slowly drowning in the darkness together.

The next morning, after breakfast, Greg and Cathy shared a smile as they emptied a successful beer glass into the compost bin, the taste of that year's strawberry jam already ripening on their tongues.

slug snog

our tongues are leopard slugs;
don't mock this; full and wet
and slipping; they navigate the
moonlight in measured single
muscled movements;

not one of us know as much
as leopard slugs; of dusk; of dew;
of glittered silver trails in soil;
of tree bark texture; lick of leaf

these are kissing's masterpiece –
romance at its best.

at best
our snogs are leopard slugs mid sex
helter skelter wrapped; writhing
round each other's thirst; dangling
on midnight branch from
glistened strings of spit

come twist your slug-like tongue tonight
like slugs in moonlit tussle;

let's glide along below these stars
all dew; all moon; all muscle

STRANGERS

Avoiding Glances

I like people

HARRY BAKER, 'Paper People'

sometimes i lie and say i'm a midwife

when strangers on trains ask what i do
i want them to think *she is good*
i want them to look at my hands
and imagine those hands have held
more than a pen. i want them to think
i have run between bedsides; mermaid to ship
swam sailors to safety on shores
delivering wisdom or toast or condolences
comforting those in the midst of an earthquake
stitching up skin in light-saving tapestries
sitting for seconds; catching breaths between screams

STRANGER DANGER

Strangers: one word to divide humanity into people we know and people we don't know. It's a strange word. Strange. Stranger. It is every single person on the planet other than the minuscule proportion of people you deem to have crossed that line, a cluster of billions of potentially lovely people (or not) into one collective noun. Strangers.

When I was younger, I remember, my dad very seriously sat me down and told me to trust no one.

'Not even you and mum?' I asked.

'No,' he said.

I had no idea what to do with that.

When people say 'I don't trust strangers' I find this ridiculous, because every single day most of us put our trust in strangers in some way. We trust the strangers who we buy food from not to have laced that food with poison; or spat in it; we trust the strangers who fix our cars not to fiddle with the brakes like movie villains might; we trust strangers to deliver our letters without filling them with explosives.

I did an equally bad heart-to-heart with my daughter when she was having a frightened 'I can hear footsteps' sort of bedtime.

I tried to ease her fears about the stranger she was sure she'd heard, but who I was assuring her was not 'in here, or here, or here' as we walked around the house, switching on the lights in each room. I was, if I'm honest, bricking it a bit more with each door I forced myself to calmly open, each time a little more certain that she was right or perhaps had the same kind of ability as the little boy in *The Sixth Sense*. After we'd checked the house and I was sweating like a zumba crotch and I thought my daughter was now settled again and sleeping, she stumbled, ten minutes later, back into my bedroom and said, 'I'm still scared, Mum.'

So I gave up on the creeping round the house method and tried the 'rational thinking' method. I told her that it was normal to be scared of strangers but that statistically strangers were the least likely people to harm you, that people were much less likely to be attacked or hurt by a stranger than by someone in their actual family and that, aside from heading directly into a war zone, the most dangerous thing you could do as a woman was to marry someone and then try to divorce them. It was meant to soothe her, but it came out all wrong. She stared at me, scared I was going to kill her too. It took a while to back-pedal. She finally fell asleep and I, grumpy from losing my slither of free post-bedtime time, went to sleep too, thinking what an arse of a mother I was.

It's bloody hard knowing what to say to kids.

I remember my mum talking to me about it too. I was scared because my mum loved walking in the woods near our house with the dog in the evenings. In the winter, it was dark when she left. To me, it was *night* night and I remember once when I was little telling her not to in case there was a murderer waiting in the woods for her. I always used 'a murderer' as a noun in itself. I didn't think of a murderer as having any other sort of identity; a murderer was a murderer at all times of the day. A murderer was a murderer at all times of their life.

My mum corrected this assumption by saying, 'Murderers are people too. They're not going to wait in the freezing cold just in case someone happens to come past them. They get bored as well. You're more likely to be attacked in a city in the daytime than in a forest late at night.'

Just like with my daughter when I warned her to be more scared of her family than anyone else, my mum's 'talk' didn't make me feel any better because no matter how hard I tried, I could not separate forests at night from danger and now I was scared of daytime walks too. I say *was*, but really, this isn't a thing of the past. I am still fairly scared of walking anywhere alone, especially in the countryside.

I know many people love walking but I don't. I always cycle because when I cycle, in my head, I can outrun a possible attacker. I said this to a friend once and they laughed, as if it was ridiculous I was so scared of simply going to the local park for a walk. I wasn't always scared to do this, but strangers, one by one, slowly and surely, without laying one hand on me, have fucked up my alone experiences so many times, I just can't any more. I don't find it beautiful to be in a forest or to gaze at the stars or to walk along the riverside *lonely as a cloud* because all I am thinking about is whether I am safe.

I have never been attacked. But I have been intimidated by so many strangers in so many different settings that I am now frightened by things I would desperately love to enjoy. I've also never related any of these experiences to anyone, because I thought I'd be seen as making a fuss about nothing. A few of the more memorable ones:

1. On the London Underground at night after work. About 11 p.m. I'm the only person in the carriage. A man gets in. Sits on the seat right next to me, despite the whole carriage being empty. Says nothing, looks straight ahead but just presses his thigh against mine until I sprint off at the next stop and then miss my train home because I don't want to get on the tube again until there's a busy carriage.

2. I think how nice it'd be to take my work to the local country park on a sunny day. I go, get a tea from the café and find a small clearing in the woodlands, get out my books and sit down. A man comes over after about half an hour and starts chatting to me. Asks my name. My age. After about ten minutes, tells me it's his birthday. Starts circling me. Asks me to

stroke his hair for his birthday. Asks if I like his hair. I pack my bag and he offers to walk me to the café. I let him because, like so often, the idea of angering a man like this is worse than being nice to him so that he maybe doesn't hurt you.

3. I pull over my car whilst driving on a long journey on tour because I see a bench beneath a tree in an avenue of forest and think it'd be nice to sit and get some air for a minute. A man cycles past, looks back, turns his bike round, cycles across to where I'm sitting and just sits on his bike two metres from me, looking at me and saying nothing. I leg it to my car and he turns and keeps staring at me as I start the engine.

4. A man, walking ahead of me at night as I was walking from New Malden station to my friend's house, keeps turning round looking at me as we both go into a pedestrian/cycle path away from the main road. He then hides behind a bush about ten metres in front of me and pokes his head back so I can see him hiding there. I run back to the station and call my boyfriend who runs from the house to meet me.

There are numerous more mere followings. Turning up roads I'm walking up. Speeding up towards me when I start running, still often wondering if I should run or if that will be a) aggravating to someone who is following me or b) insulting if it's just coincidence that this guy has about-turned to walk behind me down an isolated street.

My friend once said how annoying it is that, as a guy, he's seen as a possible attacker all the time, and how it's a bit upsetting seeing women cross the road away from him. I find it annoying too. Seeing every guy as a possible attacker. Yes, I find it really annoying too. It reminded me of a study I heard related by Gillian Anderson's character in Netflix series *The Fall*: A group of men are asked what scares them most about women. They answer: being humiliated by them. A group of women are asked the same question about men. They answer: being killed by them.

449

strange man

what was it you wanted, that day, strange man
on the underground train; empty as breath
stealing my space, staring ahead
your leg gently kissing my leg
no witness but stifling air?

were you trying to scare me?
well, well done, i was scared

how many journeys you've spoiled, strange man,
how much longer it takes to get home now
waiting for carriages face full enough
till i'm certain you're gone

to never take short cuts
to never take back streets

how much time i waste
avoiding your footsteps
how much money i've spent

what did you want, that day, strange man in the forest;
it could have been glorious; rain moist with
chestnut drops crackling in air as
you circled and circled and circled
and asked for my hands in your hair?

were you trying to scare me?
well, well done, i was scared

i don't wander the parks any more, strange man
don't pace through the forests; the woods;
don't lie in a meadow
make angels of rare settled snow

how many nights i long just to walk out my door
on my own
to gaze at the stars; how many stars i've not seen
how many wishes you've stolen;
how many places you've stained:

the night bus; the tube; the river; the train;
the meadow, the street; the walkway; the bus stop;
the nightclub; the parks; the forests; the moonlight;
the sunshine; the snowfall; the silence; the shadows
the daytime; the daydreams; the night

what i don't tell you (my child)

for any other parents who pretend to be braver than they are

i am scared of all those things
you are scared of

once i've turned down your light;
pulled back the curtains to show you
those shadows scaring your walls
are nothing but branches and leaves
storm winds and streetlight

once i've kissed you, again
convinced you no fires will find us tonight
moved the dressing gown
hanging suspiciously full on the hook of your door
once i've told you once more how
houses snore too, that creaks are not killers
sneaking upstairs; that cooling pipes chatter
that i'm here that i'm here that i'm here
you have nothing to fear

once i've stood by your bed for another ten hugs
as your eyelids drop dreams in your pockets
convinced of my strength to vanquish
all of the monsters that tiptoe the earth
once i blow out your lamp, turn away
from your breath, unbutton my bravery,
step back into the silence of night;

now
i am petrified too;

leave your room; tiptoe the floorboards; check every door twice;
keep my curtains wide open for streetlight protection;
move the dressing gown shaped like my imminent murder;
let mascara clog soot thick on my lashes,
too scared of two minutes of soap-sudded blindness;
run under the covers; keep my feet firmly
in the warmth of the tuck so the monsters i still search the
cupboards for too, can't peck at my toes while i sleep

vanishing companions

you're worried about the day your toys no longer talk to you
you're not sure they don't already
but there's still that piece of maybe
stuck between your baby teeth
and the rising crag of adult cliffs
cutting through your gums;
your gut still harbours something.
dreams not quite disintegrated. still in peter pan space.
you worry about the age when tinkerbell
won't wake up with claps
when you'll tell yourself for definite that stuffed teddies are
not stuffed with anything but cotton;
those best friends in the world;
the ones who have sat around your bedside
fighting off the monsters,
easing you to sleep, nodding at your problems,
offering the best advice,
sipping on translucent tea on towel picnic patches; that they
are nothing but woollen
patterns; stomachs padded soft
eyes bought in button shops,
smiles stitched in ribbon. blind. and deaf. and dumb.

thing is. when you're away from home
i still peek into your bedroom.
pull your blind down at night
as if your eyes will feel the sunrise here
and if your sheets have slipped away
from the friends who sit and
wait for you as impatient as i am.
paws colder than they should be.

i tuck them in again.
watch the thread across their lips twitch.
see their button eyes wink. tell them you'll be back soon.
feel their fluff hearts beat.

SPIT

There's a Colombian philosopher called Antanas Mockus who I was slightly obsessed with in my twenties. He was a philosophy lecturer who then became Mayor of Bogotá and leader of the Colombian Green Party for a while. He came to Cambridge to give a lecture and I went wet-panted to listen. He was talking about laws and why people don't break them. He gave three reasons:

First, morality. You agree that the illegal thing is morally wrong and so you don't do it.

Second, fear of punishment. This speaks for itself, I think.

Third, fear of social isolation; being shunned from family, society because of what you've done because it's socially frowned upon.

He was talking specifically about Bogotá, focusing on the inequality involved in monetary punishments, because these punishments only act as an incentive to poorer people and do nothing to dissuade the richer members of society from breaking laws.

The part of the lecture I mainly remember was this. He asked everyone to write down why they generally do not commit serious crimes. The majority of us wrote down 'morality' or some variation of this: we don't do things that we think are seriously wrong, and often (though not always) that aligns with the law of the land. Then he asked us to write down why we think most *other* people do not commit serious crimes. Here, the majority wrote down a different reason: fear of punishment.

He told us that this is a very common assumption. Me, good. Them, bad. Or at least, them, different to myself. He also said that a lot of law enforcement measures spring from this same philosophy, the idea that most *other* people are immoral bastards and only deterred from doing 'bad' things by fear of fines or prison or brutality in some cases, whereas *you* are deterred from doing them because you are an angel.

There was a similar lecture a few years later as part of my Master's degree. I was studying Development Economics and one of my chosen modules was Forced Migration. It went along the lines of: *If you could move to any country in the world with no migration restrictions whatsoever, what would you do?* According to this lecturer's research most people in the world would choose to stay roughly where they were born and raised, surrounded by the culture and language they know and the people they love and a life they are comfortable with and used to. Most people in the world don't move a lot; many not even from their towns or villages or cities, let alone a whole country.

After this, the same question was asked of other people: *If anyone in the world could move anywhere in the world without any restrictions, what would they do?* The answer was resoundingly, 'They'd all come here.' This answer cut across countries and cultures. In the UK, everyone assumed everyone would flock to the UK, in Zimbabwe that everyone would flock to Zimbabwe, in Germany that everyone would flock to Germany and so on and so on. Our judgement of other people's actions and mindsets compared to our own are so often filled with this sort of suspicion, fear and negativity, whether that relates to crime, migration or simply passing someone in the street we don't know. Like the white people who move to other countries and refer to themselves as ex-pats, almost unaware that they are immigrants, I often forget that I am 'a stranger' to most of the people who will ever see me in my lifetime.

All this said, I also really fucking hate the phrase 'strangers are just friends you don't know yet'. Someone said this to my daughter once and I hastily replied, 'Yes, but they are also possibly murderers too – so don't go with any stranger, ever.'

I don't just hate the phrase for this reason, I also hate it because, though I don't think every stranger is necessarily a cunt, this opposite version is just too positive for me to deal with for anyone not on MDMA saying it. A bit like the phrase 'turn that frown upside down' which one of my teachers used to say in class as the pupils all sat there, imagining possible assassination scenarios.

I have three games I played a lot with strangers as a teenager.

One was with my friend Julie. We'd stop on the street and choose something in the sky to stare at, normally in the middle of town. We'd talk about it and keep pointing and staring and count how many strangers we could get to try to look at what we were looking at. I loved how shy most people were about it. How cool they'd pretend to be. Look like they didn't give a shit then quickly try to glance without anyone noticing. Once, a man stopped and looked and looked amazed and then kept staring. I still don't know if he actually saw something we didn't or if he was playing us at our own game.

The game I played with a friend Nicola was to see how many strangers we could make smile. At the time I lived in an area where everyone always looked fucking miserable. Just small things like smile on the street or drive round in my car for hours stopping at every zebra crossing as people from quite far away made their way towards it just so we could let people across and get a smile. We were working as language assistants at the time and, by law, only allowed to work fifteen hours per week, so we had quite a bit of free time.

Then there was the game I played with friends in the one local nightclub near us when we were about eighteen. I thought it was amazing at the time but looking back it was fucking rank. I would get a pint glass from the bar then we'd choose the drink we wanted and run round the club seeing how many people we could get to put a bit of their drink into our pint glasses until we had, ta-daa, a whole pint of free booze. I always chose the people with blue WKD as it was easy to spot people drinking it and I never thought about all the strangers' phlegm or germs until much later on in life. I would like to be able to blame my gran's love of freebies for this, but even my gran wouldn't sink that low.

I never quite realised how much I actually liked most strangers until the coronavirus crisis. I didn't miss strangers tipping blue liquor and spit into my glass, or strangers following me in parks, but I did miss other strangers, faces I didn't recognise, lives to guess at, overheard conversations, unexpected interactions. I felt a bit guilty missing strangers. At some points I missed strangers more than seeing people I did know; craving being in a café or a bar or a park just surrounded by people I didn't know and who didn't know me. When I did manage to catch a smile or chat or glance from a stranger – some people doing road repairs, the postman, a smile from someone in the local shop, the elderly woman who waved from her front garden as we walked past – it was a thrill I'd never realised I'd be so grateful for.

to the seventy-eight-year-old woman chatting to me on the train the entire way from london to liverpool, which is almost a four-hour journey

there was no need to apologise
for taking up my time
with talk about your grandsons
and how you had to catch the train alone now
since your husband died
and how you do not really like it
but how it's nice to get a tea
and when the trolley comes again
perhaps you'll treat me to a biscuit
how you met him at a dance
how well he did the two step
how you still turn your head
when something funny comes on telly
as if he's still sat on his chair
though it's been empty near ten years
how I remind you of your daughter
how nice to still be young
how your children think you're daft
how your hips have given up
how cheap you got your coat
in the discount winter sale

truth is, i spied you first
and, desperate for company
i took that table seat
in the hope you'd be
as talkative as me

making maps

*for the person who worked in the café on the Manchester train
and was also a beauty blogger, who cheered up everyone on
the commute when she came over the tannoy system selling the
coffee, making ridiculous claims about how fresh it was and
how she'd just roasted a batch picked out the fields this morning
and who, by the end of her announcements, had the whole
bored-as-shit commuter carriage pissing themselves laughing. I
started imagining the effect of that one person each day on all
those people on the train and then all those cheered up people
on all the people they passed that day, now brighter because of
this one person working in the LNER café on the London to
Manchester line.*

So this is for her. I don't know her name.

*And it is for Helen, a brilliant friend who once bought me a
book called* The Pig of Happiness *by Edward Monkton*

he didn't know her
but she smiled
and he needed that today
and he smiled back
and she walked past
and carried on the other way
and he walked on

and he kept pace
and other people passed his way
and he smiled
and they smiled back
and they needed that today
and they walked on
and he walked on
and other people passed their ways
and they smiled
and they smiled back
and others walked towards
and then away
and she got home
and she won't know
how many
lives were changed
because she smiled
and he smiled back
and she needed that today

things that make me question whether i am who i think i am

a police car close behind me in the slow lane on a motorway
the person at the pharmacy asking when i last had sex
'if anyone can show just cause' objection speech at weddings
a stranger walking past me who stares but won't smile back
'all tickets and railcards, please' inspector stopping at my seat
the bank clerk double checking where i got my cash from
the sign with all the sharp things i don't have in my suitcase
the tick box on the aeroplane which reads: terrorist? no/yes
a party guest enquiring if i made the sausage rolls myself
the missing cat poster asking if i've seen this cat
my daughter checking sleepily if i'm actually a spy

NEON LEGGINGS BITCH
AND STINGY BASTARD SANTA

There are a few strangers I have hated for a long while who I need to forgive now, or they'll keep nagging at my brain until I die, bitter and ridiculous.

The first, I call neon leggings bitch. I think about her every Easter and I hate her every Easter and she makes me think about neon leggings when I should be thinking about small yellow chicks and daffodils. She is my perennial nettle. There are not many people I hate. There are definitely people I should hate more than her. People who have done terrible things in the world. But at the back of my mind I hate this woman more. The same way that people should be enraged by, I don't know, systematic economic inequality, but know that the sound of their partner chewing with their mouth slightly open actually annoys them more. As you will be able to tell from this most traumatic tale, I had a very good childhood with minimal trauma.

It was Easter. I was nine years old on holiday in Florida; a once in a lifetime Disney trip. I am prejudiced against both the US accent and neon leggings because of this woman. I know she does not represent her country. Or wearers of neon leggings.

The hotel noticeboard declared an egg hunt at 1 p.m. in the garden. A bunny had left chocolate for all the children on their holidays. We gathered.

The whistle went. All the spoilt children with baskets clutched in hands fired into the grounds. I was littler than most of them. They were teenage giants with accents I'd heard before on every television programme I watched. Chocolate eggs were dotted around the grounds, prevalent as rabbit shit to woodland groves. My face was a blend of burnt lobster, striped with green sunscreen like Braveheart on a holiday. I wanted to find a chocolate egg.

Eggs were hidden everywhere but I was little and I was slow. Big kids pushed past me. I stopped believing in the tortoise and the hare. Then, I saw it. I stood below the tree staring enough not to garner suspicion but to make sure it was really as good as I thought. A boxed egg. A huge one. I looked around to check no one was watching. I tried to climb and slipped. I tried to jump and missed. Then I saw an angel wearing neon leggings and a visor, her hair spilling out the top. An adult.

Do not talk to strangers, Hollie. I knew this rule. This, however, was hotel entertainment and my mum and dad were still in sight. I put on my politest voice:

Excuse me, would you reach that egg for me, please, I can't get it.

She smiled. She reached. She smiled again. She turned away. She took the egg. She called to her teenage son. She put it in his basket. They walked away.

I sat below the tree and cried.

The other strangers I need to forgive are two children, whose parents, not them, were to blame for my tears one Christmas, and then hundreds of other strangers who buy their kids too many Christmas presents and fuck it up for everyone else. I seem to hold a grudge over presents and the holiday season more than anything else.

As a kid, between the ages of about four and twelve, I was often taken to the local hockey club by my dad on a Saturday. The clubhouse looked like an oversized wooden shoebox and served orange squash when the bar at the back of the main room inside it was open. The entranceway smelled of muddy boots and chatter and there was a river at the end of the pitches that we kids could run to and play near when we got bored. It was great.

Every December, the hockey club put on a Christmas party – the clubroom was filled with plastic pop-up tables coated in paper-patterned Christmas cloths, covered in bowls of crisps and ham and jam sandwiches and see-through plastic jugs of the strongest, most delicious orange and blackcurrant squash. At about six o'clock on one of those yearly party nights when I was five, maybe six, once we'd all downed twenty cups of squash, party poppers had been popped and sniffed and faces stuffed with as much sliced Battenberg as we could manage, a tinkling of tiny bells started ringing outside. One kid noticed first, then a whisper to other little ears and the news spread quick as chickenpox from kid to kid, until we'd hurled ourselves in group frenzy towards the slightly open back doors.

Peering a glimpse, which as a short kid I didn't find easy, we could just about see Santa. We watched in amazement, pushing for a better view, as black boots and belt and buckle approached from the car-park shadows. Santa had arrived; sat on a wooden sleigh filled with a huge sack of presents, pulled by two 'reindeer'.

We kids did not notice the reindeer accessories: not the elastic string from Rudolph's 'nose'; not the hairband holding the 'antlers' in place; not the small rickety wheels underneath the 'sleigh'; nor the dad who had downed his beer and dashed to the changing rooms minutes before the bells began to chime.

Instead, we stared and we screamed; those honest, jubilant, joy-fuelled screams which so many of us lose the ability to release in adult life. We were told to *keep calm* by those same larger humans, to *be quiet*, *to behave*, threatened with make-believe tales of Santa's dislike of loud noises from children or claims that we'd *frighten the reindeer*, and then, all threats failing to contain our bursting, we were simply dragged back into the clubroom by slightly pissed adults and told to sit on the big rug and wait.

The Santa who came to my local hockey club was not the *real*

Santa of course – but I didn't know that at the time. I assumed, as many others did, that this *was* the real Santa. This belief was the reason why, when the presents were dished out, I cried a lot and asked to go home and then cried the whole way home in the car.

I remember a girl sitting next to me on that rug, dressed in a purple dress, neat as Laura Ashley violin lessons. Long plaits likely plaited with silken ribbons, perfectly bowed, sweetly smiling at me as I sat cross-legged in the pink velour tracksuit and blue wellies I refused to change out of for about the first eight years of my life. I smiled back at her, pleased to make such a glamorous new friend.

Santa paced the room, ho-ho'ed and ho'ed some more, dished the presents out one by one, built the tension terrifically, eventually stopped in front of me and my new best mate. He said our names. He said our first names *and* our second names and I couldn't believe that Santa knew my second name. I wiggled, butt clenched on the floor.

Santa pulled out two presents: the first, a huge cube-shaped package wrapped in paper patterned with silver swirls and silver baubles, as big as the biggest Barbie Dreamhouse box I'd spied the day before in SavaCentre. Santa pulled out a second parcel, a smaller rectangular-shaped gift, wrapped in paper patterned with smiling snowmen, the package this time perhaps the size of the Christmas Edition Cadbury's selection box that they sold in our local newsagent.

He passed us our gifts. The girl next to me unwrapped her Barbie Dreamhouse-sized package. It was a Barbie Dreamhouse. I unwrapped my Christmas Edition Cadbury's selection box-sized package. It was a Christmas Edition Cadbury's selection box.

I looked at it and looked at the girl next to me, and attempted to kill the girl with my frown. I looked around, grumpy as a Monday school run. I watched my brother unwrap his Christmas Edition Cadbury's selection box whilst peering incredulously at the boy beside him, who was throwing lashings and lashings of Bubble Wrap out of a big box, shaped the exact size of a brand new remote-controlled car.

When my mum and dad, having failed in their pleas that I should be grateful for this Christmas Edition Cadbury's selection box, and guilt-ridden when I asked why Santa brought other kids better stuff even though I'd been so well-behaved, informed me later that that was not the *real* Santa but merely an imposter hired by the club and that the parents had been told to buy the presents for the kids and that there had been a £5 limit, *a bloody £5 limit!* my mum would repeat for the fiftieth time twenty years later as I told this same story, pissed, at yet another family Christmas do, I still did not forgive them.

I ate the contents of the Christmas Edition Cadbury's selection box. My parents were the only parents in the whole clubhouse who had stuck to the £5 limit.

When my daughter, at five years old, came home from school and asked why Santa gave rich children more presents; why Santa had only got her one gift and a stocking, but had paid for her friend's entire bedroom to be redecorated plus their whole family to go to Spain, I finally forgave my parents.

I told my daughter that those people were lying: that Santa Claus did not have time to redecorate children's bedrooms en route around the world and that he definitely did not buy package holidays. Which is true, he doesn't.

So in the end this is a thank you more than a fuck you; a thank you to my mum and dad for sticking to the stingy rules with that delicious Christmas Edition Cadbury's selection box, and a winter plea to any fellow Santa-loving strangers for next year: if you would like to buy your beautiful little children five hundred presents for Christmas, which you are by all means entitled to do if you want them to grow up as greedy shitbags, at least give yourself the credit for the four hundred and ninety-nine of them which are not from Santa and please, please give Santa the credit only for what he deserves.

SHORT STORY: THE TWO NEIGHBOURS

The day I moved into the new house, a quiet middle terrace, pushed between two other ex-workers' cottages in a village so silent you could hear the sheep sleep, the neighbour to my left walked through my back garden, knocked on my back door and asked if she could be my friend.

She was lonely, she said.
　She didn't have many friends, she said.
　She would love to be my friend, she said.
　It was so nice to have a young neighbour, she said.
　'Can I be your friend?' she said.

I thought of the time Kelly gave me a note at school. At the top it said, *Will you be my best friend?* underlined. Below, there were two options – yes or no – and a wonky square box drawn to the left of each, waiting for my tick. I felt sick when I got the note. I didn't want to be anyone's *best* friend. Her older sister was the toughest girl in the year above. I told her that I couldn't because I didn't believe in best friends. That's true, but it was also an easier and less upsetting way out. I have never been proposed to. I imagine that can be similar. I called up my mother and told her that I thought my new neighbour to the left might murder me in my sleep. 'She has a key to the house,' I said. The landlord told me he had left a key *with the neighbour to your left, just in case*. 'Should I ask her for it back, or do you think

469

she is more likely to kill me if I ask for it back? She said she wants to be my friend, Mum.'

'What did you tell her?'

I told her yes.

I told her *I can be your friend.*

The neighbour to the left beamed.

Then she went home.

Then she came back two minutes later.

She knocked on my door and she came in.

She came in with a cup of tea for me and a bag of sugar.

'Not sure if you take sugar,' she said. 'Do you take sugar?' she said.

She stayed and chatted as I unpacked a kettle.

She stayed and chatted as I unpacked a cheese toastie maker.

She asked if I would have tea with her again.

She was lonely, she said. She didn't have many friends.

She asked if I would like to come for a cup of tea tomorrow.

She told me about her two daughters, now grown-up and left home long ago and the crush she has on her line-dancing instructor who teaches in the village hall and how all the women have a crush on him but how he dances with her the most she thinks and that they kissed once but only once and that she hadn't had love in twenty years and that her husband tried to force her to abort their second child and that she told him to fuck off and never come back and that he didn't and good riddance because she did just fine on her own.

The next day at dinnertime, she knocked on the back door again.

My daughter screamed into her soup.

'There's a woman standing at the back door,' she said, 'just standing in our garden, Mum!'

'That's our neighbour to the left,' I said.

I opened the door.

She said, 'Do you have time for a tea?'

I said, 'Yes, come in.'

She said it was lovely having a new friend.

She asked me my name again and she asked my daughter her name and she said *hello* to my daughter.

She told us about her two daughters, now grown-up and left home long ago and the crush she has on her line-dancing instructor who teaches in the village hall and how all the women have a crush on him but how he dances with her the most she thinks and that they kissed once but only once and that she hadn't had love in twenty years and that her husband tried to force her to abort their second child and that she told him to fuck off and never come back and that he didn't and good riddance because she did just fine on her own.

The next afternoon, my neighbour to my left knocked on the back door and I said sorry I was working. She said that was fine, she didn't want to trouble me. She said did I have ten minutes only ten minutes for a tea later. I did, I said. In three hours.

Three hours later she knocked on my back door.

I opened the door.

She said, 'Do you still have ten minutes for a tea?'

I said, 'Yes, of course, come in.'

She said it was lovely having a new friend.

She asked me to remind her of my daughter's name and she told me about her two daughters and the crush she has on her line-dancing instructor, *have I told you about my line-dancing teacher?* she said and I said *yes, you have*, and we laughed, and she told me how all the women had a crush on him but how he dances with her the most she thinks and that they kissed once but only once and that she hadn't had love in twenty years and that her husband tried to force her to abort their second child and that she told him to fuck off and never come back and that he didn't and good riddance because she did just fine on her own.

Have I told you? she said.

She said it was lovely to have a new friend.

The day I moved into the new house, a quiet middle terrace, pushed between two other ex-workers' cottages in a village so silent you could hear the sheep sleep, the neighbour to my right walked up to my car.

I was parked in the single space at the back of the terrace, car heavy with boxes I didn't know how I felt about unpacking, sobbing into memories and tissues. She knocked on my window and I quickly fixed my smudged mascara, looked up, smiled and opened the car door.

'What are you doing here?' she said.

'Oh, I just moved in,' I said, 'I just moved into the middle terrace.'

They owned this bit of car-park space at the back, she said.

You have to park on the pavement out the front of the row of houses because that space was only for their use, she said. *It was their space, not communal space*, she said.

'Oh,' I said.

'Sorry,' I said.

'The estate agent said I could park here to move my things in,' I said.

'No,' she said. 'This is our space.'

Then she walked away.

The day I moved into the new house, a quiet middle terrace, pushed between two other ex-workers' cottages in a village so silent you could hear the sheep sleep, I cried for an hour in the car after meeting the neighbour to my right. I cried for an hour in the empty house unpacking boxes.

I cried for an hour in the empty house unaware that the back door was about to sound three knocks and that the neighbour to my left, the neighbour who I didn't know had two daughters and a crush on her line-dancing instructor; the neighbour to my left who dances most with him she thinks out of all the other women; the neighbour to my left who kissed her line-dancing teacher once but only once, who hasn't had love in twenty years; who told her husband to fuck off when he said she'd better abort their second child and good riddance because she did just fine on her own; the neighbour to my left who brought me tea and biscuits and asked to be my friend; the neighbour to my left who the other neighbours tilt their heads at and ask me, sympathetically, *if she's knocked for me again today.*

Yes, I say. *She has.*

I say *she told me about her two daughters and the crush she has on her line-dancing instructor; have I told you about my line-dancing teacher?* she said and I said *yes* and she told me how all the women have a crush on him but how he dances with her the most she thinks and that they kissed once but only once and that she hasn't had love in twenty years and that her husband tried to force her to abort their second child and that she told him to fuck off and never come back and that he didn't and good riddance because she did just fine on her own.

'Have I told you this story before?' she said.

'Yes,' I said. 'But please tell me it again. It's the best story I've ever heard.'

ACKNOWLEDGEMENTS

Thanks to my mum, firstly, who has told me and taught me so, so much – in a good way, not in a 'things i've been told to hate' way – and who I'm addressing here first because she thinks this book makes her seem a bad mother, which she is the very opposite of (except for labelling my vulva 'a bald eagle' in childhood, which she still denies). Thank you to Becky, once again, for your huge support and unrivalled negotiating skills and cracking outfits and bar choices and to Rhiannon for your continuing belief and brilliance as an editor and a person. Thank you to the blinding work of Clara, and Emily, Sophia, Mary, Ursula and Nico, and all the others at Fleet who have helped edit this book into better shape, and remove mistakes I've made which would have made me look like a total arse. Thank you to Helen Mort for the tea and chat and for agreeing to take on the poetry editing, which has helped so much. Thanks to Esa, Francis, Iain, Marjorie and Michael for being my first and only and brilliant poetry group. Thank you to my absolutely gorgeous daughter, for putting up with me being tired after editing during the night and for making me tea in bed at weekends and for listening to three of the poems in this book and then going 'ugh you're so soppy'. (Sorry to diss the magician) – thank you for your jokes and hugs most of all. Thank you to the Royal Society of Authors for a grant to give me more time to interview people about sex and blood and grief and for all the people I've spoken to about these topics, especially certain groups of drunk people after gigs in Liverpool, Glasgow, Cardiff,

Chester, Leeds, the Outer Hebrides, Norwich, Galashiels and many more. Thank you to all the people who wrote all the books and tv shows and films and music lyrics that inspired this one. Thanks to all my friends for the years of inspiration, and well, friendship and love and for letting me write about you sometimes and for letting me put your names into my dream sexual dictionary definitions in here. Thanks to my dad for all the memes and jokes and for buying sanitary towels without a fuss, and for my sister too, and for family up in Scotland for all your support and piss-taking and pancakes and tea breaks (Tracy) and soups and music (Kit) and cheesy puffs (Nikki and Lesley) and Aunty comfort and eye-rolling and love. Thank you to Michael, for being you and for being there, and for your words and kindness and other obvious things. Thank you to anyone who reads this book. Thank you to all the birds who give me something to watch from the desk in my bedroom as they fly back and forth from their nests to the holly berry tree and remind me to look up once in a while.

READING LIST

Despite there being so many brilliant books for children, I found that, simply flicking through the library shelves, I had to make a concerted effort to find any where the main character wasn't white, able-bodied, with two white heterosexual parents and a white cat and a white picket fence. So, I would highly recommend @diverse_kids_books, @thisisbooklove and @hereweread for loads of great suggestions of books which don't, in particular, whitewash childhood so much.

In terms of adult reading, the below is less a recommended reading list and more a list of books I read in the last few years while writing and editing these poems; the books which have stayed with me in various ways.

Juno Dawson, *What's the T?*
Lemn Sissay, *My Name is Why*
Jackie Kay, *Red Dust Road*
Irvine Welsh, *Glue*
Daniel Mason, *The Winter Soldier*
Darren McGarvey, *Poverty Safari: Understanding the Anger of Britain's Underclass*
Simon Van Booy, *The Secret Lives of People in Love*
Gael Faye, *Small Country*
Elaine Feeney, *As You Were*

Shere Hite, *The Hite Report*

Uju Asika, *Bringing Up Race: How to Raise a Kind Child in a Prejudiced World*

Gavin Preto-Pinney, *A Cloud A Day*

Emma Dabiri, *Don't Touch My Hair*

Richard Powers, *Overstory*

Gaston Dorren, *Lingo*

Nimco Ali, *What We're Told Not to Talk About (But We're Going to Anyway): Women's Voices from East London to Ethiopia*

Megan Hunter, *The End We Start From*

Amelia Abraham, *Queer Intentions*

Mervyn Peake, *Gormenghast*

Sabrina Mahfouz, *The Things I Would Tell You: British Muslim Women Write*

Nina Leger, *The Collection*

Amy Benson Brown, *Breastfeeding Uncovered: Who Really Decides How We Feed Our Babies?*

Akala, *Natives: Race and Class in the Ruins of Empire*

Anna Kessel, *Eat Sweat Play: How Sport Can Change Our Lives*

Isobel Losada, *Sensation: Adventures in Sex, Love & Laughter*

Laura Dodsworth, *Womanhood: The Bare Reality*

Laura Dodsworth, *Manhood: The Bare Reality*

Maisie Hill, *Period Power: Harness Your Hormones and Get Your Cycle Working For You*

Emma Flint, *Little Deaths*

INDEX OF POEMS